The Government
and Politics of Israel

About the Book and Author

The Government and Politics of Israel
Don Peretz

What is the role of Israel's Arab minority and Oriental Jewish majority in relation to the Ashkenazi, or Western, Jewish establishment? Who governs Israel today, how is its government chosen, and how does it make its policies? Is the military establishment an influential factor in politics? How have the 1977 elections in Israel changed its politics? These are some of the questions addressed by the author in his approach to the broader topic of how the government and politics of Israel have been created, what forms they have assumed, and in what directions they are now moving. Dr. Peretz also considers the relationship of Israel's political system to world Jewry and the Zionist movement, the prestate roots of Israeli institutions in Ottoman-Turkish and British-Mandatory precedents, and the evolution of the Jewish community of Palestine from a minority to a majority in the country. His book is an excellent introduction for the student of Israel's government and politics.

Don Peretz, professor of political science at SUNY-Binghamton, received his M.A. and Ph.D. at Columbia University. A member of the Board of Advisory Editors of the *Middle East Journal,* he is a frequent contributor of articles on the Middle East to a large variety of journals and magazines. Among his books are *Israel and the Palestine Arabs, The Middle East Today,* and *A Palestine Entity?*

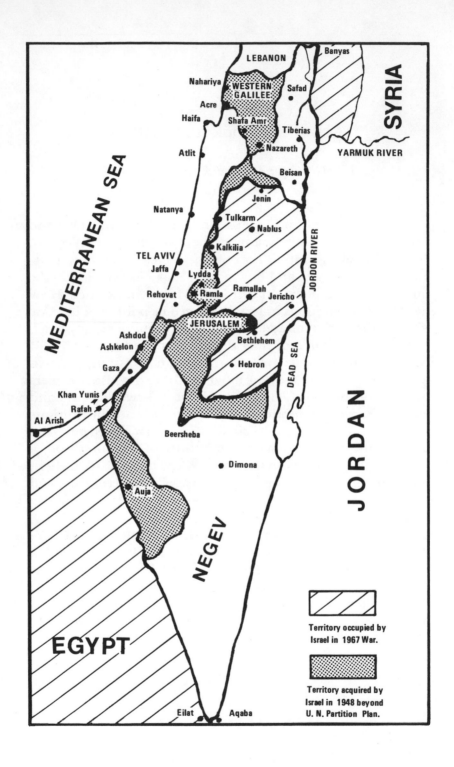

LEBANON

Banyas

Nahariya

WESTERN
GALILEE

Safad

Acre

Haifa

Shafa Amr

Tiberias

SYRIA

YARMUK RIVER

Atlit

Nazareth

Beisan

Jenin

Natanya

Tulkarm

Nablus

Kalkilia

TEL AVIV

Jaffa

Lydda

Rehovat

Ramla

Ramallah

Jericho

MEDITERRANEAN SEA

JORDON RIVER

JERUSALEM

Ashdod

Ashkelon

Bethlehem

Gaza

Hebron

DEAD SEA

Khan Yunis

Rafah

Al Arish

Beersheba

Dimona

Auja

JORDAN

NEGEV

EGYPT

Eilat

Aqaba

Territory occupied by
Israel in 1967 War.

Territory acquired by
Israel in 1948 beyond
U. N. Partition Plan.

The Government and Politics of Israel

Don Peretz

Westview Press • Boulder, Colorado

Dawson • Folkestone, England

Copyright © 1979 by Westview Press, Inc.

Published in 1979 in the United States of America by
Westview Press, Inc.
5500 Central Avenue
Boulder, Colorado 80301
Frederick A. Praeger, Publisher

Published in 1979 in Great Britain by
Wm. Dawson and Sons, Ltd.
Cannon House
Folkestone
Kent CT19 5EE

Library of Congress No.: 78-2239
ISBN (U.S.): 0-89158-086-7 (hardcover)
ISBN (U.S.): 0-89158-087-5 (paperback)
ISBN (U.K.): 0-7129-0881-1

Printed and bound in the United States of America

Contents

Preface

This survey of the government and politics of Israel is intended as an introduction to the study of the country's political system for those who are not specialists. It should be useful in survey courses of Israel's politics and as a supplementary reading for courses on Middle East government and politics. During the past decade there have been no new surveys of this type to bring up to date earlier political studies such as Leonard J. Fein's *Israel: Politics and People*, Marver H. Bernstein's *The Politics of Israel*, or Nadav Safran's *The United States and Israel*, all of which are now out of print. Since the 1960s, Israel has gone through another war and approached a peace settlement. The political system has been shaken by the Labor party's stunning defeat in 1977 and the accession to power of the right-wing opposition for the first time in the country's history. With a population increase of nearly one-third, new political, economic, and social problems have emerged in addition to those faced a decade ago. New and different ways of meeting these problems have evolved and new institutions have developed to cope with them. While this book does not pretend to be a detailed study of changes in Israel's government and politics since the 1960s, it examines the way some institutions, practices, and traditions have evolved. The purpose of the book is to give those interested in Israel's government some familiarity with its origins, the way in which it has evolved, and how it works today. Several individuals have been helpful in commenting on the manuscript, although no one other than the author is responsible for the contents. Special thanks are due to Professor Gideon Doron of the SUNY-Binghamton Political Science Department for his suggestions, some of which were accepted, and others not.

CHAPTER ONE

Historical Origins of Israel

A CHANGING SOCIETY AND ITS PROBLEMS

For a country so small in area and population, Israel has become the focus of unusual world attention. Its conflict with the surrounding Arab states, its central role in major Middle Eastern issues, and its social, economic, and political development have aroused international interest. Probably no other nation of Israel's dimensions is so well known throughout the world nor is as influential in its relationships with other countries near and far.

Israel's population of 3.5 million is smaller than that of at least a dozen of the world's largest cities, including New York; it is equivalent to about 15 percent of California's population, or a little over 1 percent of that of the United States. Israel is considerably smaller than middle-sized European countries like Belgium or Holland. Among the Middle Eastern countries, Israel is far from the largest in either area or population. It ranks with its smaller neighbors like Lebanon or Jordan in population. There are several states with populations at least ten times as large, such as Egypt, Iran, and Turkey, all with over 30 million people. Middle-sized states such as Syria, Iraq, or Saudi Arabia have two to four times Israel's population. Though not a mini-state like Abu Dhabi, Bahrein, or Kuwait, Israel is definitely among the smaller political entities of the region.

Despite its size, Israel is of prime importance to American foreign policy. It has a special relationship with the United States government and with many Americans, both Jewish and non-Jewish. What happens in and to Israel is often considered more significant, and more vital to American interests, than what happens in and to other countries in the Middle East and Europe. The country has acquired a prominence in Western consciousness that is unique.

Israel is the world's only Jewish state. There are many countries whose populations belong to the Muslim, Christian, Buddhist, or other religious faiths and ethnic groups. But Israel is the only one where the majority of the population is Jewish and where the national institutions are Jewish. Only one in seven of the population is not Jewish. This identity, religious, ethnic, and cultural, cuts across every aspect of life. It influences government, foreign affairs, internal political organization, education, the mass media, business, trade, and economics. It affects the life of every resident of the country, whether Jewish or not.

Demographically, Israel differs from its neighbors and nearly all other states because until recently most citizens had been born beyond its borders. After thirty years of independence, only about half of the Jewish population was native to Israel. The majority of Jews were immigrants from scores of Western, Asian, and African countries. Since Israel's beginnings, the population has been in flux. At first, waves of European Jewish immigrants moved into the country. After independence, large numbers of Jews from Asian and African countries replaced Arab inhabitants, who became refugees in the 1947-48 Arab-Israeli war. Later, there was a trend back to predominantly Western Jewish immigration.

Politically, Israel is unique in the Middle East, and not only because of its multiparty system and elections based on proportional representation. Although its political outlook and orientation are Western, its fundamental ideology is Zionist. Through this ideology, Israel claims close ties with large numbers of Jews who are not Israelis and who have never been to Israel. Most political parties in Israel are Zionist. These parties dominate the government and control about 90 percent of the seats in the Knesset or parliament. They include militant nationalist, Orthodox religious, bourgeois, moderate, and Marxist Socialist groups. Through membership in the world Zionist movement, nearly every party has overseas affiliates—in the United States, Great Britain, Canada, South Africa, and most other parts of the Western world. In countries where Zionist organizations are illegal, such as in the Arab and Soviet blocs, there are, of course, no such formal links.

These characteristics contribute to Israel's unique role in the Middle Eastern context and in Western consciousness. Its distinct character has been a major cause of tension with the surrounding Arab countries. Arab perceptions of Israel have in turn been transmitted to many other Third World nations, with the result that Israel, although located in Asia, is not perceived as an Asian country.

Although Israel became independent in 1948, its modern antecedents go back to the end of the nineteenth century; its ancient links with the region reach back to biblical times. Since independence in 1948 the country and its people have experienced tremendous changes. The population has increased by more than five times, and it has experienced four major wars and many more small guerrilla encounters. The economy has gone from agricultural to industrial, and expanded several times to become one of the largest in the region. Demographically Israel has been transformed from a country whose Jewish citizens were largely European to one in which Jews of Afro-Asian origin are predominant. The basic political and cultural institutions and the military establishment, which existed in embryo during 1948, have acquired firm foundations. A lively and diverse modern press and publishing industry have developed along with other communications media such as cinema, radio, and television. Until recently a minority, the native-born generation has begun to assume leadership in the mainstream of life—in politics, in cultural and scientific fields, and in economic and commercial dealings.

European Zionist leaders who had immigrated to Palestine before Israel was established dominated Israeli leadership in the first traumatic years of Israel's independence. Those who came to the country as youthful idealists before and soon after

World War I remained Israel's leaders until the early 1970s. Not until after the disaster of the fourth Arab-Israeli war in 1973 was there a native-born prime minister. Even though the new generation of young leaders has made its entry into the halls of power, the gerontocracy of early twentieth-century Zionists is still influential; they are prominent in party leadership, in the Knesset, and in other important aspects of Israeli life.

Despite the change from a European to an Afro-Asian majority, the leadership in most aspects of life is still either European or of European origin. Most members of the cabinet, parliament, political party leadership, and government administration, and most leaders in other areas are European. Economic differences separate the Europeans from the Afro-Asians, most of whom do not have the Western lifestyle and standard of living for which European Israel is known. Tensions created by the resulting economic and cultural disparities have not yet had serious political repercussions, although an Israeli Black Panther movement made its appearance during 1970. The problem of a socio-economic gap characterized by differences in national origin was then recognized and Israelis began to be concerned about it.

Not all citizens of the Jewish state are Jewish. By 1978 there were over 500,000 Israeli Arabs. This minority presents another series of dilemmas to Israel's leaders. After the 1948 war and the flight of most Arab inhabitants, a non-Jewish, mostly Arab minority remained. Largely concentrated along the borders of the adjoining states with which Israel had been at war, the Arab minority was perceived by many as a security problem. The fact that Israeli Arabs have one of the world's highest birth rates has increased their number by 400 percent since 1948, from about 10 percent of the population to over 15. Some demographers estimate that Israeli Arabs will equal the number of Israeli Jews within a century. Socioeconomic, cultural, linguistic, and political differences between Israeli Jews and Israeli Arabs have increasingly politicized the issue and raised serious questions about the future of Israel as a Jewish state.

This dilemma intensified after the 1967 war, when Israel occupied those remaining parts of mandatory Palestine not yet within its borders. In acquiring the West Bank from Jordan and the Gaza Strip from Egypt, Israel became responsible for an additional million Arabs in these territories. For historical or sentimental reasons, during a decade of occupation, many Israelis came to regard the occupied or administered territories as parts of their country. Government policy has been ambivalent about their eventual fate, partly because of the large Arab population and its high birth rate.

The continuing state of war with the surrounding Arab countries has been a decisive factor in shaping Israel's economic structure and policies. The geometric escalations in the cost of security after the 1973 war, worldwide inflation, and the increased capacity of the Arab states to outspend Israel in the arms race because of their large oil revenues have taxed the Israeli economy and created serious internal problems. Even within the labor movement there was reevaluation of the Socialist doctrines that were its driving force. These doctrines were the basis of the welfare society, which provided Israeli citizens with an extensive network of modern services including high-level education, subsidized medical care, unemployment compensation, and other well-developed social programs. Living standards were maintained at a Western level through government subsidy of many necessities such as food, housing, and education. As inflation and soaring defense costs increased the economic pressure on the government, many leaders began to reappraise the Socialist doctrines that were the foundation of Israel's social programs. A major result has been increased tension between organized labor and the government, demonstrated by the frequent outbreak of strikes.

Closely related to the dilemmas of economics and ethnicity already mentioned is the question of class relationships in Israel. Since establishment of the Jewish state, class distinctions have not only become more visible, they have acquired increasing political significance. At independence in 1948, the Jewish community of some 650,000 was relatively close-knit and homogeneous. There were no great discrepancies between rich and poor or between upper and lower classes. Since 1948, a new bourgeoisie has emerged and enough people have become millionaires to almost constitute a class. On the other hand, with large-scale immigration of Jews from countries in which they were at the bottom of the social and economic scale, problems of poverty have become commonplace. Urban and rural slums have sprung up and tension has grown between the poor and the increasingly affluent middle class. The problem has intensified because the largest percentage of poor are Jews from Africa and Asia and the most affluent are mostly Jews of Western origin.

Established with the goal of becoming the Jewish homeland, Israel has been an immigrant society since 1948. During its first years, massive waves of Jews immigrated, mostly from Europe, emptying the post–World War II displaced persons camps and the internment centers on Cyprus, where Great Britain had managed the annual arrival of hundreds of thousands of Western Jews during 1948 and 1949; tens of thousands also came from Asia and Africa. Since the late 1950s and early 1960s, immigration has declined precipitously. In some years, the number of Jews leaving Israel has been greater than the number entering. Since Israel was established to "ingather" the Jewish exiles, decline in immigration has been a major concern of Zionist leaders.

In recent years there has been a slight increase in the number of Jews coming from the Soviet Union. Some observers believe that if Moscow lifted all restrictions on Jewish emigration from Russia there would be a substantial increase in Israel's Jewish population; others have doubts about the magnitude of the increase. Generally speaking, however, most other potential large sources of Jewish immigration have been tapped. Few people from the large Jewish communities in the West, such as the United States, Great Britain, and France, have been willing to leave their homes for Israel. Yet the Jewish state was established with the goal of a homeland in mind, and ingathering is a fundamental principle of Zionism. So the question arises, how can this vital role of the state be continued? The problem acquires greater urgency in view of the rapidly increasing number of Israeli Arab citizens.

The Jewish community in Israel has diverse conceptions of the meaning of "Jewish state," ranging from the secularist perception of Jewish identity as ethnic or national to the

Orthodox religious Zionist belief that the Jewish religion should be the foundation of the state. Since Israel was established, questions of how Jewish and what kind of Jewish the state should be have been at the heart of political life. Although only a minority of Israelis belong to the religious political parties or regularly observe Orthodox customs and traditions, the question of the relationship between state and religion has been among the most controversial. Should Sabbath observance be compulsory, restricting public transportation and other services? Should the Jewish dietary laws be required in the army and in other public facilities? Should personal matters such as marriage, divorce, inheritance, and adoption be controlled by religious or secular authorities? Does the Orthodox Jewish rabbinate have exclusive authority over Jewish observance or should Reform and Conservative rabbis also be given religious authority in Israel? There is also difficulty in defining just who is a Jew. The answer to that problem determines citizenship and a variety of other rights and prerogatives in Israel.

Questions of state and religion are complicated by the political situation. No single party has ever won an absolute majority in national elections. Thus all governments have been formed from coalitions of parties with the socialist-oriented Labor party as the base until 1977. It has usually been necessary to include religious parties in government coalitions to achieve a parliamentary majority. Thus, despite their relatively small size, the Orthodox parties have made the issues of state and religion central to Israel's political life.

THE GEOPOLITICAL SETTING

Israel's borders were carved from mandatory Palestine in a series of international agreements and wars. Prior to the First World War, Palestine itself was an integral part of the Ottoman Empire; thus, although both the terms Palestine and Israel have ancient historical antecedents, they were new political entities created during the twentieth century. Since the establishment of the Jewish state in 1948, it has had no permanent, generally recognized international boundaries.

The area of the Jewish state partitioned from Palestine by the
United Nations in 1947 was approximately 6,000 square miles.
This was increased to nearly 8,000 square miles during the first
Arab-Israeli war in 1947-48, which was terminated by armistice
agreements between Israel and Egypt, Syria, Jordan, and
Lebanon. After the June 1967 war with Egypt, Syria and
Jordan areas under Israeli control within the new cease-fire
lines totaled nearly 35,000 square miles. The sparsely settled
desert of the Sinai Peninsula captured from Egypt constituted
more than two-thirds of this area. Also included were the Syrian Golan Heights and those remnants of former mandatory Palestine held by Egypt—and Jordan—the Gaza Strip and
the West Bank.

Although the area under Israel's control has increased, its
borders with the neighboring Arab states have diminished. The
cease-fire lines of 1967 shortened the borders to 523 miles,
compared with the 1949 armistice frontiers, which were 570
miles long. The new lines were of great strategic advantage to
Israel. Before 1967, most large population centers were only a
few miles from the bordering Arab states. After 1967, most
Jewish settlements and large cities like Jerusalem and Tel Aviv
were no longer within easy reach of neighboring armies. The
1967 war created large buffer zones between Israel and those
neighboring Arab states with which it was still at war: Egypt
in the southwest, Jordan on the east, and Syria to the northeast.
The international border established between Palestine and
Lebanon after World War I still remains intact in the north, despite Israel's brief occupation of southern Lebanon in 1978.

The diverse climates, land forms, flora, and fauna within
these territories are similar to those of Southern California.
The Mediterranean coastal plain has mild winters with
moderate rainfall and hot, dry summers. The mountain and
hilly areas running from Lebanon in the north through central
Palestine and the Negev Desert in the south are sparsely settled
and not very productive. South of Beersheba and Gaza, the
Negev and Sinai deserts and the Jordan Valley in the east are
arid and dry throughout the year, although with irrigation they
can produce high-quality crops.

As in most other Middle Eastern countries on the edge of

the desert, lack of water in Israel is a major restraint on growth.
Rainfall is uneven, with adequate quantities in the north and
almost none in some of the southern regions. Periodically there
are droughts which cause extensive damage to the country's
agriculture. Throughout history, there have been quarrels
among the countries of the region over water. They continue
today. Disputes over the main water system, the Jordan River
and its tributaries, have caused frequent clashes between Israel
and Syria and Jordan.

The Jordan and its tributaries including the Dan and
Hasbani rivers in the north, Lake Tiberias (also called the Sea
of Galilee or, in Hebrew, *Keneret*), and the Dead Sea in the
south are important not only for their economic value to Israel
and the other riparian countries; they also have strategic,
political, and historico-religious significance.

Light rainfall, dry climate, sparse water sources, and the
sandy soil of the region produce a Mediterranean-type
agriculture with emphasis on field crops (cereals and grains),
fruits, and vegetables. Beginning early in the century before
Israel's establishment, Jewish farmers introduced extensive
irrigation and scientific agricultural methods, which greatly
increased the productivity of the land. Development of the
citrus industry became a major element in the Jewish economy.
Since 1948 other specialized crops such as bananas, strawberries
and avocados have been raised for export to Europe. With
expansion of other sectors of the economy and decline of
manpower requirements in agriculture, farming has diminished in relative importance, providing only 6 to 7 percent of
the national product and employing less than 15 percent of the
work force. Natural resources are modest. They include
mineral deposits such as potash, phosphates, and copper ore,
which is exploited commercially. In recent years, commercial
oil deposits have been discovered.

More than 85 percent of the total population and over 90
percent of the Jewish population live in urban localities.
Nearly one-third of the Jewish population lives in the three
largest cities: Tel Aviv–Jaffa—350,000; Jerusalem—355,000;
and Haifa—230,000. The proportion of Arabs living in rural
areas is much larger—nearly 50 percent. The coastal area

between the ports of Haifa and Ashdod contains the greatest concentration of Jewish inhabitants, as well as the greatest concentration of industry, commerce, and other vital sectors of the economy.

Most of the country's Arab minority is geographically separated from the Jewish population. This is more a circumstance of history than planning. In the Middle East, diverse ethnic and religious groups have traditionally lived apart. In urban centers where there were mixtures of Jews, Muslims, Christians, and their respective subgroups, each group often had its own "quarter" or city district. During the first Arab-Israeli war in 1948, most Arabs left their quarters in the large urban areas such as Jerusalem, Haifa, and Jaffa, where they had lived alongside the Jews. Today most Israeli Arabs live in the villages of Galilee and along the pre-1967 frontier with Jordan.

Since 1948, the Israeli government has attempted to disperse the Jewish population more widely. Aside from the nearly 100,000 Jews living in the city of Beersheba, the southern Negev region, which constituted about one-half the area of Israel before 1967, had less than 1 percent of the population. In the strategic Galilee region of northern Israel, less than one-half the population was Jewish. Concerned for both security and ideological reasons, the government offered incentives to Jewish settlers in these sparsely inhabited regions. New immigrants, a large proportion from Asia and Africa, were directed to development towns to establish a Jewish presence outside the urban areas. Since 1967, the government has also encouraged Jewish settlement in several dozen new villages and towns in the occupied areas, a fact that complicates future policy regarding their return to the Arab states.

ORIGINS OF MODERN ISRAEL

Before Great Britain assumed the Mandate for Palestine after World War I, there was a Jewish presence in Palestine, but those associated with Zionist institutions and settlements were few. By 1914, the forty-four Jewish settlements with a population of at least 12,000 constituted only 14 percent of the Yishuv (Jewish community). Most lived in cities and towns such as Hebron, Safed, Tiberias, and Jerusalem, where Jews had lived for centuries. In the city of Jerusalem, Jews had constituted the majority of the population since the middle of the nineteenth century.

How was it possible for so small a group of people to establish a country that became a regional power within a single generation? The question is even more provocative considering Israel's sparse natural resources and scarcity of water, its relative smallness and precarious situation in a region that is not only geographically hostile, but is also surrounded by an Arab population—with much more extensive territories, vaster numbers, and richer natural endowments—that regards the Jewish state with deep animosity.

Modern Zionism, still less than a century old, was a European nationalist movement linked by history, tradition, and mythology to the land of Israel. After Roman conquest of the Jewish community in Palestine during the first century, destruction of the second temple, and forceful dispersion of a large part of the Jewish population in A.D. 70, Palestine was no longer the center of organized Jewish life. But Jewish communities continued to survive in Galilee, parts of the coastal plain, and Judea. One version of the Talmud (studies of Jewish history and law), compiled in Palestine between 200 B.C. and A.D. 500, mentions over 400 Jewish settlements there. The Bar Kochba Rebellion against Rome (A.D. 132-135), although suppressed, became a major event in Jewish history.

Separated physically from "the Land of Israel," Jews scattered in the diaspora retained close traditional and emotional ties with Palestine, chiefly through the Bible and other Jewish religious literature which became the basis of communal life for 2,000 years. Some historical theories maintain that through conversion many non-Semitic peoples became Jews and that there are today few direct descendants of the ancient Hebrews. However, the question is more one of historical significance than of immediate political relevance, since most Jews are strongly attached to their Jewish identity regardless of their past origins.

The largest Jewish communities were established in Europe, although they were dispersed as far as China, Ethiopia, and Central Asia. Jews continued to live in separate communities where life was based on the laws, traditions, and customs of ancient Israel. In the Byzantine, and in the Catholic and Protestant nations of medieval Europe which had state religions, Jews were prevented from participation in national life. They could not hold public office or own land and were usually excluded from the mainstream of social life. Frequently they were expelled because of religious differences or when they became the victims of political persecution. Nearly every major European nation—Spain, France, Portugal, England, Poland, Rumania, and Germany—exiled its Jewish community at one time or another.

Jews were thus a people apart, until the nineteenth century; they never really became Frenchmen, Englishmen, Poles, Germans, or Russians. Not only were they regarded as a distinctive people by those around them, they thought of themselves that way. Jews and non-Jews (Gentiles) came to regard each other with mutual suspicion, Gentiles because they perceived the Jews as a foreign element in their midst, and Jews because they believed that the Gentiles were determined to persecute them, if not eliminate them altogether. As a result of their exclusion from landholding and such primary occupations as agriculture, Jews often gravitated toward work which others would not do. Frequently they became skilled middlemen, merchants, and bankers, or, at intermediate and lower levels of the economy, craftsmen, tailors, and the like, and a number of characteristically Jewish occupations developed. Social isolation and economic exclusion became hallmarks of the Jewish condition in Europe, phenomena that were later to become significant in Zionist ideology.

These conditions intensified the closeness within the Jewish communities and their inner-directed perceptions of the world. They also strengthened the emphasis on ancient Israel and glories of the past. Jewish tradition, observance, and custom were central to the lives of nearly all Jews until modern times. There were no distinctions between Reform, Conservative, and

Orthodox Judaism. All abided by Jewish law and followed the leadership of their rabbinical elders. The finer distinctions between Judaism as a religion and as an ethnic or national identity had not yet developed. Reform and Conservative Judaism were developments of the late nineteenth and early twentieth centuries.

Most aspects of Jewish life in the diaspora were intimately linked with Palestine. Jewish rabbinical law favored the settler in the ancient homeland. Religious literature echoed with such sayings as: "It is better to dwell in the deserts of Palestine than in palaces abroad," "Whoever lives in Palestine lives sinless," and "The air of Palestine makes one wise." There was no distinction between the spiritual and the physical Palestine in the minds of most Jews. Although separated from the Holy Land by thousands of miles, to most it seemed closer than the neighboring Christian communities, which were regarded with hostility and fear. Holidays, feasts, and fasts commemorated events in the Bible such as Moses' flight across the Sinai Desert from Egypt to Palestine, the destruction of the first and second Jewish temples in Jerusalem, and the harvest season; events that did not take place in Russia or Poland, but in the Holy Land. The annual passover festival commemorating the exodus from the pharaoh's Egypt ended with the hopeful prayer "Next year in Jerusalem!" Jewish religious ties with Palestine were more than formal or ritualistic. Heightened by the conditions of the Jewish exile, there was a mystic quality about them that was more intense and deeper than the attachments of the average Muslim or Christian.

After the French Revolution, new ideas swept across Europe, and the life of European Jewry was transformed. The most important changes were the destruction of the ghetto walls that had physically isolated the Jews and the growing acceptance of Jews as equal citizens in Western Europe. By the middle of the nineteenth century, many of the restrictions on Jews had been removed. In varying degrees, they were permitted to own property, practice law, teach in universities, and be employed by the government. Jews became involved in political life, stood for office, and entered military service.

Integration into the mainstream of civil life led to new forms of Judaism. Notable was the rise of Reform Judaism, seeking to separate religious practice and observance from the requirements of daily life. As Jews integrated with others and became accepted, it became increasingly difficult to observe all of the customs and practices required by Orthodox observance. Reform Judaism was an attempt to modernize the faith and adapt it to lifestyles and manners of the predominantly non-Jewish environment.

The French Revolutionary and Napoleonic concept of equality for all citizens, regardless of religious practice, was not accepted in tsarist-controlled Eastern Europe. There, response to Western reform was to impose new restrictions and intensify the fight against subversive liberal ideologies. The Jew in tsarist domains became the chief victim of these reactions, and fresh restrictions were imposed on Jewish movement, places of residence, and employment. In the 1880s, Russian anti-Semitism broke out into sporadic pogroms, with officially sanctioned attacks on Jewish lives and property. Anti-Semitism reached such proportions in Russia by the end of the century that the Jewish community was thrown into turmoil. Reactions to tsarist persecution took diverse forms. The most frequent was through immigration to the West. Most of the large Jewish communities in the United States, Great Britain, and France increased vastly during this period.

Some Jews joined indigenous protest movements including Social Democratic organizations, labor unions, and radical secular movements. Other Jews preferred distinctively Jewish organizations in which they could cooperate in a common struggle against reactionary forces. Jews also formed secular Socialist parties like the Bund, or labor groups in which they retained their distinctive Jewish identity.

A smaller number was attracted to Jewish nationalism. In many ways it resembled other nineteenth-century nationalist movements, some of earlier and some of later origin. Like other nineteenth-century nationalist movements, it was the product of both negative and positive forces: a response to Jewish oppression and a revival of Jewish pride in ancient culture. Jewish nationalism also had deep religious roots and affinities with the organized religious institutions of the community.

Although there was no Jewish national church similar to the Greek, Rumanian, or Bulgarian Orthodox Church, many Eastern European rabbis played a prominent role in the revival of Jewish nationalism.

Identification with a specific historical territory was an integral part of all nineteenth-century national movements. One major difference between Jewish nationalism and the others was that its followers were far removed from the land with which they identified. Most had never seen, and would never see, their "homeland." However, this did not diminish the fervent attachment of the religious Jews and Jewish nationalists to the Holy Land. Separation not only intensified their longing for and their emotional involvement with the Holy Land, it often resulted in unrealistic images and false perceptions by Jews abroad of realities in Palestine. To some it was a "land of milk and honey"; to others "a land without a people waiting for a people without a land." Many believed it had been abandoned since biblical times.

The reality, as the first Zionist settlers were to find out, was quite different. There was a substantial Arab population in Palestine at the end of the nineteenth century, with a peasantry cultivating large stretches of the land. In the villages and larger towns such as Jaffa, Hebron, and Nablus, local gentry were quite visible, many in leadership of a nascent Arab nationalist movement. True, much of Palestine was abandoned desert, and cultivation was primitive by European standards, leaving most of the villagers in dire poverty.

Initially Jewish nationalism was poorly developed and loosely organized. There was no central movement or leadership. Jewish intellectuals in various parts of Europe wrote tracts propounding a Jewish homeland as the answer to the Jewish condition. Among them were Moses Hess (1812-1875), author of *Rome and Jerusalem* (1862), and Leo Pinsker (1821-1891), author of *Autoemancipation* (1882); these works were to become the foundations of later Zionist writings. Moses Hess, a German Socialist, was inspired by Italian nationalist reunification of Italy in 1857 to propose a similar Jewish "national renaissance." He believed in the "creative genius of the nation," and called the Jewish cause "the last national problem." Later, Pinsker, a Russian physician, stirred by the pogroms of the 1880s, gave currency to a new term, "anti-Semitism," which he described as "Judeo-phobia." The Jews—everywhere a minority, nowhere a majority—were a "ghost-nation," an abnormal phenomenon, always "guests" and never "hosts." No matter how hard they tried, the Jews would be unable to become like their Gentile neighbors and gain acceptance. Forever alien, the Jews were unassimilable, hated, and thus forced to find their own homeland.

Asher Ginsberg (1856-1927), who Hebraicized his name to Ahad Ha'am ("One of the People"), emphasized the cultural aspects of Jewish nationalism. He envisioned Palestine as the center of Hebrew literature and learning, "a true miniature of the people of Israel as it ought to be which will bind all Jews together." His emphasis on Jewish ethics led him to deemphasize Zionist political aspiration for a national state.

One of the first movements to evolve from early Jewish nationalist writings was Hoveve Zion ("Lovers of Zion"), established in Russia during the early 1880s. Its members, striving for a cultural revival and self-determination, advocated Jewish settlement in Palestine as a practical relief measure rather than as a religious ideal. Inspired by Pinsker, they argued that legal emancipation in Russia, even stemming from humanitarian motives, was useless. Only a "land of our own," whether on the banks of the Jordan or the Mississippi, was the true solution.

One student member of Hoveve Zion traveled through Russia recruiting 500 fellow enthusiasts who were determined to settle in Zion. The group, called the Bilu, from the Hebrew initials of their rallying call in the Old Testament, "O house of Jacob, come, let us go forth," succeeded in sending a few youths to Palestine, where they established one of the first Zionist towns, Rishon le-Zion ("First in Zion"), in 1882. By the end of the century, a few dozen other small Jewish settlements, or colonies, had been established by Jewish intellectuals from Russia and Poland.

Only a handful of early Zionists went to Palestine, but millions of Russian Jews immigrated to America and Western Europe. Among these immigrants were many Zionists and members of other Jewish national or social movements fleeing tsarist persecution. Difficult living conditions in Palestine, the problems of obtaining entry into the Ottoman Empire, and the uncertainties of life there were deterrents to a mass movement of people to the East. Economic difficulties and problems of adjustment to the arduous pioneer life stunted the new Zionist colonies so that few ever developed into major Jewish centers. Though Zionism advocated return to the land in a physical as well as a historical sense, it was not easy for lower-middle class Jews unaccustomed to rigorous toil to work the land. Many of the Bilu settlers preferred to hire Arab labor rather than to dig the earth with their own hands. Thus many of the early efforts were not only unsuccessful economically but ideologically as well, as far as Zionist theory was concerned.

THE ZIONIST MOVEMENT AND POLITICAL ZIONISM

Within fifteen years after establishment of Hoveve Zion, the diverse groups coalesced into a single, large, and unified world Zionist organization. Ironically, its founder was not from the ghettos of Eastern Europe. Theodor Herzl, born in Budapest in the Austro-Hungarian Empire during 1860, was an assimilated Western Jew. In his youth, Herzl admired Prussian culture and Teutonic might. He found little to attract him in Jewish tradition and was, throughout his life, quite ignorant of its customs and practices.

As a correspondent for a Viennese newspaper, Herzl attended the 1894 trial in Paris of Captain Alfred Dreyfus, a French Jewish army officer falsely accused of selling military secrets to Germany. Dreyfus was sentenced to imprisonment on Devil's Island. His trial stirred humanitarian protest in Western Europe, and sparked waves of anti-Semitism in France. Herzl was deeply affected by the virulent manifestations of hatred of Jews during the trial such as the cry of "Death to Jews!" at the ceremony stripping Dreyfus of his rank. The affair aroused Herzl's memories of the anti-Semitism he had experienced as a youth attempting to become part of Germanic society.

Shortly after the Dreyfus trial, Herzl began work on a pamphlet that was to become the basic document of the new

Zionist movement. Written in 1896, *Der Judenstaat* ("The Jewish State") laid out Herzl's perception of the Jewish problem and his proposals for a solution. Although he had never read Moses Hess or Leo Pinsker, his analysis and proposals were similar to theirs. He too believed that the Jew was a unique part of society, alienated from the mainstream. The Jew would never be accepted and was destined to be universally hated. Where the Jew goes, Herzl argued, he carries the virus of anti-Semitism; therefore he must either leave non-Jewish society or totally assimilate. Even immigration to supposedly friendly nations would not exempt Jews from eventual anti-Semitism. Perhaps, if not persecuted or discriminated against for two generations, Jews might become part of a new liberal society, Herzl added, but it seemed unlikely that they could be free from persecution for so long. The Jewish problem was not religious or social, he concluded. The Jews were a "nation without a land." Therefore they should be granted a territory by the world powers to fulfill the needs of a nation. "Let sovereignty be granted us over a portion of the globe large enough to satisfy the rightful requirements of a nation," he wrote, "and the rest we will arrange ourselves."

In his book, Herzl presented an action plan to establish a Jewish state. A "Society of Jews" would organize the Jewish masses for emigration from Europe and would negotiate with the European powers for acquisition of a national territory. No specific territory was demanded, provided it met the requirements for a Jewish national home. Herzl, who had none of the deep religious attachments of Orthodox Jews to the Holy Land, suggested either Palestine or Argentina—the latter because of its rich undeveloped area. Jewish public opinion and the Society of Jews would make the final determination.

After publication of his small volume, Herzl traveled through the Jewish communities of Eastern Europe to propagate his ideas. He also sought audiences with the most powerful political figures of the day, attempting to persuade them to support him. Most Jewish leaders in Western Europe and America, who felt secure in their liberal environments, were skeptical. They believed Herzl's program was unrealistic and that it would jeopardize their own integration into

Western society. His approaches to Jewish financial magnates such as the Rothschilds and Hirsches were unsuccessful, providing little, if any, of the funds required for the venture.

The masses of Eastern European Jewry, on the other hand, lionized Herzl as a new Moses. He, in turn, was driven by a frenzy of compassion for the oppressed Jews of Russia and Rumania, frequently warning that disaster awaited them within a generation if nothing was done about their plight. The most orthodox rabbis attacked his ideas as blaspheming the "mission of Israel" and the Messianic hope which would be fulfilled by the hand of God, not by man. Western European Jewish liberals and Eastern Socialists believed that their fate lay with non-Jewish compatriots. They opposed adding still another to the already proliferating array of national movements. Instead, they looked forward to a new internationalism.

In his efforts to convince the powerful of his scheme, Herzl gained access to the German kaiser, the Ottoman sultan, the pope, and the chief political figures of Great Britain. Unable to convince imperial Germany to become protector of the Jewish state, he turned to Great Britain. Rejected by the sultan, he tried to negotiate for other territories in the British Empire—East Africa, Sinai, or Cyprus.

Enthusiasm for the Jewish state among Jews in Russia, Poland, and Rumania was so great that Herzl was able to convene the First World Zionist Congress in Basle, Switzerland, during August 1897. It was an international gathering of over 200 delegates from all over the world, with the largest representation coming from Eastern Europe. Those attending were a cross section of Jewish society representing Orthodox and Reform sects, Eastern and Oriental Jews, and a variety of political persuasions and social classes.

The major accomplishments of the First Zionist Congress were organization of an official Zionist movement and establishment of a formal credo which was to become the foundation of Zionist nationalism and of the state of Israel. It stated that: "The aim of Zionism is to create for the Jewish People a home in Palestine secured by public law." To attain this objective, all Jewry would be organized, as in Herzl's

Jewish State, to promote the systematic settlement of Jewish farmers, artisans, and craftsmen in Palestine. Jewish consciousness and national identity were to be strengthened, and efforts made to raise the funds necessary to achieve Zionist objectives. A Zionist was thereafter officially defined as a dues-paying member of the organization who supported the Basle program.

Shortly after the congress, in late 1897, Herzl wrote in his diary:

> If I were to sum up the Basle Congress in one word—which I shall not do openly—it would be this: at Basle I founded the Jewish State. If I were to say this today, I would be met by universal laughter. In five years, perhaps, and certainly in fifty, everyone will see it. The State is already founded, in essence, in the will of the people of the State.

In 1902, Herzl persuaded the British government to offer Uganda for Jewish settlement. The offer nearly split the new movement between those inclined to accept any territory and those, mostly from Eastern Europe and with deep religious ties to the promised land, who would accept only Palestine. Because of his support for the Uganda project as a temporary shelter for the Jewish oppressed, Herzl, respected leader that he was, fell victim to the sharp disputes within the movement, although he remained its leader until his death in 1904. His greatest achievements, aside from publishing *The Jewish State,* were the Basle congress and its organization of Zionism into an effective and coherent political movement. Herzl is regarded as the founder of modern Jewish nationalism as expressed in the Zionist idea and as the father of modern Israel. His picture is still in Israeli government offices, schools, and public places; it adorns Israel's postage stamps and currency.

Herzl's *Jewish State* and the Basle congress planted the seeds from which have grown organizations and ideas which are still vital to the movement and to Israel. They include organizations for fund raising and mass recruitment; representative bodies such as the Knesset; and the concept of proportional representation in the Israeli electoral system and in the World Zionist Congresses.

After the Basle congress, Jewish nationalism in its Zionist form entered a new era. Jewish nationalism became identical with Zionism and to most Jews Zionism meant Herzlian Zionism as expressed in the Basle program. New leaders with a great variety of views about the Jewish state emerged inside the movement. In less than a decade, a wide range of viewpoints, representing diverse social, economic, and religious philosophies, developed. Some became distinct groups or parties. Others were merely philosophic trends unrepresented by any formal organization. Most are represented in Israel today either in political parties or in the country's intellectual and political journals. The common denominator of all Zionist parties and groups, whether religious, Socialist, radical, secular, militant, or moderate, is the Basle program conceived by Herzl in 1897.

Despite many controversies around and within the Zionist movement, it became the strongest unifying force among world Jewry. Until World War II, it had to compete with other Jewish movements such as the Jewish Socialist Bund *(Der Algemeyner Yiddischer Arbeter Bund)*, or the General Jewish Workers Union also established during 1897 in Eastern Europe. The Bund, strongly anti-Zionist until after the holocaust in Europe during World War II, emphasized Jewish working-class collaboration with other European Socialist movements. It underscored retention of Jewish culture, but with Yiddish rather than Hebrew as the basis. Other influential groups, like the American Jewish Committee, called themselves non-Zionist and were cool to the idea of Jewish nationalism. By the end of World War II, most organized opposition to Zionism and establishment of a Jewish state dissipated when the full dimensions of the holocaust became clear. Zionism's major strengths in overcoming opposition were the simplicity of its fundamental creed and the extent to which its followers could, within that creed, maintain a wide variety of interpretations.

Among the early divisions within Zionism were those between the cultural and the political Zionists. The "culturals" were less concerned about the establishment of a political entity than with revival of Hebrew identity. In the words of Ahad Ha'am, one of the cultural leaders, the crux of the problem was less "the need of the Jews" than "the need of Judaism."

Zionism's task was to devise new structures to contain the separate identity of the Jews. In Ha'am's view, the Jewish "national spirit" was more important than the God of Israel. Religion was merely an instrument to preserve Jewish national identity and the special role of the Jews in society. Jewish identity was to be expressed through revival of Hebrew as a modern tongue, and through the establishment of a Hebrew university where the finest of Hebrew culture in literary, scientific, humanistic, and other fields would be preserved and developed. Palestine was seen by the culturalists as the spiritual center of Jewish culture rather than as a political state.

Political Zionists emphasized the immediate need for a physical refuge for Jews, a territorial solution of the Jewish problem. A few were willing to accept any land where large numbers of Jews could be settled; but, for the overwhelming majority, only Palestine was acceptable, because of its centrality in Jewish consciousness. Herzl was the political Zionist par excellence. He conceived of a Jewish state with institutions including an army, parliament, constitution, and the other trappings of Western nations. Throughout his career, his driving ambition was to obtain a charter giving international recognition to Zionist claims. A handful of "territorialists" were so determined to attain a piece of exclusive Jewish national property that they severed relations with the Zionist movement when it rejected Great Britain's Uganda offer in 1903. They all but disappeared within a few years leaving only a few hundred followers.

Another group of Zionists stressed practical achievements in Palestine. Their emphasis was on developing sound economic and social institutions, and on "creating facts," in the form of new Jewish settlements, with expanding agriculture and industry, ports, roads, transportation and communication, and other aspects of a national infrastructure which would give viability and validity to Jewish identity in Palestine. In the words of Chaim Weizmann, Israel's first president, the goal was to create "absorptive capacity" for new Jewish immigrants on the land and in the cities. The "practicals" placed less emphasis on political achievements than on physical expansion of the Jewish presence in Palestine.

Still other trends developed, some shaped by political philosophies like Marxism and socialism, some by controversies between secularist and Orthodox Jews. One of the strongest movements was the Zionist labor movement which developed several political parties. Religious Jews, less strong than the Zionist Socialists, also formed their own parties.

As distinctive political parties emerged within the movement, different aspects of Zionism were stressed. Parties in the militant nationalist wing were more inclined to strive for realization of international political acceptance than on developing new settlements or expanding Jewish agriculture.

As the nationalist ideology solidified, a Zionist organizational apparatus developed along with other permanent institutions. At the apex was the World Zionist Congress, which met every year or two, depending on international circumstances. The congresses represented Zionist groups, national federations, and other subsidiary affiliates like political parties of religious, labor, or general Zionists; these meetings set the general outlines of policy. Dues-paying members could vote for representatives from their respective countries to the world congress. Most countries in Europe and the Americas had federations of Zionist groups affiliated with the world movement. The number of members expanded rapidly, from over 164,000 in 1907 to more than 2 million by the late 1960s.

Between congresses, affairs of the movement were carried out by an institutional bureaucracy and by subgroups such as an Actions Committee, later called the Zionist General Council, and its executive, first known as the Small Actions Committee. In accord with Herzl's blueprints, the Zionist organization established its own bank in 1899, called the Jewish Colonial Trust, and registered in England. It became an Israeli company in 1955. The Jewish National Fund was founded at the Fifth Zionist Congress in 1901 to acquire, develop, and afforest land in Palestine. A substantial part of its funds were collected in small contributions from world Jewry in blue and white boxes, later a common feature in Jewish homes and synagogues. Herzl and his associates also founded a newspaper in 1899, *Die Welt*, which became the movement's official organ.

Since its inception, the Zionist movement and its organizations have been international in character, representing Jews from dozens of different countries, with headquarters and offices in several places. Although the focus of Zionism was on establishment of a Jewish home in Palestine, its presence in that country was hardly more than token during the first twenty years. Zionism's leaders and followers, its headquarters and offices, and the greater part of its activities were not in Palestine but in the countries of the diaspora. Few Zionists visited Palestine until after World War I, and thus their conceptions of the country and its indigenous inhabitants were often highly romanticized if not inaccurate.

Herzl dominated the Zionist congresses and the interim administrative and political activities of the organization until he died. Zionist headquarters were in Vienna, where Herzl lived. After his death, they were transferred to Cologne, the residence of his successor from 1905 to 1911, David Wolffsohn. With the next president, Otto Warburg, head of the organization between 1911 and 1920, Berlin became the center. During World War I, the movement was divided, and an Allied branch with offices in London was set up. A liaison office was organized during 1915 in neutral Copenhagen to facilitate contact across the battle lines. During the presidencies of Chaim Weizmann and Nahum Sokolow, spanning the years from 1920 to 1946, London became the capital of world Zionism. In 1936, many activities of the organization were transferred to Jerusalem, although the presidential organization and several members of the executive remained in London.

While great activity and large membership were generated in Europe and America during the first twenty years of Zionism, the situation in the Middle East was different. There was still no political entity called Palestine. It was merely a vague geographic term indicating the area where the ancient Philistines and later the Jews had lived. The largely Arab population were not yet known as Palestinians, but referred to themselves as Syrians. After the Ottoman conquest in 1517, the land had been divided and redivided among several provinces until, in 1864, it was partitioned between the two Ottoman *vilayets* ("provinces") of Beirut and Syria and the smaller *sanjak* ("administrative subdivision") of Jerusalem. Its special status was guaranteed by the European Christian powers after their intervention to protect Christians in the Levant during the 1860s.

Despite Herzl's fervent pleas to the sultan, the Ottoman authorities were reluctant to grant any special political consideration to Jewish settlers. They were suspicious of Zionist connections with the Western powers and feared any further European intervention in their already disintegrating empire. When the Turks did intervene, it was not to the advantage of the new Jewish settlers, who were perceived by the indigenous Arabs as infidel intruders.

Jewish presence in Palestine had continued since the Roman dispersion, although the number of Jews had greatly declined. When Napoleon invaded the area early in the nineteenth century, there were only 5,000 Jews. By mid-century the number had doubled, and it doubled again by the 1880s, when the first Zionist settlers arrived. Between 1882 and 1914, the number grew from 24,000 to 85,000, most of whom were pious elderly Jews who had come to die in the Holy Land. By 1914, some 12,000 Jews lived in one or another of the forty-four Zionist agricultural settlements. Most Jewish residents of the country were protected by various European powers. Only 10 percent were Ottoman subjects.

The 600,000 Christian and Muslim Arab inhabitants had not yet developed a strong nationalist sentiment. Ethnic identity was based on religious affiliation to Islam, Judaism, or one of the many Christian bodies recognized as a *millet* ("national community") by the Ottoman authorities. Arab nationalism as an organized movement was not a significant political factor until World War I. There was little Ottoman intervention in the lives of most Arab villagers and practically none among the roaming Bedouin in the south and along the edges of the cultivated areas. Periodic Bedouin raids on both Arab and Jewish villages met little response from the Ottoman authorities.

Contacts between Jews and local Arabs were rare. Few of the early Zionist leaders recognized the significance of Arab-Jewish relations. Instead, they concentrated on contacts with the European powers who they believed would further their goals. After Herzl's visit to Palestine, there was barely any mention of the Arab population in his diary or written reports.

Because a large number of Jewish settlers were Russians or citizens of other Allied powers at war with Turkey, many were deported, imprisoned, or executed during World War I. The Zionist movement was charged with subversion and intent to dismember the Ottoman Empire. Institutions like the Jewish Colonial Trust and Anglo-Palestine Bank were banned, and public use of Hebrew was forbidden. Natural disasters including drought, a locust plague, and famine added to the miseries of the populace. By the time General Edmund Allenby, commander of British forces in the area, entered Jerusalem in 1917, the total population in Palestine had diminished by nearly one-fifth and the Jewish population by about one-third to only 55,000.

THE BALFOUR DECLARATION

In the international political arena, the war was the occasion for spectacular Zionist advances. Despite division of the movement into Allied, Central Power, and neutral camps, it achieved the recognition Herzl had striven for but never acquired. Both Germans and Britons sought the support of their own Jewish communities and those on the other side through statements recognizing Zionist aspirations. Jewish leaders in Allied capitals pressed their claims to Palestine by organizing special Jewish units to assist the war effort. Joseph Trumpeldor gathered 900 men into the Zion Mule Corps, which served with the British in Gallipoli against the Turks. Another Russian Zionist, Vladimir Jabotinsky, later to become leader of the nationalistic wing, headed a campaign to create a Jewish legion. Although never organized on the scale conceived by Jabotinsky, two battalions of Jewish volunteers from Russia, England, and America were formed as the Judeans and attached to Allenby's forces. Another volunteer battalion brought Jewish strength among the British forces in Palestine to about 5,000.

The major political efforts were made in Great Britain and the United States, where Zionism won official approval. Dr. Chaim Weizmann, a Russian-born chemistry lecturer at Manchester University, became the focus of these activities. After settling in England and becoming a British subject, he became an active leader in the Zionist movement. As a young man he attended the Basle conference, and he remained active in the Zionist organization. Next to Herzl, Weizmann is probably the individual most associated with the establishment of modern Israel.

Among his scientific accomplishments was development of a process to produce acetone, an essential ingredient for manufacturing the cordite required in British artillery shells during World War I. Weizmann's scientific work brought him into close contact with high-level British officials whom he persuaded to support Zionism.

After months of lengthy discussions, and despite divisions in the British cabinet and in the Jewish community, a compromise formula was reached in which Great Britain officially recognized and supported Jewish aspirations in Palestine. Some cabinet members were reluctant to adopt this stance because of fears that support for Zionism would alienate Arabs and Muslims in the Middle East and elsewhere in the British Empire. Non-Zionist Jewish leaders were apprehensive about repercussions on their identity as loyal British subjects. But expectations that support for Zionism would win large Jewish support finally led to the Balfour Declaration, published on November 2, 1917.

It was a watered-down version of what Weizmann and his colleagues desired. Its wording was sufficiently vague to become the subject of numerous future debates. The declaration took the form of a public letter from Lord Alfred Balfour, British foreign minister, to Lord Rothschild, a prominent British Zionist leader. It stated that

His Majesty's Government view with favour the establishment in Palestine of a national home for the Jewish people, and will use their best endeavours to facilitate the achievement of that object, it being clearly understood that nothing shall be done

which may prejudice the civil and religious rights of the
existing non-Jewish communities in Palestine, or the rights and
political status enjoyed by Jews in any other country.

In deference to non-Zionists, wording of the declaration was
changed to call for establishment of "a national home" in
Palestine rather than *"the* national home of the Jewish
people." The existing communities in Palestine, as well as
Jewish rights in the diaspora, were to be safeguarded.

The British Information Ministry created a special Jewish
department to follow through. It prepared leaflets containing
the Balfour Declaration to drop over enemy territory, and
spread word about it both in Eastern Europe and in the United
States, where Jewish sentiment was strongly antipathetic to
tsarist Russia, Great Britain's ally until the 1917 revolution. If
an alliance could be contracted with a variety of Jewish interest
groups, it might strengthen the pro-Allies sentiment of many
influential Jews and weaken those opposed to the war. Some
British officials even hoped to win German Jewish support.

In other statements, agreements, and contractual arrangements with France and Arab nationalist leaders, Great Britain
made a variety of promises about the future of the Ottoman
Empire after an Allied victory. Some British leaders asserted
that the diverse promises could be reconciled, while to many
they seemed to conflict.

Conflicting or not, British involvements in the Middle East
became even more complicated after General Allenby's
conquest of Palestine. Zionist leaders demanded and received
from London permission for a Zionist Commission of Jews
from Allied countries to visit the occupied areas. At the same
time, the Arabs were beginning to ask embarrassing questions
about Jewish activities.

The Zionist Commission was the first official activity of the
Zionist movement undertaken in Palestine with international
recognition. Established as an advisory body to the British
occupation forces, it was to represent both Palestinian and
world Jewish concerns. From the beginning, the commission
was at odds with British officials. The latter saw their primary
responsibility as the maintenance of a politically stable

environment in which British interests could flourish. The Zionists believed that Great Britain was obligated to implement the Balfour Declaration, with its emphasis on development of the Jewish national home.

Following an interruption during the war, meetings of the World Zionist Congress were resumed in 1921, and functions of the Zionist Commission were absorbed by the Zionist executive of the congress. Major decisions for the Jewish community in Palestine, the Yishuv, as well as for the world Zionist movement, continued to be made at European headquarters by leaders like Weizmann who were resident in Europe. The Yishuv was viewed as the "vanguard of world Jewry," laying the groundwork for the Jewish state which in the future would hopefully absorb most of the world's Jews. According to Zionist dogma, Jews in the diaspora were obliged to back the national home with financial and political support.

Locally, the Yishuv attempted to organize its own representative bodies. After the British took Jerusalem in 1917, the Jews, a majority of the city's population, set up a city council. Later a countrywide provisional council was organized to prepare the way for an elected Jewish constituent assembly; however, it was blocked by the British authorities as premature. By 1918, when the rest of Palestine was captured from the Turks, a national conference representing several Jewish settlements chose Weizmann and his Russian Zionist colleague, Nahum Sokolow, to represent them at the Paris peace talks. However, not until British military authorities turned the country over to civil rule in 1920, was there a Jewish constituent assembly formally recognized.

By the end of World War I, Dr. Weizmann had become the real successor to Theodor Herzl as the world Zionist leader. Although he still lived in England, the Yishuv and Zionist Congress called upon him to negotiate the future of Palestine with Great Britain and Arab nationalists. Through British intercession, Weizmann conducted several parleys with the new King Faisal of Syria to mollify growing Arab concerns about his plans for Palestine. At meetings in London and Aqaba in southern Palestine, Faisal recognized the Balfour Declaration, and the need for cooperation with the Zionists, and he encouraged Jewish immigration provided it did not jeopardize Arab rights. In return, Weizmann promised Jewish economic and technical assistance in development of an Arab state. Both agreed that the British would arbitrate disputes. In a caveat to their written protocol, Faisal insisted that if Arab nationalist aspirations were not fully realized, he would "not then be bound by a single word of the present Agreement which shall be deemed void and of no account or validity, and I shall not be answerable in any way whatsoever." This appended clause was later cited by Arab nationalists as justification for breaking the agreement. They argued that the French conquest of Syria and the fall of Faisal invalidated the pact with Weizmann.

At Paris, it soon became evident that Faisal did not represent an Arab consensus concerning Palestine. Syrian nationalists warned that Palestine was incontestably part of their country. Jews would be permitted to settle in an autonomous Palestine, but they would be tied by a bond of federation with Syria. By 1918, nationalism was also stirring Palestinian Arab consciousness. Sparked by repressive Ottoman war measures and Allied promises of self-determination, associations of Christian and Muslim notables were formed during 1919 and 1920 in several Palestinian towns. They were sent to the nationalist congresses in Damascus to introduce anti-Zionist platforms. During this era, most Arabs in the 850 villages of the country did not yet consider themselves Palestinian, but saw themselves as part of the new Syrian Arab kingdom.

Zionist leaders urged the Paris peace conferees to turn Palestine over to the newly created League of Nations. The international community, they argued, was obligated to consult world Jewry concerning the future of Palestine, and to support its establishment as an autonomous Jewish commonwealth. In return, they promised full religious freedom to Muslims and Christians and protection of sites sacred to all religions.

Palestine's immediate fate was determined by neither Zionists nor Arab nationalists. British and French negotiations over their respective imperial interests in the Middle East were decisive. New Palestinian borders were the result of compromises based on demands by France in the north and promises to Arab nationalists in the south. Since there was no previous international frontier defining Palestine, the British felt free during 1921 to subdivide their area into Transjordan and Western Palestine.

Transjordan was turned over to Faisal's brother, Abdullah, as a reward for services rendered during the war. Faisal was compensated for loss of Syria to the French with the new kingdom of Iraq. Transjordan and Palestine were both governed by a single British high commissioner under the Colonial Office after the military occupation, but the east bank was excluded from commitments related to establishment of a Jewish national home. This unilateral British separation of Palestine from Transjordan raised no strong protests among mainstream Zionist leaders, for there were no Jewish settlers on the East Bank. However, more militant nationalists, especially Jabotinsky's followers, strenuously protested the division of the country into the East and West Banks. Their objections later became the basis for a new Zionist political party of Revisionists, whose chief raison d'etre was revision of Palestine's borders to include both the East and West Banks of the Jordan River.

THE MANDATE FOR PALESTINE

After Great Britain and France agreed on the frontiers of Palestine at the San Remo Conference in 1920, Palestine received its first civilian high commissioner, Sir Herbert Samuel, an English Jew who was a leader of the Liberal party and an avowed Zionist. He had played a significant role in framing the Balfour Declaration and was at first considered sympathetic to development of the Jewish home. Zionists were enthusiastic about his appointment, believing that he would carry out mandatory policies favorable to them.

While administered by Great Britain, the Mandate for Palestine was, according to international law, the ultimate responsibility of the League of Nations. The mandate system established by the League was intended to avoid quarrels over colonial territory conquered by the Allies, and to replace imperialism with a more enlightened policy. Each of the Allied victors entrusted with former German colonies or pieces of the Ottoman Empire was to assist those countries in developing self-governing institutions leading to eventual independence. In the Middle East, France was entrusted with Syria and Lebanon, while Great Britain received Iraq, Transjordan, and Palestine.

The Mandate for Palestine was unique because it gave special recognition to Zionist claims. Throughout the document, emphasis was on rights and privileges of the Jewish community. The preamble incorporated the Balfour Declaration verbatim. There was no specific reference to the country's Arab population by name. Instead they were called "the inhabitants of Palestine." While Great Britain was vested with "full powers of legislation and administration," special emphasis was placed on British responsibility "for placing the country under such political, administrative and economic conditions as will secure the establishment of the Jewish national home. . . ." Local autonomy was to be encouraged "so far as circumstances permit. . . ."

The Mandate formally recognized the Zionist movement. The Zionist organization was declared the appropriate Jewish agency in matters affecting establishment of the national home and the interests of the Jewish population in Palestine. Outside Palestine, the Zionist organization was authorized to take steps "to secure the cooperation of all Jews who are willing to assist in establishment of the Jewish national home."

Among the tasks assigned Great Britain were to "facilitate Jewish immigration . . . and encourage, in cooperation with the Jewish agency [Zionist organization] . . . close settlement by Jews on the land, including State lands and waste lands not required for public purposes." The nationality law was to include "provisions framed so as to facilitate the acquisition of Palestinian citizenship by Jews who take up their permanent residence in Palestine." Hebrew, English, and Arabic were recognized as the official languages: "Any statement or inscription in Arabic on stamps or money in Palestine shall be repeated in Hebrew and any statements or inscriptions in Hebrew shall be repeated in Arabic."

Requirements protecting the civil and religious rights of "existing non-Jewish communities in Palestine," as stated in the Balfour Declaration, were reemphasized in the Mandate. Respect for the religious practices "of the various peoples and communities" in Palestine was to be guaranteed. Foreign relations were entrusted to control of the mandatory authority, as was protection of Palestinian citizens when abroad. In all matters of responsibility related to the "Holy Places and religious buildings or sites in Palestine, including that of preserving existing rights and of securing free access to the Holy Places, religious buildings and sites and the free exercise of worship," the mandatory authority "shall be responsible solely to the League of Nations. . . . " A special commission was to be appointed by the mandatory authority "to study, define and determine the rights and claims in connection with the Holy Places and the rights and claims relating to the different religious communities in Palestine." Freedom of worship and conscience were guaranteed. "No discrimination of any kind shall be made between the inhabitants of Palestine on the ground of race, religion or language. No person shall be excluded from Palestine on the sole ground of his belief."

The Mandate for Palestine was sufficiently vague to stimulate years of controversy over its intent. Zionists insisted that it obligated Great Britain to further development of their commonwealth with all due haste. Arab nationalists protested that, if not an outright violation of the League of Nations covenant guaranteeing their independence, the Mandate was discriminatory because it emphasized Jewish rights and failed to even mention Arab rights. Furthermore, they argued, it could not be carried out evenhandedly because of internal inconsistencies. On the one hand, the Mandate prohibited discrimination against any group in Palestine, yet it clearly guaranteed certain economic and political advantages to the Jewish community.

The British, caught on the horns of this dilemma, improvised a wide range of devices to reconcile their policies with the demands imposed by both Arabs and Jews. The fact that there were three tiers of responsibility for administration of the Mandate added to diffusion of responsibility and lack of clarity about final authority. British colonial administrators at the local level in Palestine often differed with each other in carrying out their tasks. Some were sympathetic to Jewish aspirations; others favored the Arabs. Both groups frequently were at odds with or received unclear signals from London, where officials in the Colonial Office or the military frequently differed with the policies laid out by Parliament. Finally, the British government, ultimately responsible to the Permanent Mandates Commission of the League of Nations, was determined to devise policies in Palestine consistent with its larger imperial interests in the Middle East.

Throughout the mandatory era, Palestine was run like a British crown colony. The high commissioner, appointed by the British crown, had all the power and authority of a colonial governor or viceroy in India. He was responsible only to London, not to the population of Palestine or to any world Jewish organization. Authority delegated by him through his staff or executive council of mostly British officials was also legally unchallenged. District commissioners ruled the three principal subdivisions of the country; they too were British. After Herbert Samuel there were six more high commissioners, nearly all generals who had served in other colonial posts.

Of the 10,000 or so employees in the Palestinian civil service, apart from the police, only about 250 were British. By the end of the Mandate, about one-third of the civil service was Jewish and two-thirds Arab, although proportions varied from department to department. While major decisions were made by high-ranking British officials, the day-to-day implementation was carried out by Palestinian Jews and Arabs. At first, all the district officers responsible to the three district commissioners were also British, but later several were chosen from the local Arab and Jewish populations.

The legal basis of British authority was the 1922 Palestine Order in Council passed by Parliament in London. In effect it was Palestine's constitution during the mandatory era, supplemented by laws published in the *Palestine Official Gazette*. This legislation, mostly based on English law, pertained to administration, crime, commerce, labor, and other such matters. Other legislation pertaining to land and personal status was taken over bodily by the British administration from the Ottoman rulers.

Ottoman law relating to personal status matters including marriage, divorce, inheritance, and provision for orphans, was continued under the British administration. It assigned jurisdiction in these affairs to the recognized Jewish, Muslim, and Christian religious courts. The British, reluctant to surrender their political authority, recognized the communities in Palestine as religious rather than political entities. Under the Religious Communities Organization Ordinance, Muslims, Jews, and Christians were identified with their respective religious communities. Land law was also borrowed from the Ottomans; thus various categories of property, and their use, taxation, and inheritance, were prescribed according to Ottoman tradition.

Under the Mandate there was major progress in development of the country. New roads and railways extended the communications network and linked many formerly isolated regions of the country. Health and educational facilities were expanded by the British in the Arab sector, and by the institutions of the Yishuv among the Jews. Agricultural and industrial productivity increased substantially in both sectors. Zionist leaders claimed credit not only for growth of the Yishuv but for development of the rest of the country. The British credited their own administration. Arab nationalists discounted any advance, asserting that the country could have achieved far greater progress had it been independent. Less·important than the statistical evidence were the perceptions of each group. These self-images were a major factor in creating separate national identities and driving the ethnic groups apart.

The mandatory government's efforts to create self-governing institutions were defeated by the conflicting objectives of the three major communities. At stake were the Yishuv's Zionist nationalism, the Arab fear of the Yishuv and escalating demands for self-determination, and British efforts to balance their obligations to both Jews and Arabs with their own imperial concerns.

Initially, Sir Herbert Samuel formed an advisory council of

British officials, Palestinian Jews, and Arabs. It was to have been replaced by an elected legislative council that was stillborn. Until 1936 there were several more efforts to form a legislative council, all aborted by differences between Jews and Arabs. In the earlier proposals for local representation, the Jews would have been outvoted. Arab nationalists, nevertheless, charged that because they were the majority, they were underrepresented. The most militant refused to recognize any British authority. Consequently there was little local input into major government decisions. Most were taken by the high commissioner and his staff, restricted only by directives from London, or by popular outbursts.

THE YISHUV IN PALESTINE

Within this system, the Yishuv was able to lay the foundations of the future Jewish state, to establish its presence in Palestine as a viable and powerful entity, and to achieve national recognition from Jewish communities abroad and from the Western world as a whole. The various factions within the Zionist movement continued their ideological disputes during the Mandate, but all made progress. The "politicals" achieved the international recognition for a Jewish national identity that Herzl had struggled for. The "practicals" saw expansion of the Yishuv from a tiny minority of the population and development of a Jewish economic infrastructure with its own agriculture, industry, trade, and commerce. The number of Jewish settlements increased tenfold. "Cultural" Zionists could boast that the Hebrew language had taken root, the number of newspapers and publishing houses had multiplied, and an educational system capped by the Hebrew University in Jerusalem had developed.

By the end of the Mandate, the Jewish population had increased, largely through immigration, from 65,000 in 1919 to about 650,000 in 1948. Territorially the Yishuv still occupied less than 10 percent of Palestine. By far the largest areas were lands belonging to the government, including nearly the whole southern half of the country, called the Negev.

The majority of the Yishuv were Eastern European Jewish

immigrants, mostly from Poland and Russia, although smaller groups came from Rumania, Bulgaria, and Hungary. There were also a few Middle Eastern immigrants, mainly from Yemen. After Hitler's rise, a new wave of refugees arrived from Germany and Austria. In 1948, more than two-thirds of the Jewish population were recent immigrants, who had come since 1919. Of these, 90 percent were European. Immigration was caused by the push of anti-Semitism in Poland after World War I, and from Nazi-ruled areas after 1933; and by deteriorating economic conditions in Central Europe. During the interwar period, most Jewish migration still flowed westward toward the United States and Western Europe. Despite development of the Yishuv, life in Palestine was still difficult and political unrest there caused frequent "troubles" or "disturbances," as the British called the strife with Jews and Arabs.

The Yishuv referred to the successive waves of migration as *aliya* ("ascent"), since the arrivals were "going up" to the Holy Land. An immigrant was called an *oleh*, and the five successive waves of migration before 1948 were *aliyot*. The first *aliya* consisted of small groups of Bilu from Russia who founded the early Jewish colonies during the 1880s and other Jewish settlers before 1905. In July 1882, fourteen Biluim arrived in Jaffa to start the process. By 1903, the Bilu had established a score of new settlements and brought some 10,000 Jews to Palestine. Only half became farmers. The others began new Jewish urban settlements, notably in Jaffa, where there were 3,000 settlers.

Failure of the 1905 Russian revolution caused a somewhat larger *aliya* of young workers and Socialist Zionists. They placed more emphasis on realization of Zionist-Socialist goals, especially the use of Jewish labor on Jewish land. This contrasted with the Bilu, who often followed the traditional colonial pattern of using local Arabs to farm their fields. Many of Israel's founders, including the first prime minister, David Ben-Gurion, were from the second *aliya*. They played a major role in establishment of the original collective agricultural settlements *(kibbutzim)*, which symbolized Zionist activity in the country.

The third *aliya*, between 1919 and 1923, came from Poland

and other Eastern and Central European nations where economic pressures on the lower-middle-class Jewish communities and increased anti-Semitism made life difficult. Ideologically akin to settlers in the second *aliya,* many became active in formation of labor organizations, and in providing *halutzim* ("pioneers") in agriculture and in the new industries being formed by the Yishuv. About 35,000 came during this period.

Larger numbers, about half from Poland, came in the fourth *aliya.* Many had been impoverished by economic crisis and discriminatory measures clamped on Jews by Poland's finance minister, Wladyslaw Grabski. Some called the fourth *aliya* the Grabski *Aliya* because of his role in driving Jews from Poland. America's policy of a closed door to large-scale immigration began after 1925, turning many Jews toward Palestine. A larger number of immigrants from the fourth *aliya* possessed capital which they invested in small businesses in Palestine. Between 1926 and 1929, Palestine passed through a severe economic crisis, resulting in departure of thousands of the new Jewish immigrants known as *yoredim* ("descenders," in contrast to *olim).* By 1927 there were nearly twice as many *yoredim* as *olim* and a net decline in the Jewish population.

There was no really sizeable immigration again until Hitler's rise to power in 1933 precipitated the fifth and largest *aliya.* Between 1933 and 1936, 164,000 Jews immigrated to Palestine. Nazi persecution changed both the demography and the outlook of the Yishuv.

Until the arrival of middle-class German Jews, the Yishuv was a fairly homogeneous community. There were no large class differences and no great diversity in social structure. Jewish immigration during the previous half century had come largely from an area of only a few hundred square miles in Eastern Europe. A kind of frontier camaraderie existed in which Jews addressed each other as *haver* ("comrade"). Scorn for formality was epitomized by calling the necktie a herring *(dag maluah).* Standard male dress was khaki shorts and open-necked work shirts. The work ethic, with emphasis on agriculture, was dominant, although the Jewish population was concentrated in three large cities, Tel Aviv, Jerusalem, and Haifa.

With a total population smaller than that of many European cities, the Yishuv of the 1920s and 1930s had much of the atmosphere of a town. In this small, closely knit community it was easy to develop a strong spirit of national identity. Furthermore, the community was separated from the non-Jewish population by its economic and social life. In Arab and Jewish communities alike, the average individual grew up with little outside contact. Jews were born in and used Jewish hospitals, studied in Jewish schools, and attended the Hebrew University. Social activity revolved around Zionist youth clubs or Jewish scout groups. Work was in Jewish business, trade, or public enterprise. Jews were employed in Jewish factories with Jewish bosses and a Jewish trade union organization, the Histadrut. Finally, they were buried in Jewish cemeteries.

Education played an important role in developing national consciousness. A British royal commission observed in 1936 that there emerged from the education melting pot a national self-consciousness of unusual intensity. Jewish educational institutions, from preschool to university, were conducted in the Hebrew language, fostering development of strong cultural identity and institutions.

With the fifth *aliya* and arrival of many professionals from Germany, the demographic and class structure of the Yishuv was altered. Among the arrivals from Central Europe were a high percentage of physicians, engineers, musicians, and Ph.D.s with diverse skills. The distinctively middle-class, liberal, Western European viewpoints of the German Jews helped to broaden the perspectives and outlooks of the Yishuv. The German settlers with new ideas, organizational and managerial skills, began to temper the largely Eastern European Jewish community. Most Germans were more closely identified with the mainstream of traditional European culture than were the immigrants from Russia and Poland. Among the notable cultural contributions of the Germans was development of the new Philharmonic, which became one of the most acclaimed orchestras in the world. Their distinctive German accent provided nuances to the Hebrew language, and their German customs identified them as a distinct national group. The expression *yeke* (a contraction from "jacket") was applied to German Jews because of their frequent formal attire and manners. Politically, the Germans and Central Europeans strengthened the non-Socialist liberal political orientation of the Yishuv through establishment of the New Immigrant *(Aliya Hadasha)* party, a forerunner of the present Independent Liberal movement.

During the Mandate, about 45,000 non-European or non-Western Jews came to Palestine, constituting just over 10 percent of the migrants. Many were from the ancient community in Yemen where Jews lived before the rise of Islam. Known as excellent craftsmen and arduous laborers, they did little to influence the mainstream of cultural and political development. Although the number of Eastern or Sephardic Jews was small, it was large enough to start the debate between Western and Oriental Jews that still continues. By the end of the Mandate, the 650,000-member Yishuv was definitely European in composition, outlook, and social orientation.

Under the Mandate, Jewish communal institutions established before World War I, and a variety of new ones, flourished. The most important local representative body was the National Council *(Vaad Leumi)* of between 23 and 42 members, established in 1920 under British mandatory regulations authorizing each religious community to organize its own institutions, a policy the British adapted from the Ottoman era. The council was chosen by the Elected Assembly *(Asafat ha-Nivharim)*, which consisted of between 170 and 300 representatives elected nationally by Knesset Israel, the organized Yishuv. Under mandatory regulations, membership in Knesset Israel was voluntary. Only a small number of Orthodox zealots of the anti-Zionist Aguda Israel movement opted out. To exclude oneself from the Yishuv was in effect to be cut off from community activities and services such as education, social welfare, and even normal social life.

Nearly every member of the Yishuv belonged to some organized group within the official Israeli community. There were myriad youth groups, sports organizations, labor activities, social welfare services, and political parties. Most were connected to one or another of the Zionist political parties that were part of the world movement.

The party system was unique because there were so many

parties, and because of party ties with related Zionist groups in the world movement. Parties were both national, because they were represented in the National Council, and international, by virtue of representation in the World Zionist Organization and Congress. Some Zionist parties had their headquarters abroad, some in Palestine. Most had branches in many countries, including the United States and Great Britain. Many were members of international federations or confederations; others maintained only loose ties with their associates abroad.

Rather than representing separate geographic districts in Palestine, party candidates were elected by the whole Yishuv in a system of proportional representation. When casting a ballot, the voter chose a list of candidates representing a party, not individual candidates. Party leaders determined who would be on the ballot. When all returns were in, the number of votes required to elect a candidate was obtained by dividing the total number of valid ballots cast by the number of offices to be filled. Replacements between elections were chosen by the party rather than in by-elections.

Because of the great variety of political views in the Yishuv and the world Zionist movement, representing many shades of opinion from various parts of Europe, this system of strict proportional representation produced an unusually large number of parties. By 1936, there were ten main parties, each uniting two or more subgroups. At the end of the Mandate, the total number was nearly three dozen. The main trends were then and still are: labor, centrist or bourgeois, Orthodox Jewish, and national rightist. The strongest trend was Socialist, with the labor movement in control of most political institutions like the National Council. Its base was the Histadrut, or General Federation of Jewish Workers in Palestine. It controlled the agricultural sector, the *kibbutzim*, or collective settlements, and the largest labor unions in the industrial sector. As its strength expanded, it developed its own industries, marketing cooperatives, transportation systems, banks and financial institutions, and social-service network. Most leaders of the Yishuv came from the labor movement and its affiliated institutions.

Real power in the community was wielded by the National

Council executive, a group of six to fourteen leaders who headed departments organized much like a cabinet, including education, health, social welfare, and political affairs. The council even organized the clandestine recruitment and military training of Jewish youth in the Haganah ("Defense"), later to become the basis for Israel's national security forces. By 1936 there were about 10,000 well-trained and relatively well-equipped Haganah members. Some of its components were organized with British assistance during the Arab revolt against the Mandate between 1936 and 1939.

Deliberations of the National Council, its executive, and diverse operational or cabinet departments reflected the major issues of the day inside the small Jewish community. Relative homogeneity and a large measure of social equality notwithstanding, there were many controversial questions during the quarter century of prestate political existence. While the great majority favored obligatory membership in the Yishuv because of its small numbers, some dissidents wanted membership to be voluntary. The small Communist movement opposed direction by the "bourgeois" National Council. Was the nature of identity in the community to be personal or territorial; that is, would membership automatically include all who lived within the boundaries of the Jewish community? Should the growing numbers of local settlements, *kibbutzim* and *moshavim*, and the new towns have greater authority, or should control be centralized in the National Council? What was to be the position of women in this largely egalitarian society? Debates over such issues continued after the state was established, and some have yet to be resolved.

One of the most strenuous debates was over the role of religion. The Zionist religious parties placed strong emphasis on the Jewish content of the Zionist movement, while, at the other end of the political spectrum, Marxist Zionists perceived class struggle and rights of Jewish workers as elemental. Zionist Socialists advocated establishment of a welfare system, a planned economy, and greater equalization in society, in contrast to non-Socialists, who believed that a major responsibility of the Yishuv was to concentrate on economic expansion by encouraging private investment in agriculture and industry.

Zionist interests abroad were sustained and developed through the World Zionist Organization and Jewish Agency for Palestine. When Israel was established, the Zionist organization and its institutions had become a far-reaching network with branches in some fifty nations and approximately a million members. The Zionist executive established its seat in Jerusalem by the late 1930s, with departments handling immigration and absorption, youth and immigration, education and culture, settlement, and information. These departments supplemented the local activities of the National Council, for which the Yishuv was responsible.

To rally support of non-Zionist Jews in building the national home, Zionist President Chaim Weizmann urged the movement to establish the Jewish Agency for Palestine in 1929. The agency was established on the principle of parity between Zionists and non-Zionist Jews, who supported building a national home without accepting political aspirations of the movement (i.e. establishment of a Jewish state). The Jewish Agency assumed the activities of building the national home in which all Jews, even non-Zionists, could participate. It conducted negotiations with the Palestinian mandatory government, with Great Britain, and with the League of Nations. However, its attempts to negotiate with Arab leaders were unsuccessful. The most important offices of the Jewish Agency, including its presidency and heads of political, finance, labor, trade, industry, and statistical departments, were held by Zionists. Only those offices concerned with agricultural settlement and the problems of German Jewish immigration were directed by non-Zionists. Both Zionists and non-Zionists shared direction of the important immigration department, whose task was to determine which Jews could come to Palestine within the strict quota system laid down by Great Britain.

With growth of the Yishuv, its leaders attained positions of increasing influence in the World Zionist Organization and in the Jewish Agency. By the 1930s, most affairs of importance concerning the Jewish national home were directed by Jews from Palestine. Differences between Zionists and non-Zionists gradually disappeared. In 1947, after resignation of the last non-Zionist, the Jewish Agency and World Zionist Organization were merged. Participation in the National Council, the World Zionist Organization, and the Jewish Agency gave hundreds of Palestinian Jews experience in the theoretical and practical problems of statecraft. It also helped create the cadre for the extensive civil service that was to become part of the new Israeli government in 1948.

Israel's first four prime ministers, most of its cabinet members during the first generation, and a large number of its top officials, party leaders, and members of parliament received their experience in the politics of the prestate Yishuv and in the Zionist movement.

Only at the peripheries of society and in the mixed cities like Haifa and Jerusalem was there any extensive contact between Jews and non-Jews. More often than not, contacts with Arabs or British officials were business rather than social occasions. Language also divided the groups from each other. Hebrew was the chief means of communication in Jewish educational and cultural life. Yiddish was considered the language of the diaspora, and its use was discouraged for public purposes, although it continued as the home tongue of many Eastern European families. With thousands of Jews working for the British mandatory government, English became the second language for many. Only a handful of Jews knew more than a few words of Arabic. A parallel situation prevailed in the Arab community, where English, not Hebrew became the second language.

A major characteristic of this system of Jewish political and social organization was its isolation from non-Jewish life. Under British rule, the Palestinian Arabs also organized their own separate and distinctive communal establishments, although the Arabs were not as well financed, cohesive, or closely knit as the Yishuv. By the end of the Mandate, the Arab two-thirds of the population were more spread out geographically and more divided politically and socially than the Yishuv. However, the regional class, religious, and familial or clan differences within Arab society did not prevent it from uniting in its opposition to Jewish immigration and settlement in Palestine. The country's history during the Mandate was one of strife and dissension between Jews and Arabs, and between each of them and the British mandatory government.

Each community perceived the other as a threat to its existence and to its national aspirations. Both Arabs and Jews in Palestine also perceived the British as antagonistic to their respective goals.

FROM MANDATE TO JEWISH STATE

At the end of World War II, several factors converged to end the British Mandate in Palestine, leading to establishment of the Israeli republic. Most powerful was the wartime experience of European Jewry. After the outbreak of World War II in 1939, anti-Semitism in Hitler's Germany became increasingly virulent. Nazi policy changed from persecution to outright liquidation of Jews. Hitler's goal was no longer merely to uproot, but to totally exterminate them. The result was the Holocaust, in which 6 million Jews were slaughtered, or about 90 percent of the Jews in German-controlled Europe and about one-third of the world's Jews. Had the war continued beyond 1946, Hitler may well have achieved his goal of totally destroying all Jews in Europe.

When the first word leaked out about the death camps, most Westerners, including many Jews, received it with disbelief. By the end of the war, the truth of these rumors was all too apparent. The Holocaust intensified Jewish nationalistic fervor and galvanized most organized Jewish communities behind Zionist demands for a Jewish state in Palestine. Competing Jewish nationalist ideologies such as the Bund lost most of their supporters. Most opponents of Jewish nationalism abandoned their opposition, and lukewarm supporters or those who had been indifferent rallied to support the Jewish state. Influential non-Zionist Jewish organizations in the West, like the American Jewish Committee, not only abandoned their opposition but actively supported creation of Israel.

Within the Zionist movement, the trend was toward more militant activism. Organizational aims were sharpened and focused on the immediate needs of European Jewry. At an emergency meeting held in the Biltmore Hotel in New York during May 1942, the Biltmore Program was adopted; it became the basis of mainstream Zionism until the establishment of Israel in 1948. It urged "that the gates of Palestine be opened; that the Jewish Agency be vested with control of immigration into Palestine . . . and that Palestine be established as a Jewish Commonwealth integrated in the structure of the new democratic world. . . . "

In the face of conflicting promises and responsibilities, British power and prestige declined precipitously. Plagued by war weariness and financial pressures, Great Britain began to withdraw from its most troublesome and expensive imperial outposts. India, Pakistan, Burma, and Ceylon became independent. In the Middle East, British control in Egypt, Iraq, and Transjordan was loosened. There was also great pressure in England to give up the Mandate in Palestine. Intensification of Jewish nationalism and demands that restrictions on immigration and physical expansion of the Jewish homeland be removed led to clashes between British forces and the Yishuv. In desperation, Great Britain turned the problem over to the new United Nations organization in 1946.

The United Nations, successor to the League of Nations, was still Western dominated. Asian and African members were then a minority and the concept of a Third World bloc was not yet envisaged. In an attempt to deal with Arab opposition to the establishment of a Jewish state occupying all of Palestine, the General Assembly recommended a compromise partition resolution dividing the country into a Jewish state, an Arab state, and an international enclave around Jerusalem. In a rare display of unity, the United States and the Soviet Union both supported partition. The ten Arab and Muslim members of the assembly voted against the resolution. Great Britain, the mandatory power, refused to support partition because of disagreement from Arab opponents.

The partition resolution precipitated a civil war in Palestine. The Yishuv, elated with the result of the UN debate, demonstrated its joy with victory celebrations and parades. Many who had never expected to see a Jewish state realized were astonished at the haste with which their dream seemed about to be fulfilled. For the Arab community, the UN resolution was a nightmare. They poured into the streets in demonstrations of opposition. Inevitably, tensions escalated between the two communities, quickly erupting into violent incidents. Jews quickly retaliated against Arab attacks, and within days the country was plunged into civil war.

Great Britain still refused to cooperate in implementing the partition resolution. Its official goal was to leave Palestine by May 15, the last day of the Mandate, with as little trouble as possible. Local British commanders aided Arab forces or Jewish forces, as expediency dictated. No effort was made to effect an orderly transition. Instead, thirty years of British administration ended in total chaos. Government offices, equipment, and records fell into the hands of whatever forces happened to fill the vacuum left by departing British officials.

Between November 30, when the partition resolution was passed by the UN, and May 14, when the Mandate officially ended, Arab leaders in Palestine organized local militia forces to prevent establishment of a Jewish state. They were aided by guerrillas from the surrounding Arab countries; on May 14 the armies of Egypt, Syria, Lebanon, Jordan, and Iraq officially joined the battle. This first in a series of wars between Israel and the surrounding Arab states was called the War of Liberation by Israelis. It ended in 1949, when Israel signed separate armistice agreements with Egypt, Syria, Jordan, and Lebanon. Although the armistice agreements did not lead to the envisaged peace treaties, they established Israel's frontiers with its Arab neighbors for nearly twenty years, until the third Arab-Israeli war in 1967.

The state of Israel was declared and its first government established amidst war and chaos on May 14, 1948. Actually, a de facto government had begun to function several months earlier, anticipating the end of the Mandate. The United Nations had sent a Palestine commission to implement the partition plan. Since neither Arabs nor British were willing to cooperate with it, the commission worked exclusively with the Jewish community through the National Council and the Jewish Agency to establish the Jewish government described in the UN resolution. A Jewish Provisional Council chosen from

National Council and Jewish Agency executive members was
organized in March 1948. It assumed control in many Jewish
areas as they were abandoned by the British. When the British
withdrew, the Provisional Council provided the services and
administrative apparatus necessary to maintain a semblance of
normal life. Thus education, sanitation, social welfare, and
public law and order were maintained in Jewish-controlled
regions. The Jewish Agency even organized a provisional post
office to replace the mandatory service.

As the date for termination of the Mandate and departure of
the British grew closer, opinion was divided in the Provisional
Council as to whether to declare independence. Many
countries, including the United States, which had supported
the partition resolution only a few weeks earlier, now urged the
Zionist leaders to postpone independence. They wanted to
avoid further escalation of the war, fearing the consequences
that struggle might have for the entire Middle East. In the end,
David Ben-Gurion, chairman of the Jewish Agency and leader
of the Yishuv, carried the day, insisting that the opportunity to
declare independence not be lost. The council decided to issue
its Declaration of Independence on May 14, the last day of the
Mandate.

In a theater on the Tel Aviv waterfront, the council issued the
declaration and transformed itself into the new Provisional
Council of State, Israel's first government. No definite
decision was made about the name of the Jewish state until the
last moment. Various suggestions had been made, drawn from
ancient Jewish sources, including the name Judea. Finally the
name Israel was chosen, since it was closest to the Hebrew term,
Eretz Israel ("Land of Israel"). The letters EI had appeared on
mandatory coins and stamps and had been used to stand for
Palestine during the Mandate and before.

The Declaration of Independence became the statement of
principles for Israel's new constitutional system. As in Great
Britain, there is no formal written constitution in Israel; rather,
an accumulation of basic laws form the legal basis of the
government and the constitutional system. The Declaration of
Independence emphasized the historical claims of the Jewish
people to the Land of Israel. These received international

confirmation, the document stated, in the Balfour Declaration, the League of Nations Mandate, and the United Nations partition resolution. Israel was defined as a Jewish state "representing the Jewish people in Palestine and the World Zionist movement." Israel would "be open to the immigration of Jews from all countries of their dispersion." The "Jewish people all over the world" were called "to rally to our side in the task of immigration and development, and to stand by us in the great struggle for the fulfillment of the dream of generations for the redemption of Israel."

Special emphasis was placed on Israel's relationship to the survivors of the Holocaust and "the need to solve the problem of the homelessness and lack of independence of the Jewish people."

Non-Jewish rights were guaranteed and it was promised that the country would be developed "for the benefit of all its inhabitants . . . on the principles of liberty, justice and peace as conceived by the Prophets of Israel." All citizens were guaranteed "full social and political equality . . . without distinctions of religion, race, or sex." The declaration also guaranteed "freedom of religion, conscience, education and culture; [it] will safeguard the Holy Places of all religions; and will loyally uphold the principles of the United Nations Charter."

Arab inhabitants of the state were called upon "to preserve the ways of peace and play their part in the development of the State, on the basis of full and equal citizenship and due representation in all its bodies and institutions—provisional and permanent." Cooperation "with the independent Jewish nation for the common good of all" was offered "to all the neighbouring states and their peoples." Israel offered to "make its contribution to the progress of the Middle East as a whole."

The National Council was designated as the Provisional State Council and the National Administration was to constitute the provisional government of the Jewish state. These arrangements were to take effect from termination of the Mandate at midnight on May 14, until the establishment of duly elected bodies set up in accordance with a constitution "to be drawn up by the Constituent Assembly not later than the than the 1st October, 1948."

The Declaration of Independence reflected a number of ideological and political compromises among the diverse factions of the Yishuv and the Zionist movement. It made no reference to boundaries or frontiers. Although the Jewish Agency and National Council had accepted the UN partition plan, all of Palestine was considered the land of Israel. The Revisionist trend within the Zionist movement still regarded the East Bank of the Jordan as a rightful part of the Jewish patrimony. Furthermore, Israel was in the midst of a war with surrounding Arab states in which the outcome was yet to be determined.

Another major dilemma was the role of religion in the Jewish state. Orthodox Jewish leaders wanted the declaration to emphasize clearly the role of formal religion and to recognize explicitly not merely its Jewish ethnic character but its intimate ties with the Jewish faith. At the other end of the spectrum, Marxist-oriented members of the Mapam party opposed any deference to Orthodoxy. They wanted a Jewish secular state in which religion would be separated from politics, with no mention of God. A compromise was reached by using Old Testament phraseology in which signers of the declaration placed their "trust in the Rock of Israel."

The state of Israel and its new government replaced the British mandatory government in most of Palestine. Areas not under Israeli control by the end of the war were divided among various Arab armies, principally those of Jordan, Egypt, Syria, and Lebanon. When the 1949 armistice agreements were signed, Israel controlled four-fifths of Palestine's 10,000 square miles, Jordan held the largely Arab regions west of the Jordan River, and Egypt occupied the Gaza Strip.

CHAPTER TWO

Political Culture

ISRAEL: AN IMMIGRANT SOCIETY

Immigration is the lifeblood of Zionism, for years its raison d'etre, and a major objective in the establishment of the Jewish state. A jocular definition of a Zionist in the diaspora used to be "a Jew who collects money from another Jew to send a third Jew to Eretz Israel."

The Zionist Congress spent much time discussing immigration and settlement of the *olim* in Palestine. Throughout the mandatory period, disputes over Jewish immigration were a chief cause of tension between the British and Zionist leaders. Arab nationalists during the Mandate demanded that Great Britain cut the flow of Jews into the country. Had immigration not been so crucial, relations between the Yishuv and the British and Arabs would not have been so strained. Fear of being outnumbered was a primary factor in development of the Arab nationalist movement. And Zionist fears that the Yishuv would remain a small and beleaguered enclave was a driving force leading to demands for a Jewish commonwealth free to determine its own immigration policies.

British restrictions on Jewish immigration and land purchases in Palestine, imposed in the 1939 White Paper, were a decisive factor intensifying Zionist militancy and leading to the 1942 Biltmore Program. Immigration was essential, not only to save Jews from anti-Semitism in Europe but to continue development of the Jewish national home. One of the first official acts of the new government in 1948 was to repeal the 1939 restrictions on immigration and to enact the Law of Return.

Passed unanimously by the Knesset on July 5, 1950, the Law of Return is considered one of the country's basic constitutional documents, perhaps second in psychological importance only to the Declaration of Independence. The law confirms provisions of the declaration by guaranteeing that "every Jew has the right to immigrate to the country." Any Jew expressing a desire to settle in Israel is guaranteed an immigrant visa with the exception of one who "acts against the Jewish nation" or who "may threaten the public health or State security."

In presenting the law to the Knesset, Prime Minister Ben-Gurion observed: "This law lays down not that the State accords the right of settlement to Jews abroad but that this right is inherent in every Jew by virtue of his being a Jew if it but be his will to take part in settling the land. This right preceded the State of Israel; it is that which built the State."

Since 1948, the volume of immigration has varied from year to year. About 1.6 million Jews have entered Israel from all over the world—more than twice the number in Israel at independence, and about four times the number who came during the Mandate.

By far the largest number came during the first four years after independence. The Jewish population nearly doubled as a result of this immigrant tidal wave. The all-time high was in 1949, when there were 240,000 immigrants. During this early period, the largest number came from Eastern Europe, with Poland, Russia, and Bulgaria leading, although immigrants came from more than forty countries. "Ingathering of the exiles" emptied the displaced persons camps in Europe, which housed refugees from the Nazi concentration camps, and closed the internment centers on Cyprus, where the British kept "illegal" Jewish immigrants.

By the early 1950s, most of the European refugees were resettled, and a new wave of immigration began from Asia and North Africa. During the next twenty years, these immigrants nearly equalled the European arrivals. As a result, the majority in the Yishuv is no longer European Ashkenazi, but Sephardi, or Oriental.

Oriental Jewish immigration began on a large scale with Operation Magic Carpet from Yemen. Nearly all that country's Jews, about 47,000, were flown to Israel during 1949 and 1950. When the operation ended, only a few hundred Jews remained in Yemen. Iraq suddenly enacted a law in 1950 authorizing Jewish emigration, and Iraqis too were flown to Israel "on eagle's wings" in Operation Ezra and Nehemia (two Old Testament patriarchs who migrated to the Holy Land from Mesopotamia). After the departure of 121,000 Iraqi Jews, only a handful were left in this ancient center of Jewish settlement. The series of wars between Israel and the Arab states intensified anti-Zionism and caused frequent anti-Jewish riots in several Arab countries. Growing political unrest and increased economic insecurity finally led to the departure of most Jews from the Middle Eastern and North African countries where they had lived for centuries. By the 1970s, nearly all Jews had left Syria, Lebanon, Egypt, Tunisia, Algeria, and Libya. Many migrated to Europe and the Americas; the total reaching Israel was some 750,000. Morocco contributed the largest number of refugees from this area, about 255,000. Only 30,000 Jews remained in Morocco, 10 percent of those living there when Israel was established.

Between 1947 and 1977, the number of Jews in Israel increased fivefold, to more than 3 million. Sixty-two percent of the increase was from immigration. Israel had become the second-largest center of world Jewry after the United States, which had 6 million Jews. Eighteen percent of world Jewry now live in Israel, an increase from 0.3 percent when Zionist settlement began in Palestine less than a century ago. Removal of immigration restrictions to Israel did not end the flow of Jews to other parts of the world. Between 1948 and the early 1970s, less than one-third of world Jewish migration was to Israel. The largest movement was from east to west, with North America still drawing the most immigrants.

By 1952, Jewish immigration to Israel had declined sharply. Economic recession and difficult living conditions in Israel between 1952 and 1955 caused an even steeper decline. Fewer than 12,000 immigrants entered Israel in 1953, a smaller number than during many years of restrictive mandatory controls. Immigration patterns were influenced by Israel's relations with the countries from which people emigrated and by world economic conditions. The highest annual immigration figure was 70,000 in 1957. After 1964 the trend was downward again, with a low of 14,000 in 1967, when there was another economic recession in Israel. In 1975 and 1976 immigration was disappointingly low, about 17,000 in each year. Many Jewish emigrants from the Soviet Union who had applied for Israeli visas decided to go elsewhere after leaving Russia. The result was the loss of thousands of potential new settlers.

CHANGING CLASS STRUCTURE

It is difficult to characterize the "average Israeli" because the country's class structure is so diverse and the ethnic composition and value systems are so varied. Israel is several societies, Jewish and Arab, Oriental and Western, cosmopolitan and parochial, rich and poor. However, to the extent that demographic, social, and economic data can offer some insight into the life of the country, the following statistics are informative. The "typical" Jewish family in Israel during 1976 consisted of 3.5 persons, including 1.5 children. Among those born in Asia or Africa the average number of children per family was 2.1, three times the average of those from Europe and America. This compared to an average of 3.6 children among Israeli non-Jews (mostly Arabs).

Just over one-half the population was native born, about 12 percent were born in Africa, 10.4 percent in Asia, and 27 percent in Europe or America. More than 90 percent were town dwellers, and the rest lived in rural settlements including over 300 *kibbutzim*.

More than 75 percent of the gainfully employed were wage earners, as opposed to self-employed. The average Jewish family's monthly income was about $300, with one and one-half family members employed. Among these, 33.8 percent were in public and communal service; 28.6 percent in industry; 7.8 percent in trade and tourist industries; 7.7 percent in business and finance; 7.3 percent in transportation and communications; 6.3 percent in building and construction; 1.9 percent in agriculture; 1.3 percent in electricity and water works; and 0.5 percent in personal services.

A little over half the families lived at a housing density of one person or less per room; 28.7 percent lived two per room; and 18.9 percent lived at the highly crowded rate of more than two per room. Household and personal possessions have increased greatly since 1948. As of 1976, 98.5 percent of families had a refrigerator; 85 percent owned a television; 65 percent had a washing machine; and 8.3 percent owned an automobile.

Nine percent of the Jewish population was illiterate; half had a secondary education; one in six had completed education above the secondary level.

The shift in immigration from Western to non-Western Jews changed not only the demographic composition of Israel but also its social structure. Before discussing these changes the differences between the two groups should be clarified.

In Israeli documentation such as the government's annual *Statistical Abstract*, the population is divided between Jews from "Europe-America," and those from "Asia-Africa." However, in much of the literature about Israel and among many Jews, these groups are identified as "Ashkenazi" and "Sephardi." The Ashkenazi are Jews of European, mainly Eastern European, origin. Most of them come from Russia, Poland, Hungary, Rumania, and Lithuania. A smaller but influential group is of German and Austrian origin. Of the other Ashkenazi in Western Europe and North America, few have immigrated to Israel. "European" does not necessarily designate geographic origin; Jewish communities, mostly Ashkenazi, in South Africa, Argentina, and Brazil are also considered "European." Historically, the distinguishing feature of Ashkenazic Jews was use of Yiddish, or "Jewish," as it was sometimes called.

When Israel was established, nearly one-half the Jewish population spoke Yiddish in addition to Hebrew. In Israel there were many disputes over use of Yiddish. The language, written in Hebrew script, is based on German and mixed with words and phrases from Hebrew, and includes some Polish, Russian, Hungarian, or Rumanian in regional dialects. During the latter part of the nineteenth and early twentieth centuries, an extensive literature, press, and theatre used Yiddish.

Although they spoke it themselves, most early leaders of the Yishuv discouraged the use of Yiddish for official purposes. To many it was a diaspora tongue and a badge of inferiority. Furthermore they feared it would compete with, and perhaps displace Hebrew, the official language of the Zionist movement. As the Ashkenazi assimilated, they became less attached to Yiddish and its use declined. Few *sabras* (native-born Israelis) speak it, and of course it is foreign to Jews from Asia and Africa.

Since 1948, the Ashkenazi community in Israel, which was almost synonymous with the Yishuv, has become much more diverse. As Ashkenazi have immigrated from many areas, they have formed communities reflecting the cultural outlooks, preferences, and prejudices of the countries from which they have migrated. Traditional national animosities, such as those between Hungarians and Poles or Czechs and Slovaks, are sometimes reflected among these Jewish immigrants. The rich cultural heritage of Europe runs deeply through the emerging culture of the Jewish state. It is evident in Israeli music, cuisine, art, drama, and humor. Despite powerful pressures to assimilate—to learn Hebrew and adopt *sabra* manners and customs—the mainstream of cultural and social life is still European.

The Sephardi are an equally diverse group. Their linguistic base is Ladino, a language of Spanish origins spoken by Jews whose descendants were expelled from Spain and Portugal during the fifteenth and sixteenth centuries. Sometimes called Judeo-Spanish, Ladino also uses Hebrew script and has assimilated parts of Hebrew, and Turkish, Greek, and other languages in local variants.

Sephardic Jews have lived in Palestine longer than any other Jews, since the end of the fifteenth century. When expelled from Spain and later Portugal, most Sephardic Jews settled along the shores of the Mediterranean, establishing large, influential, and flourishing centers in Morocco, Greece, Turkey, and the Levant. There were also Sephardic communities in Western Europe and North America, where they were sometimes regarded as a Jewish "aristocracy." In Palestine, many of the Sephardi, who had been there since Ottoman times, also regarded themselves as an elite. The community included many professionals and successful businessmen, and an unusually high percentage of the Jewish employees in the mandatory government. Old Sephardic families often regarded the Ashkenazic newcomers as abrasive or harsh in their manners, overzealous in their dedication to the labor ideal, and ignorant of the local traditions. Because many Sephardim from the old Yishuv had had good personal relations with local Arabs before 1948, and served as intermediaries with the Arabs, some Eastern European Zionists zealots regarded them as less patriotic.

The dichotomy between the Sephardi and the Ashkenazi is institutionalized in Israel's religious organizations, a heritage from the Ottoman era, when each group had its own chief rabbi. It is perpetuated through appointment of a chief rabbi for each community and maintenance of separate synagogues. Actual religious differences, however, are based less on fundamental dogma or interpretation of Jewish law than on minor issues—the tunes in which the same prayers are sung, the dress of clerics, and synagogue architecture and decor. Recently the latent hostility between the two groups was demonstrated in clashes between the two chief rabbis, expressed in such minutiae as whether or not grass should be permitted to grow on the Wailing Wall in Jerusalem.

Often all non-Western Jews are erroneously regarded by the Ashkenazim as Sephardim. Perhaps their darker skin, use of Middle Eastern languages—Arabic, Persian, or Turkish—and Eastern value system and lifestyle made all Afro-Asian Jews appear Sephardic. In fact, a large percentage of Jews from Asia and Africa have no Spanish ancestry and know nothing of Ladino culture. Most Jews from Yemen, Iraq, Persia, India, or China are not Sephardic, they are Oriental. Within these diverse Eastern communities, national differences are as great as among the Europeans.

In addition to the cultural differences, there are class distinctions between the Europeans and the Afro-Asians. Some Afro-Asians are affluent and university educated. But most are relatively poorly educated, unskilled, and economically deprived by comparison with the European community. The problem has been the subject of several official inquiries.

Education is a key indicator because it is required to attain skills for upward economic and social mobility in a highly industrialized society. Disparities in educational levels remain great. Over 20 percent of the Jews born in Asia and Africa, compared to less than 3 percent from Europe and America, had no formal education as of 1974. There are twice as many Ashkenazic high school graduates as Sephardic and five times as many in higher education.

While larger numbers of Oriental Jews now achieve a higher education than during the 1960s, the gap remains. A 1971 study by David Horowitz, former governor of the Bank of Israel, entitled "Income Distribution and Social Inequality," reports that the number of fourteen- to seventeen-year-olds from Oriental communities who attended secondary school had increased from 46 percent in 1963-64 to 59 percent in 1970. This compared to a rise among Westerners from 61 to 77 percent. In universities Oriental enrollments increased from 0.8 percent of the relevant population in 1948 to 1.6 percent during the 1960s. Among Western youth there was an increase from 4.1 percent to 6.4 percent during this period. By the mid-1970s fewer than 10 percent of university graduates came from Oriental homes.

Afro-Asian Jews have larger families. Among the 40 percent of Israeli children under eighteen who had three or more siblings, 57 percent were Afro-Asian, 11 percent European-American, and 17 percent native Israelis, according to the Horowitz study. (A high percentage of the native Israelis are also of Afro-Asian origin.) Fifty-five percent of family heads who did not finish elementary school were Afro-Asian, 16 percent European-American, and 16 percent native Israeli. Orientals' housing density is also much greater, but has been improving. During the 1960s, 37 percent of Oriental families lived three or more to a room, though the figure had declined to

12 percent by 1970. Despite improvement in many sectors of Oriental Jewish life, built-in handicaps to upward mobility continue. Among Orientals, in the early 1970s, 80 percent had at least one learning disability compared to 33 percent among European-Americans.

Differences in educational levels are translated into differences in occupational attainment, income, and living standards. As Israel has become increasingly industrialized, achieving a Western European or North American standard of living, the gap between the Western and non-Western population has not closed.

In 1971, the average income of a European-American family was 2.09 times higher than that of an Afro-Asian family. By 1974, the ratio was almost unchanged, although both groups had acquired increased incomes. The per capita difference was, in fact, greater than the statistics indicate, since Oriental Jewish families are about three times as large. The gap in incomes was not overcome by length of residence; *sabras* were included in the calculations above.

In general, Oriental youth are simply not trained for the more prestigious, better-paying occupations. In the early 1970s about one-half of the Israelis of Western origin were in whitecollar jobs compared to less than a quarter of the Orientals. Even within white-collar fields, Western workers had higher incomes than the Orientals. A much higher percentage of Jews from Afro-Asian countries were in farming, factory work, and other blue-collar occupations.

The economic gap between the ethnic groups is reinforced socially. Each group has a perception of the other that makes it difficult to bridge differences and to integrate the groups into a common Israeli society. Oriental Jews are often looked down on by Western Jews because of their origins in Islamic societies, their frequent physical similarity to Arabs, and their Eastern cultural values. Many Ashkenazim perceive Orientals as less industrious, technologically inept, and "hot blooded." A deprecatory expression for poorly executed manual or semi-skilled work is that it is *avoda aravit* ("Arab labor"). Jews from Yemen are often excluded from these stereotypes because they are seen as skilled craftsmen and have acquired a reputation for being industrious.

Social distance between the two groups accompanies these stereotypes. Studies by Israeli sociologists indicate that many European Jews are less willing to accept Orientals as marriage partners or even neighbors than Orientals are to accept Europeans. Ironically, evidence shows that negative stereo-typical images prevailing among the Europeans are frequently adopted by Orientals. In effect, these negative images become self-fulfilling when Orientals begin to believe in their own inferiority. Another indicator of social distance is the endogomy index or rate of intermarriage. There has been a gradual increase in the number of intermarriages between the two groups from 11.8 percent in 1955 to 19.2 percent in 1975.

After the 1967 war, there was a major change in the attitude of Westerners toward Orientals. Because of their active role in the war, Orientals were said to have accepted Western values and adapted to modern technology. Reaction among Oriental Jewish leaders was less flattered than resentful. Many regarded it as a put-down of non-Western Jewish culture. One Oriental Jewish intellectual, Nissim Rejwan, a native of Iraq, charged that the country's establishment was seeking to absorb Oriental Jews into its own European culture based "on the assumption that there exists in Israel a fairly well-defined 'native' culture to which these immigrants have to adapt and into which they can and have to be fused."

Rejwan observed that

> the declared goal of "remoulding" the Oriental . . . was pursued with a vigor and a self-assurance that in retrospect seems truly staggering. . . . Using a variety of threadbare excuses and rationalizations, the dominant group practiced a systematic policy of exclusion and incapacitation, a policy which did not leave unaffected even the country's institutions of higher learning.

Citing Ben-Gurion's attitudes toward Orientals as typical, Rejwan recalled an interview in which the former prime minister stated: "We do not want Israelis to become Arabs. We are duty bound to fight against the spirit of the Levant, which corrupted individuals and societies, and preserve the authentic Jewish values as they crystalized in the Diaspora."

"Our suspicion," Rejwan commented, "is that the authentic Jewish values which Mr. Ben-Gurion is so eager to preserve have just about nothing to do with Jewish values and Jewish culture as, say, a Yemenite, Moroccan, Persian, or Iraqi Jew would understand the term."

The solution to this dilemma, Rejwan believed, was not necessarily opposition to integration. However, it must not be one-sided "in the sense that members of the weaker groups are integrated *into* rather than *with* the dominant group." Acceptance by the more powerful Western Jewish community of democratic pluralism "must obtain in Israel before the stage can be set for genuine integration. It is a pity, and not a little surprising, that some Israelis should feel somewhat bewildered about the prospect of a pluralist society. In the circumstances, such development offers the only alternative to Levantiniza- tion—or something far worse."

Consequences of class differences in Israeli society have been both social and political. They are most evident in develop- ment of ethnic neighborhoods in the larger cities, and in concentrations of Oriental Jews in certain development towns. At first, the Jewish Agency attempted to establish new immigrant settlements from mixed ethnic groups, but sociolo- gists and anthropologists advised that there were advantages to preserving already existing communal structures. *Olim* were thereafter settled in national groups. This often reinforced ethnic separateness and concentrated less affluent settlers in distinctive neighborhoods. Oriental Jewish neighborhoods are thus poorer than others, with greater need for social welfare services. The result of these ethnic/class differences shows in the country's police records. In 1973, by far the largest number of convicted adult offenders were Oriental. Only a small percent were of European-American origin.

Orientals provide the largest share of recruits to the armed forces, considered Israel's major socializing institution. In the army they receive basic Hebrew education, learn technical skills, and become more closely acquainted with the norms of the society. However, after leaving military service it is often more difficult for them to find a place in civilian society than it is for Westerners.

As latecomers to the Yishuv, Oriental Jews found themselves outside the political establishment. Europeans who immigrated after 1948 and *sabras* were also underrepresented in the political elite, having been unable to obtain leadership positions in the various party machines during the early period. Of the sixty-four Israeli cabinet ministers who served during the first twenty-five years of the nation's existence, only three were of Oriental background. As of 1973, there were only fifteen Oriental Jews in the 120-member Knesset, compared to sixty-eight from Eastern Europe and twenty-eight *sabras* (seven of whom were Arabs). Similar patterns exist in the upper ranks of the party leadership and among heads of the civil service. The number of Oriental Jews serving as low-level civil servants is much higher. The police force, for example, includes a very high percentage of Oriental Jews.

As they became more "Israelized," the Orientals became more politically active at the local level, assuming leadership positions in municipalities, local councils, and local trade union organizations. Between 1950 and 1965, Oriental representation in local-government bodies increased from 13 percent to 44 percent. By 1970, 30 percent of the Jewish mayors in Israel were from Oriental communities. Israeli political scientist Shlomo Avineri compared this development to the rise of American ethnic groups like the Irish and Italians through local politics to positions of influence in the American political hierarchy. Beersheba, one of the largest cities in Israel and considered the capital of the Negev region, illustrates the rise of the Orientals to political power. During the Mandate, it was a small backwater town inhabited by Arabs, with only a handful of Jews. The first Jewish settlers sent by the government after 1948 were Europeans, who controlled the municipality. Since 1948, the population has grown from 2,000 to nearly 100,000, a large number of whom are Oriental. As they increased in numbers they also gained in political influence, taking over the local Labor party executive committee, the party secretariat, the secretariat of the Histadrut, and the mayor's office.

Oriental settlement patterns have been urban rather than rural. Only a small number of Orientals have gone to *kibbutzim*. Their social organization, close-knit family patterns, and emphasis on individualism in work have made it easier for them to adjust to life in towns and villages than to collective agriculture.

The government has made strenuous efforts to narrow, if not overcome, the gap between Oriental and Western Jews. It has developed an extensive network of social services with special emphasis on integrating Orientals. In secondary and higher education, special scholarship funds have been established, and in the army much time is spent in education to overcome environmental obstacles. But efforts to attack such an enormous problem are frustrated by many factors. Limited resources are another important obstacle. As Israel finds it necessary to invest an increasingly large share of its resources in defense, austerity measures force sharp cuts in social services. Perhaps most important are the intangible psychological obstacles—the cultural differences and disparate value systems that separate Western from Eastern communities. The Yishuv as a whole is being pressed internally and externally to face the problem of reassessing fundamental values. This task of dealing with social change, modernization, and value reorientation is exceedingly difficult.

NON-JEWS IN ISRAEL

There is another rift in Israeli society, that between Jews and non-Jews. The latter, nearly all Muslim and Christian Arabs, made up about 15 percent of the total population as of the mid-1970s. At the end of the Mandate, Arabs constituted two-thirds of the population in Palestine as a whole and nearly one-half in the area designated as the Jewish state by the UN partition plan. Their number greatly decreased during the 1948 war, when more than 700,000 became refugees in the neighboring Arab countries. Under the armistice agreements with the neighboring states, about 125,000 Arabs remained within Israel's jurisdiction. Since 1948 their number has increased due to one of the world's highest birth rates. In addition, East

Jerusalem, with its 75,000 Arabs, was incorporated into Israel after the 1967 war.

Except for residents of East Jerusalem, the Arabs in Israel are Israeli citizens. (After annexation of East Jerusalem, its Arabs were given the option of becoming Israeli citizens, but most preferred to retain their previous citizenship, expecting that the city would return to Arab rule.)

Relations between the country's Jews and Arabs have been complicated by the state of war with surrounding Arab countries since 1948, and by social and economic differences between the two peoples. Continued belligerency has created serious strains, marked by mutual suspicion, deep antagonism, and the imposition of special security arrangements on Israeli Arab communities during the first two decades of independence. Incidents of Arab disloyalty or treason against Israel have been few, but because most Arab families have close relatives living in "enemy" territory, the government's security forces have remained apprehensive.

Israeli Arabs were victims of deep trauma resulting from the 1948 war. The economic and political organization of the indigenous Palestinian Arab community was devastated. Most Arab towns, villages, farms, and property in Israel were destroyed or taken over by the new Jewish government. Palestinian Arab intellectual, political, and religious leadership fled, leaving behind only a remnant of the communal structure developed during the Mandate. Those remaining in Israel were confused and uncertain about their future.

Guarantees to the Arab population in the UN partition resolution and in Israel's Declaration of Independence were undermined by the war. Arabs were considered a security problem and the areas where they lived were placed under military rule. During the first years of independence, Arabs, while they were Israeli citizens with full legal equality, were subject to military-government controls. They were required to obtain passes for travel within and beyond certain points. They were also subjected to army search and seizure, arbitrary arrest, expulsion from the country, and banishment to other villages in Israel.

As security conditions improved and evidence of Israeli Arab loyalty increased, military-government control was relaxed. Growing numbers of Israeli Jews pressed first for relaxation, then for total abolition of military government. Many feared that the restrictions would alienate the Arab citizenry and undermine democratic institutions, a possibility which threatened dissident Jewish groups as well as Arabs. In the late 1950s, it became easier for Israeli Arabs to obtain travel permits and to move from their homes to other areas. Most restrictions were lifted on Arabs in the large Jewish population centers such as Jaffa and Haifa. In 1966 the Knesset abolished the military government altogether, and controls on Arabs suspected of subversive activity were transferred to civil police authority.

During the first decade of Israel's existence, the government expropriated a substantial proportion of Israeli Arab agricultural land. Land along the frontiers with Arab states or in other strategically located areas was seized by Israeli forces during the 1948 war. Later, additional thousands of acres were taken for national development and settled by new Jewish immigrants. Although intended to deal with the property of Arabs who had fled Israel during 1947-48, the Absentee Property Law was frequently applied to Israeli Arab citizens. It authorized the seizure of land, buildings, and other possessions belonging to anyone who was in "enemy territory" during the period specified in the law. Because many Arab areas did not come under jurisdiction of the Israeli government until after this period, Israeli Arabs who were residing, or even visiting, these areas were subjected to the confiscatory legislation. By the 1960s, it was estimated that Israeli Arabs had lost about two-thirds of their agricultural land through the Absentee Property Law and other legislation. Many Arabs were compensated for their property losses, but disputes about the equity of these payments continued for several years.

Loss of agricultural land radically altered the social and economic structure of the Israeli Arab community through changes in occupational distribution and landholding patterns. During the Mandate, 76 to 80 percent of Palestine's Arab community lived from agriculture, but the proportion declined to 40 percent after the foundation of Israel. As a result of diminishing agricultural employment, large numbers of

former villagers are now employed in Jewish urban sectors of
the economy. The shift from agricultural to urban pursuits
changed consumption patterns and lifestyles.

The official government portrait of the Arab in Israel depicts
well-being and prosperity despite necessary inconveniences to
which the minority must unfortunately be subjected because of
the war with the surrounding countries. In its official
publications, the government asserts that Israeli Arab income
and living standards are higher than those in other Middle
Eastern countries. Through extensive government financing of
irrigation, land reclamation, agricultural mechanization and
modernization, health services, and village reconstruction, the
Arab in Israel has achieved an economic position superior to
Arabs elsewhere. But the Arab community in Israel has retained
a distinctive character evident in its towns and villages, which
still resemble those of Palestinian Arabs living in West Bank
Jordan.

After Israel's occupation of the West Bank and Gaza in 1967,
Israeli Arabs entered another phase of change. Between 1948
and 1967, they were cut off and isolated from contact with the
rest of the Arab world. Only a small number of Christian Arabs
were authorized to visit relatives across the border in Jordan
during holidays like Christmas and Easter. No arrangements
were made to permit such visits by Israeli Muslims. Arabs in
Israel were thus separated from larger family groups and from
direct contact with political and social developments in the
Arab world, although they could listen to radio broadcasts
from surrounding countries. After the war and occupation of
the West Bank and Gaza, another 1 million Arabs were added to
the 400,000 then under Israel's jurisdiction. When barriers to
the occupied areas were removed, Israelis and Arabs from the
occupied territories established direct contact. Those from the
West Bank and Gaza could visit Israel, and Israelis were free to
travel in the occupied regions. Gaza and West Bank Arabs were
also permitted to cross the bridges over the Jordan River, and
many traveled to capitals of the Arab world, bringing back
direct word of events in Cairo, Beirut, Damascus, and the Gulf
states. Israeli Arabs were put into direct contact again with
families from which many had been separated, and with the

pulse of social and political life in the Arab world.

A humiliating defeat in 1967, an apparent victory in the 1973 war, and six years of direct links to the Arab world politicized many Israeli Arabs. A strong Arab consciousness was revived, and Palestinian nationalism was reborn. Larger numbers of Israeli Arabs began to identify with the militant themes of the Palestinian movement. Before 1967, there was no extensive Israeli Arab political opposition other than through the Communist party. The largest number of Arab votes went to the Labor party or to its Arab affiliates.

The first explicit political expression of Arab nationalism emerged in 1965. At that time the Israeli Communist party split into two factions: the New Communists (Rakkah), most but not all of whom were Arabs; and the parent Israeli Communists, nearly all of whom were Jewish. The split was caused by differences between Jewish and Arab Communists over the Middle East policies of the Soviet Union and the Arab states. After 1967, differences between the two groups became more pronounced.

A survey by Israeli sociologists showed a startling increase in the number of Israeli Arab school children who thought it would be necessary to wage still another war despite defeat in the previous three. Many fewer Arabs felt at ease in Israel than in the past, according to the survey. By 1973, the number voting for Rakkah had increased to 37 percent from 23.6 percent in the 1965 Knesset election. Rakkah received about one-half the Arab votes in 1977. Municipal elections in 1973 also showed a more militant attitude; voters in Nazareth, Israel's largest Arab town, chose a Rakkah mayor and a leftist municipal council for the first time.

The Israeli Arab is caught between his identity as an Arab and his status as a citizen of the Jewish state. He is plagued by a feeling of uncertainty and marginality. In the words of a participant in one of the post-1967 surveys: "I sometimes think that we are neither real Arabs nor real Israelis because in the Arab countries they call us *traitors* and in Israel—*spies.*"

Ethnic distinctions between Arabs in Israel and Jews are reinforced by economic differences, which place the Arab in a lower social stratum. After the 1967 war a large percentage of

Israel's unskilled labor in agriculture, construction, and service industries was provided by Arabs from the occupied areas and from Israel. By 1976, they provided more than half the work force in agriculture and construction and more than 10 percent in industry. About one-half of all unskilled workers in manufacturing were also Arab, and they dominated such fields as hotel and garage work.

Poor living conditions and lack of opportunity for upward mobility have been a radicalizing force among these laborers. While Arabs are employed in the civil service and police force—according to some estimates as many as 2,500 Arab citizens work in the government—fewer than two dozen were among the several hundred top officials listed in the Israeli *1975 Government Year-Book*. No Arabs were in the cabinet in 1977, although 2 served at subcabinet level. Nor were they among the directors and assistant directors for Christian, Muslim, and Druze affairs in the ministries for minorities.

Much of the existing suspicion toward Arabs would presumably dissipate and many security restrictions be removed if there were peace between Israel and its neighbors. However, problems of social integration would likely remain. While Israeli Arabs can vote, are represented in the Knesset, serve in increasingly higher government offices, and prosper materially, like Oriental Jews, they will doubtless encounter many problems in adjusting to a modern technological society. Many Arab villagers still wear traditional dress, live in modest one-room houses, and follow the tempo of life set by the agricultural seasons. Superficially, life may seem the same as it always has been, but the tremors caused by Israel's new ways and Western orientation have shaken the foundations of the patriarchal structure, and it too is in transition. Leadership is no longer an exclusive prerogative of a relatively small landowning group. Government confiscation of large agricultural areas and flight of the traditional estate owners during or before 1948 started a leveling process. By 1950, over 65 percent of the approximately 15,000 Israeli Arab farms were fully owner operated, over 30 percent partly owned and partly rented, and less than 5 percent operated on totally rented land. Expressed another way, nearly 80 percent of the 250,000 acres of

Arab farmland was farmed by the owner himself.

There is little love lost between Israeli Arabs and Oriental Jews, despite similarity in attitudes toward women, child-parent relations, and family life, and in other values. Similar social and economic problems have not produced a common class-consciousness. Ethnic differences between Jew and Arab are still sufficiently great to prevent any common political action. Experiences in Eastern countries have made Oriental Jews most vehement in their hostility toward Arabs. Efforts by the Communist parties, pronouncements by the Israeli Black Panthers, and assertions by Palestinian nationalists that they are striving for equality, have failed to create a common class identity. Intermarriage, too, is insignificant because the ethos of both groups is strongly against such unions.

Even if Israel's position in the Middle East becomes secure and the Arab minority attains economic and political equality, the cultural and ethnic chasm will continue. A fundamental question is whether Israel's Arabs will ever be able to identify with such an exclusively Jewish milieu. Will the Jewish state concept ever have meaning to or command the loyalty of Israeli Arabs? Can the Jewish heritage and culture, developed through centuries of life in the diaspora, ever become an Arab heritage? These questions are especially critical since, according to the most optimistic estimates, the Arab minority, not including Arabs in the occupied territories, will increase from 15 to 20 percent of Israel's population by the end of the century.

CHANGING VALUE SYSTEMS

Zionist credo holds that Israel was established not only by and for the Yishuv but for world Jewry. The most optimistic Zionists dreamed that all Jews would be included in the ingathering. Those with less expansive vision saw Israel as a cultural and spiritual homeland for all Jews but residence of only some. Israel has become an emotional and ideological focus for Jewish communities in the diaspora, who have supported it financially and politically, and are sustained by cultural and emotional ties to it. But only a small number have voluntarily settled in Israel. Among those who leave the diaspora because of oppression or economic dislocation, only a small percentage choose Israel as their refuge. The largest number of Jewish emigrants, since establishment of Israel, has continued to settle in other countries.

In the prestate era, Zionist visionaries saw the Jewish state not only as a physical refuge but also as the cultural and spiritual center of Judaism. Jewish traditions and ethics would flourish and the Jewish people would experience a spiritual rebirth. This messianic vision, according to Israel's first prime minister, David Ben-Gurion,

> is not the outcome of any local or temporary conditions; it was created by the prophetic concept of the universe, the destiny of man on earth and the millenial era. It does not recognize idols of gold and silver; it does not accept the robbery of the poor, the oppression of peoples, the lifting up of swords by nation against nation or the study of war; it foretells the coming of the Redeemer whose loins are girt with righteousness; it looks forward to the day when the nations will cease to do evil. This Messianic vision depends on the redemption of Israel, which will assume two forms: the ingathering of the exiles and the creation of a model nation.

Israel's perilous environment, the pressures of massive immigration with its accompanying economic and social problems, and the tensions caused by perpetual threats of war have led the state in directions much different from those which Zionist ideologues imagined. Today's leaders explain that requirements for survival have made it necessary to postpone realization of the Zionist vision.

Compromises between the struggle for survival and aspirations to become a model nation have had paradoxical consequences. The early social ideals are often diluted. Social equality, cooperation, and pioneering are still goals but it no longer carries a stigma to be rich; competition often replaces cooperation, and more settlers strive to live in urban rather than rural settlements.

A former Histadrut secretary general, Yitzhak Ben-Aharon, described how the gap developed between vision and reality:

When Jews come here because of their conviction, they must be provided with a livelihood. To provide jobs, money is needed. This money can be obtained from certain sources with a certain character and outlook. The Jews who immigrate are themselves a factor, and the way of life here should therefore be adjusted to their habits and personalities. Consequently, planned direction, supervision, and guidance according to a social ideology must be kept to a minimum.

The influx of immigrants with few, if any skills, the need to rapidly expand the economic infrastructure and its productive capacity, and the need for massive capital to finance the rapidly growing economy all conspire against egalitarian visions. The major thrust of the economy has not been toward the land but toward rapid industrialization. An agricultural revolution brought about by irrigation and scientific farming methods increased agricultural production tenfold between 1948 and 1972. As a result, labor requirements in the rural sector have declined. Between 1958 and 1972, the number of people employed in agriculture decreased from 17.6 to 8 percent of the labor force. Despite increasing numbers of new rural settlements, the agricultural population diminished to less than 10 percent of the total. After the economic boom of 1968, labor shortages in Israel led to employment of Arab labor, even in many *kibbutzim*, which had epitomized the Zionist ideal of Jewish labor on Jewish land.

The phenomenal expansion of the industrial sector is evident in its thirtyfold (3,000 percent) growth in income from 1952 to 1972; in the 350 percent increase in industrial investment; in an 1100 percent increase in industrial exports; and in an almost 500 percent rise in value of industrial output. Although the percentage of the labor force employed in industry remained about the same, the absolute number of industrial workers nearly doubled between 1955 and 1972.

Economic reorientation from land to factory, from pioneer rural settlement to urban industry, has necessitated ideological readjustment. The ideal of an egalitarian society with a strong Socialist emphasis has been replaced by a mixed economy with special provisions to encourage private capital and foreign investment. Socialist leaders have had to compromise in coalition governments with non-Socialist groups such as the General Zionists, the Liberals, and the religious bloc.

Large-scale economic assistance from both private and government sources in the United States has also militated against Socialist dogmatism. Reparations from the West German Federal Republic for crimes against Jews added additional resources and incentives to the private sector.

An ideological transition occurred in the Labor party during the 1960s, when a group of new leaders shifted the party's emphasis from traditional Socialist goals to science and technology. These young Turks, led by David Ben-Gurion, included individuals like Shimon Peres and Moshe Dayan, who were deeply involved in developing the country's military technology. As military production absorbed an increasing proportion of the country's manpower, resources, and industrial base, the need for modern technology became obvious. For the new technocracy, pioneering no longer just meant establishing a new settlement, draining a swamp, irrigating a desert, or planting a forest. It also meant opening a new electronics plant, an aircraft factory, or a steel-rolling mill.

The pace of industrial expansion accelerated sharply after 1967. American, Canadian, German, French, and a few British companies, both Jewish and non-Jewish, substantially increased their investments in Israel. In addition to Jewish investors such as the Warburgs and the Rothschilds, there were multinational firms including ITT, RCA, IBM, Allied Chemical, Coca-Cola, Ford, ITEK, Motorola, Bethlehem Steel, and Monsanto. By 1970, these and other foreign companies were investing about $150 million a year. The process was described thus by the British Zionist writer Jon Kimche:

> The combination of this massive domestic investment and the interests of large foreign concerns linked to the large inflow of capital—donations, the sale of bonds, foreign loans and aid— created a new Israeli elite, a new establishment that to a considerable extent displaced the old, or embraced part of it into its amply financed New Deal. This resulted in a new parallel power-structure to that which had dominated Israel for the

previous 30 years, even in the days before the State was established. Thus, alongside the old establishment—the political parties, the Jewish Agency, the Histadrut, the Kibbutz organizations and the armed forces—there grew up the new elite, which was no longer dependent on the restrictive patronage of the old establishment but was strong enough and had the financial resources to exercise its own form of patronage and influence.

Kimche describes those who owned the most prosperous concerns as the "captains of industry," Israel's "hundred families," with control over a substantial share of the private sector. Most of these wealthy "captains" had served in either the military or civilian institutions of the Yishuv, and formed a bridge to the wealth of diaspora Jews, mostly American and British. In addition to this group, Kimche describes another, who had no part in industrial ownership but who carried considerable political influence. These were Israelis who had been part of the governmental or military establishments and had been affiliated with one of the major political parties. They included a former intelligence chief, a former chief of staff, a former commander of the navy, politicians, lawyers, doctors, and academics. The largest number were probably from the military services. Of seventy-five senior military officers who retired between 1952 and 1970, twenty-two assumed executive positions in industry.

These groups constituted the new Zionist elite in a movement where pioneering had shifted from land to industry, defense, and finance. After 1967, says Kimche,

the new Zionist elite was almost totally cut off from the mass of Israelis by a difference in outlook and wealth, by altogether different social aspirations and interests, and by an altogether different assessment of Israel's role in the life of the Jew. In place of the balanced society of classical Zionism came the concept of the efficient state derived from the models which owed more of their concepts to the modern supermarket and merchant bankers than to the ideologies of Herzl and Weizmann.

The contradictions created by the gap between ideology and the requirements of rapid modernization were revealed in contrasting lifestyles, living standards, and attitudes. Until the late 1970s, between 94 and 95 percent of Israeli land was publicly owned by the state, the Jewish National Fund, or some other public body. Yet private land speculation has become widespread. The State Lands Authority either sells or rents land at market prices to private entrepreneurs for agricultural or industrial purposes. While 60 percent of Israel's economy is in the public sector, the tax structure and system of government subsidies favor private enterprise, according to many Israeli economists. Large accumulations of property or capital endow the owner with privileges: higher education for his children, foreign travel, luxury housing, and a lifestyle not available to the average Israeli.

Transformations in Israeli society during the first generation have inevitably changed the perspectives and values of the population and its leaders. Many fundamental credos of the Yishuv during the preindependence era are still accepted as the basis for national ideology even though some have become anachronistic under the impact of changes after 1948. The Yishuv is no longer a small compact society with a relatively homogeneous social and economic structure. Nor could the state, with its substantial Arab minority, claim to be exclusively Jewish. Principles of egalitarianism and emphasis on pioneering, while still theoretically upheld, receive much less emphasis. In an expanding world economy dominated by industrial and technological development, both ideological and practical compromises have been necessary.

CHAPTER THREE

Political Parties and Ideologies in Israel

The political party system of Israel is a heritage of the prestate era, evolving from diverse ideological trends and interest groups within the Zionist movement. Three large party blocs dominate the system: the Labor, religious, and center-nationalist groups. In recent elections, these blocs were represented as follows: the Labor bloc by the Labor alignment (Maarach); the religious bloc by the National Religious party (Mafdal) and by a smaller, more Orthodox group called the Torah Religious Front; and the center-nationalist bloc by Likud, a coalition of Herut and Liberals called Gahal, and other nationalist factions. In the eighth national election of 1973, the three blocs combined received more than 80 percent of all votes, and won over 100 of the 120 Knesset seats. During the 1977 election, a new party, the Democratic Movement for Change, was formed by ex-members of the two nonreligious blocs, severely undermining Labor's strength in the Ninth Knesset.

THE PARTY SYSTEM

The three large blocs and the parties that comprise them have often undergone mergers, splits, fragmentations, and reunions, sometimes caused by ideological or policy differences, sometimes by personality clashes (see Figure 1). The number of

Figure 1.   The Evolution of Israel's Political Parties,
1949-1977

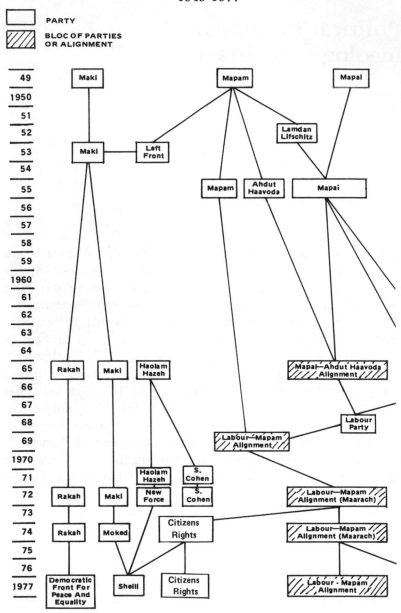

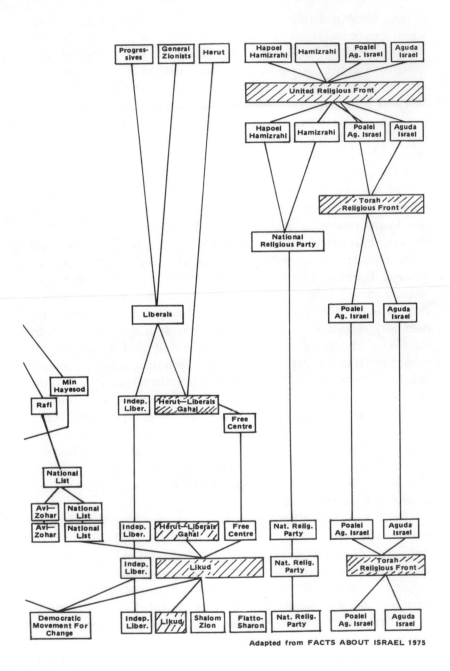

Adapted from FACTS ABOUT ISRAEL 1975

parties rises and falls with the political winds. Before 1948, when the population of the Yishuv was less than one-fifth of what it is today, there were more than thirty parties or political groups. Twenty-four parties participated in the first election during 1949. Sixteen were represented in the First Knesset. Mergers and establishment of large party blocs reduced the number so that only twenty-one participated in the 1973 election, with ten winning seats in parliament. In 1977, twenty-three entered the election; thirteen won Knesset seats (see Table 1).

Multiple parties are said to be a function of the proportional representation system in which members are elected at large, not from separate constituencies. This system originated in the world Zionist movement. All major parties in Israel descend from Zionist groups established in the diaspora, mostly in Eastern Europe. Elections to the World Zionist Congresses were determined by the nature of the World Zionist Organization, which was not a government and did not have sovereignty over any territory. Congressional representatives came from dozens of diaspora countries with small and large Jewish communities. Therefore territorial constituencies were impractical or impossible to form. A system in which constituencies were represented by whoever won the most votes would have left out a large number of significant perspectives. Many Zionists would have been unrepresented and some might have left the organization to form their own separate Zionist bodies, as when Jabotinsky followers left the World Zionist Organization in the 1930s to form the New Zionist Organization because of policy disagreements.

The Zionist movement organized congresses so that diverse trends and personalities would have an opportunity to publicize their views. Because the World Zionist Organization was based on voluntary membership, it could not impose majority rule. If minority rights were not respected, dissidents were free to leave the movement. But special efforts were made to see that all groups were represented on the Zionist executive and in the council that managed organization affairs.

As growing numbers of Jews accepted the credos of Zionism, the constituency expanded to include many political, social,

and economic orientations. There were Orthodox fundamen-
talists, Jewish modernists, secularists, and even atheists;
protagonists of conservative, liberal, radical, and Marxist
economic doctrines; some who emphasized political or
territorial problems, and others for whom development of a
national culture and language was paramount. Differences
were often so intense that followers of these diverse factions
formed their own organizations or parties to advance their own
causes within the Zionist movement and to elect their own
representatives to its governing bodies.

Most parties in areas of Europe where there were large Jewish
communities formed their own Zionist organizations. They
established youth groups, party newspapers and periodicals,
book publishing companies, financial institutions, and in a
few cases, labor groups and health services. During the
Mandate, the leaders of many of these groups moved to
Palestine and established parallel Zionist parties there. Under
mandatory law, the Yishuv could levy dues on members of the
Jewish community, which were distributed among the parties
on the basis of their strength.

Originally, the parties strongly emphasized ideological
issues, influenced by the political climate in Eastern and
Central Europe. Minutiae of ideology were discussed in party
organs, daily or weekly newspapers, and in other publications
such as the party dissertations published at election time.
Ideologues were trained at seminars, in study groups, and in
political clubs. Before coming to Palestine, these groups could
not impose levies on the community, and ideologues had to
rely on moral pressure to rally support.

Ideological consensus based on the simple fundamentals of
Zionism has held the Yishuv together despite sharp differences.
Recently, outnumbered by surrounding hostile populations,
Israelis have been brought together by the issue of national
survival, a stronger force than divisiveness between right and
left, religion and secularism. This was persuasively demonstrated on the eve of the 1967 war, when a government coalition
was formed including groups which had vowed never to work
together.

For some Jews, the Zionist movement or secular Jewish

Table 1. Knesset Election Results, 1949-1977

PARTY	First 25.1.49 Electorate 506,567 Valid Votes Cast 434,684 — %	Seat	Second 30.7.51 924,885 687,492 — %	Seat	Third 26.7.55 1,057,795 853,219 — %	Seat	Fourth 3.11.59 1,218,483 964,337 — %	Seat	Fifth 15.8.61 1,274,280 1,006,964 — %	Seat	Sixth 2.11.65 1,449,709 1,206,728 — %	Seat
MAPAI	35.7[1]	46	37.3[1]	45	32.2	40	38.2	47	34.7	42	44.6	55[7]
ACHDUT HA'AVODA					8.2	10	6.0	7	6.5	8		
MAPAM	14.7	19	12.5	15	7.3	9	7.2	9	7.6	9	6.6	8
HERUT	11.5	14	6.6	8	12.6	15	13.6	17	13.7	17	21.3[8]	26
LIBERALS[2]	5.2 / 4.1	7 / 5	18.9 / 3.2	23 / 4	10.2 / 4.4	13 / 5	6.1 / 4.6	8 / 6	13.6	17	3.8	5
NATIONAL RELIGIOUS PARTY	12.2	16[3]	8.3	10	9.1	11	9.9	12	9.8	12	8.9	11
AGUDA ISRAEL			3.7[6]	5	4.7	6	4.7	6	3.7	4	3.3	4
POALEI AGUDA ISRAEL									1.9	2	1.8	2
COMMUNISTS	3.5	4	4.0	5	4.5	6	2.8	3	4.1	5	3.4	4[10]
ARAB LISTS[4]	3.0	2	4.7	5	4.9	5	3.5	5	3.5	4	3.3	4
OTHERS (Total)	10.1	7[5]	0.7	—	1.9	—	3.4	—	0.7	—	2.9	1[11]

Eighth 31.12.73 — Electorate 2,037,478 — Valid Votes Cast 1,566,855

PARTY	%	Seats
LABOUR—MAPAM ALIGNMENT (MA'ARACH)	39.7	51
ARAB LIST AFFILIATED TO LABOUR	2.4	3
LIKUD	30.2	39
INDEPENDENT LIBERALS	3.6	4
NATIONAL RELIGIOUS PARTY (MAFDAL)	8.3	10
TORAH RELIGIOUS FRONT	3.8	5
NEW COMMUNIST LIST (RAKAH)	3.4	4
CITIZENS RIGHTS MOVEMENT	2.2	3
MOKED	1.4	1
OTHERS (Total)	5.0	—

Seventh 28.10.69 — Electorate 1,758,685 — Valid Votes Cast 1,367,743

PARTY	%	Seats
LABOUR—MAPAM ALIGNMENT (MA'ARACH)	46.22	56
ARAB LIST AFFILIATED TO LABOUR	3.51	4
GAHAL	21.67	26
NATIONAL (MAMLACHTI)	3.11	4
FREE CENTRE	1.20	2
INDEPENDENT LIBERALS	3.21	4
NATIONAL RELIGIOUS PARTY	9.74	12
AGUDA ISRAEL	3.22	4
POALEI AGUDA ISRAEL	1.83	2
NEW COMMUNIST LIST (RAKKAH)	2.84	3
ISRAEL COMMUNIST PARTY (MAKI)	1.15	1
HA'OLAM HAZEH (NEW FORCE)	1.23	2
OTHERS (Total)	1.07	—

PARTY	Ninth 11.5.77 1,747,820	
	%	Seats
LABOUR—MAPAM ALIGNMENT (MA'ARACH) ARAB LIST AFFILIATED TO LABOUR	26	32 1
LIKUD	33.4	43
DEMOCRATIC MOVEMENT FOR CHANGE	11.6	15
NATIONAL RELIGIOUS PARTY	9.2	12
AGUDA ISRAEL	3.4	4
POALEI AGUDA ISRAEL	1.4	1
DEMOCRATIC FRONT FOR PEACE AND EQUALITY (RAKKAH AND BLACK PANTHERS)	4.6	5
SHELLI (MOKED 1973)	1.6	2
SHALOM ZION (GENERAL SHARON)	1.9	2
FLATTO—SHARON	2.0	1
INDEPENDENT LIBERALS	1.2	1
CITIZENS RIGHTS	1.2	1

[1] In 1949 and 1951 Mapam included Achdut Ha'avoda. [2] Figures for first four Knessets refer respectively to General Zionists and Progressives, who merged in 1961 to form the Liberal Party. See also notes 8 and 9. [3] In 1949 these parties constituted the United Religious Front. [4] Associated with or affiliated to Mapai. [5] Four Sephardim, one Yemenite, one WIZO and one of the Fighters' (Lehi). [6] In 1951 and 1959, these constituted the Torah Religious Front. [7] The Mapai-Achdut Ha'avoda alignment, with 36.7% and 45 seats, and Rafi (7.9% and 10 seats). [8] Herut-Liberal Bloc (Gahal) [9] Independent Liberals. [10] Three New Communist List (Rakkah) and one Israel Communist Party (Maki). [11] Ha'olem Hazeh.

Adapted From FACTS ABOUT ISRAEL 1975

nationalism was often a substitute for Jewish religious identity and practice. Participation in Zionist political activity, both in the diaspora and in Israel, replaced participation in the synagogue, the traditional center of Jewish communal identity.

Ideology tends to harden at the peripheries of each major bloc. Mapam, on the left wing of the Labor alignment, adamantly resists the Orthodox and Likud blocs, but in the Labor party as a whole there are more Orthodox Jews than there are in any of the religious parties. The Religious Workers party in the religious bloc is often closer in its social and economic platforms to Labor than to Likud. On the right wing of the Labor alignment, there are several leaders whose foreign policy and social orientations are closer to Likud than to Mapam. Within Likud, there are Knesset members whose foreign policy orientations are compatible with those of the Mapam mainstream.

As parties merge into larger blocs, the tendency is to deemphasize ideology because of the need to find common ground with other groups. The larger the bloc, and the greater the number of factions which constitute it, the greater the pressure for internal ideological compromise. The small parties with the least need to find political compromises remain the most ideologically "pure." The left of Israel's political spectrum demonstrates this well. The farther one moves to the left, the larger the number of splits between parties. Israel's Communist movement has gone through extensive fragmentation because of quarrels over minutiae of dogma. After division of the Israeli Communist party into two large factions during 1965, each spawned so many offspring that it is difficult to keep up with their numbers and policies.

In the larger parties, especially in the Labor alignment, the range of activities nearly covers the gamut of daily life. The spectrum of party activities is greater than those among the large Social Democratic movements of Western Europe. Through control of the Histadrut, or General Federation of Labor, the party helps to provide housing projects, health services, vacation resorts, and cooperatives to buy and purchase foods. The Labor party–dominated Histadrut also has its own newspapers, publishing houses, schools, cultural activities including theatrical and musical groups, and a string of cooperative enterprises from bus lines to construction companies. Manver Bernstein, an American political scientist and university professor, has described what domination of the Histadrut by the Labor alignment means: a party member

> could spend his whole life within the framework of the organization. He wakes up in a house built by a Histadrut society, goes to work in a bus operated by a cooperative, spends his days in a factory owned by the Histadrut, sends his children to what used to be labour movement schools, goes to a Kupat Holim (the Histadrut health service) for medical treatment, spends his vacation at a Histadrut rest home, and finds entertainment in workers' clubs and theatres. It needs no big stretch of the imagination to say the same of the Mapai member who can, if he wishes, move exclusively within this huge, largely self-contained organization.

None of the parties outside the Labor bloc has so extensive a network of services, but most engage in activities extending far beyond those of Western political parties. The religious and right-wing parties have attempted to compete with the economic and social welfare services offered by Labor, but they never had access to the kind of resources the Histadrut was able to rally. Until 1948, some of the parties had their own military or paramilitary affiliated organizations. The IZL or Irgun Zvai Leumi ("National Military Organization") was closely linked to the Revisionist movement, and the Palmach or Plugot Mahatz ("Strike Force") with left-wing Labor *kibbutzim*. After Ben-Gurion's decision to merge all these forces into a national military organization above party politics, there were no longer any armed forces controlled by political groups.

Party dues provide only a small percentage of the funds for this diverse range of activities. Additional resources are available through contributions raised by overseas Jewish communities, party business enterprises, and banks and credit organizations belonging to the parties. A law passed by the Knesset in 1974 allows state subventions in proportion to the number of party members, provided the party receives no contributions from corporations. (Histadrut payment of election expenses was not included in this restriction.)

An unusual aspect of this system is party identification with its affiliates in Jewish communities abroad, and membership of Zionist parties in Israel and abroad in international federations or confederations. The Likud is affiliated with the Revisionist movement in the United States and with an international Revisionist association; the National Religious party is associated with the Mizrachi movement in the United States and several other countries and with an international federation; the two components of the Labor Alignment, the Labor party and Mapam, have affiliates in Western countries and are themselves members of an international federation of Zionist Labor parties.

The internal organization and structure of each party is more or less similar, marked by strong centralization and control by a few older leaders in the party executive. Until the shake-up caused by the 1973 war, most party leaders were the same individuals who had been at the helm when the state was established in 1948. Each party has a convention of representatives periodically elected by the membership; it selects the central committee, party chairman, and other officials. Before these elections, the convention composes the party platform. But the real center of power lies with those individuals at the head of the list of candidates. Until recently, these few people could dominate the party and make its vital decisions. In parties or blocs composed of several factions, bargaining similar to that in a coalition cabinet is necessary to satisfy various interest groups.

Some individuals have successfully thwarted the leadership by leaving the party to form their own separate faction or list. The Knesset has had several one-, two-, and three-person factions made up of individuals who broke with larger parties. The Independent Liberals (ILP) are a remnant of the once powerful Liberal party, which joined with Herut in 1965 to form the Gahal bloc (Gush Herut-Liberalim). The Liberals were formed in 1961 by a merger of the General Zionist and Progressive parties. Liberals who refused to combine with Herut in 1965 have successfully maintained their separate identity and independence; they were considered ideal partners in Labor coalitions because of their moderate approach to both domestic and foreign affairs. In 1977 the ILP lost three of its four Knesset seats.

The Citizens Rights movement headed by Mrs. Shulamit Aloni scored surprisingly well in the 1973 elections, winning three Knesset seats with 2.2 percent of the vote. Mrs. Aloni previously was a Labor Knesset member who lost her "safe" place on the party's list because of outspoken disagreement with Prime Minister Meir. She won a relatively large following in 1973 by appealing to women, secularists, and those discontented with government bureaucracy. After Mrs. Meir's succession by Prime Minister Rabin, Mrs. Aloni became a cabinet minister without portfolio in the new coalition. However, she was sacrificed as a partner when Rabin decided to broaden his coalition by bringing the National Religious party back into government. The three Knesset members of the Citizens Rights movement briefly combined with another independent-minded maverick, Arie Eliav, who left the Labor party in 1974, to form a Knesset faction called Yozma ("initiative"). Eliav, a former Labor party secretary general, was critical of many government policies, especially in foreign affairs. Once elected to the Knesset as a Labor representative, he could not be deprived of his seat, but lost standing in the party; he was not included on its 1977 election list. Instead he ran on a new list called Shelli ("Peace and Equality for Israel").

Within a few months, disagreements between Eliav and Aloni split their small band of four Knesset members. Eliav and one of Mrs. Aloni's former followers formed a separate two-person Knesset faction called the Israeli Socialist party. Mrs. Aloni and her only remaining partner reconstituted their Citizens Rights movement, with two seats. In 1977, Eliav joined forces with Moked, another peace group, to form Shelli, which won two Knesset seats; Mrs. Aloni's Citizens Rights party obtained one seat. The list of separate factions formed in this manner is long. It is one of the more colorful and stimulating aspects of Israeli party life.

Pressure for greater democratization of party operations has been building up since the late 1950s, when Ben-Gurion became concerned about loss of vitality in the Labor organization. Through his influence, the first Mapai party convention in seven years was convened during 1956. A new party constitution was proposed which empowered 200 district branches of Mapai to nominate two-thirds of the party's Knesset list and two-thirds of the central committee members. The Mapai old guard, reluctant to surrender its control and prerogatives fought the proposals. A compromise was reached in which one-half of the Knesset list and one-half of the central committee members would be nominated by local branches. As part of the reform, younger men like Moshe Dayan and Shimon Peres, then in their late thirties or early forties, were coopted into leadership positions. Their disagreements with the old guard factionalized Mapai, and several prominent leaders left the party to form a new Knesset list in 1965 called Rafi—Reshima Poeli Israel ("Israel Workers List").

Other parties have gone through similar internal changes. Among younger members of the National Religious party and Gahal there has been growing criticism of the old guard, and an ascent of an assertive new generation to leadership positions. Either through internal political coups or through attrition by age, the old guard is bound soon to be replaced. The irony is that when the "young Turks" in these movements reach power, they usually have passed middle age. In the Labor party, the three men who symbolized the new generation, Yigal Allon, Shimon Peres, and Yitzhak Rabin, were all over fifty when they finally took over from the party's gerentocracy in 1973.

The trend toward democratization of political parties has been strengthened by the growing influence of local branches, especially in the Labor party. There is an ethnic component to this development. Many branches of the Labor party are in new development towns with large Oriental Jewish populations. At the local level, there has already been a shift of power from the older generation of the European Yishuv to the Oriental immigrants and their children. As they strengthen their positions in local party branches and in the Histadrut, the influence of these Orientals in elections to the national conventions has increased. Their input into national politics, while still small, is now given much more consideration by party leaders of European origin.

The division of cabinet posts among diverse parties closely influences government administrations. The most strategic ministries, including the position of prime minister and the ministries of Defense, Foreign Affairs, and the Treasury, were in the hands of the Labor party and its predecessor, Mapai, from 1948 until the election of 1977. During that time, those ministries maintained continuity in administration, planning, and daily operations despite shifts in the political winds. Other ministries shifted control from one party to another and often lost momentum as projects initiated by one party were abandoned when another took over. Often there was a change in the top ministry personnel as coalitions changed.

Government agencies have also been shunted from one ministry to another depending on political exigencies. The important Social Security Administration has been annexed to the Ministry of Labor from the Ministry of Development to accommodate a new party controlling the Labor Ministry. At times new ministries have been created and old ones disbanded to accommodate the coalition. The Ministry of Information was dispensed with when the cabinet post was no longer required. Information and Tourism have been both separate ministries and offices under the prime minister. The relative importance of a ministry, and the work it carries on, are in large measure related to the party that controls it. If, say, a ministry is shifted from Labor to a minor party in the coalition, the possibility that it will be downgraded is strong. In a government that is always short of funds, projects are to receive priority in ministries controlled by the dominant partner in the coalition, especially since that party always controls the Treasury, whose influence is strong in budget planning and implementation. (See chapter 6.)

THE LABOR BLOC

Jewish socialism and Jewish nationalism fused in early twentieth-century Europe to produce the Zionist Labor movement. Socialist Zionists perceived the Jewish community as an "inverted pyramid," with few Jews in primary occupations but many as middlemen. An early twentieth-century analysis of Jewish occupational distribution showed nearly one-half the population employed in the distribution of food and liquor, the clothing trade, the manufacture of jewelry, and the operation of small print shops. Fifteen to 20 percent were employed in building and textiles. Fewer than 1 percent were in agriculture and fewer than 10 percent in basic industry. Jews were not supplying society's basic requirements; instead they were concentrated in small shops, at the end of the production cycle. Out of the mainstream of the Marxist movement, they became paupers in highly competitive sweatshops. According to theoreticians like Ber Borochov, Jews in the diaspora were excluded from the larger Socialist struggle because of their rootlessness. They needed to be concentrated in a country of their own, where they would be unhampered by nationalist competition from, and discrimination by, other groups; a place where they could develop the base of their own socio-economic pyramid. Such a land would need sparse population and great potential for agricultural expansion.

This analysis provided the ideological basis for the first Socialist Zionist group, Poale Zion ("Workers of Zion"), established in 1907. It fused Borochov's ideas with those of A. D. Gordon, who settled in Palestine in 1904 at the age of forty-nine. Regarded by his followers as a saint and mystic, Gordon made the Jewish nation the foundation of his ideology, and socialism the basis for building the nation. He was among the early Zionists who venerated physical labor for its own sake. Through physical labor on the land, the Jewish nation would regenerate its lost spiritual values. His thesis, much less Marxian than Borochov's, was that the crux of the Jewish problem was not a struggle of capital against labor but of production versus parasitism. These theories created the mystique of Jewish labor on Jewish land.

Gordon's closest followers established Hapoel Hatzair ("The Young Worker") in Palestine, a group whose goals were to drain swamps, irrigate deserts, and establish new agricultural outposts. The more Marxian-oriented Poale Zion changed its name to Achdut Ha-Avoda ("Unity of Labor"), after merging with several smaller Socialist Zionist groups in Palestine.

The two parties, Poale Zion and Achdut Ha-Avoda, established Mapai ("Workers of Israel") in 1929, combining theoretical and practical Socialist trends. During the Mandate Mapai emphasized development of Jewish land with Jewish labor. Its slogans included "Conquest of the Land," and "Conquest of Labor." Most *kibbutzim* established during the mandatory era were affiliated with the Mapai-controlled *kibbutz* federation. The party also helped to establish agricultural cooperatives or *moshavim*. Jewish labor, Jewish production of essential commodities, a Jewish cooperative movement, and attraction of Jewish youth to land settlement in Eretz Israel were the movement's chief goals.

In 1920, before fusion into Mapai, the two Zionist Labor parties formed the Histadrut, which developed a massive structure parallel to the political parties and other institutions of the Yishuv. Most leaders, activities, and policies of the Histadrut were part of or determined by the Labor parties. All large trade unions belonged to the Histadrut. By the 1970s, about 80 percent of all workers and 90 percent of all organized workers in Israel belonged to the organization. Individuals or groups who are not members of the Labor parties can belong to the Histadrut; they include Communists, members of the religious bloc and Likud, and others, although Labor has always won more than one-half the votes in the Histadrut and thereby controls the organization. There still is an interlocking directorate of Histadrut and Labor alignment leaders. Several Histadrut secretaries general have also headed Mapai and the Labor party and Histadrut's executive is dominated by individuals who are or have been on the central committee of the Labor party.

By the 1930s, about 45 percent of the Yishuv was identified in one way or another with Labor organizations. Through centralization, dynamism, and dedication, Labor carried more weight than all other political groups. Mapai's leaders, like Ben-Gurion, Sharett, and Meir, became the central figures in the institutions of the Yishuv such as the National Council and the Haganah, and were also leaders of the world Zionist movement.

Until establishment of Israel in 1948, many leaders and members of Labor organizations came from the *kibbutzim*. From 1930 to 1965, Mapai membership grew from 6,000 to over 200,000. Sixty percent of the original members were from the agricultural sector, but by 1964 only 4.2 percent were farmers. Seventy percent or more of the party is now urban; about one-half is from Israel's five largest cities. During the 1930s and 1940s, when party leaders were mostly from *kibbutzim*, there was strong emphasis on developing agriculture. The ethos of Labor Zionism was still on the land and on physical expansion of the Yishuv.

As the economic foundations of the country broadened after 1949, there was increasing emphasis on industry, trade, commerce, and services which competed with agriculture for Labor party attention. It was necessary to attract not only industrial workers and artisans, but large professional groups in the cities including physicians, writers, journalists, engineers, and others whose living was not derived from primary occupations. Expansion of the labor movement into the nonagricultural sector was evident in the change of Histadrut membership. In 1964, when about one-half of the country's population were members, two-thirds were industrial workers, and nearly one-third clerical and professional workers. The percentage of agricultural workers had become negligible.

Mapai

Mapai, the core party of the Labor bloc until 1965, mirrored the changing social structure of Israel. As the Yishuv became more complex and interest groups multiplied, Mapai had to cater to a larger constituency. Changing attitudes toward class stratification, and the growing ethnic diversity of the country were reflected in structural changes within Mapai. The Arab communities, now part of Israel, were organized into separate Arab lists affiliated with Mapai.

The growing acceptance of bourgeois values in the Yishuv after 1948 was demonstrated in changing lifestyles, values, and political attitudes. Mapai directed more attention not only to the urban worker but to artisans and professionals. Physicians, lawyers, and accountants, formerly perceived as less important to the party than farmers or industrial workers, were organized into Mapai-affiliated professional groups. Recognition of such middle-class members departed from traditional Socialist glorification of the proletariat and the tendency to downgrade so-called bourgeois occupations. With expansion of the public sector in government and in the national institutions, the value of these professionals and their contributions to the national welfare received greater recognition.

The new situation raised serious ideological problems for Labor. Physicians, lawyers, and university professors demanded higher wages than laborers, and their lifestyles created class differences within the movement. Tensions generated by diverse lifestyles appeared when the Labor party attempted to reconcile differences between its organization for professional workers and the affiliated trade unions. These were apparent in disputes over wage policies which divided the Histadrut from the Labor party leadership when union members organized strikes not authorized by federation headquarters. In times of economic crises or austerity, when the governing Labor party imposed measures such as higher taxes or reduced food subsidies in opposition to the trade union membership, the rift between party and unions widened.

Israel's changing demographic patterns show in Labor party membership statistics. In 1954, only 27 percent of the party were Oriental Jews; they were 45 percent by 1965. Socialization or integration of new immigrants became a party function through departments for North Africans, Yemenites, and Iraqis. Mapai established more than thirty of these organizations, where immigrants were taught Hebrew and Israeli culture and values. The party assisted new immigrants in adjusting to Israeli life by helping them to find jobs, housing, and bank credit, and to resolve family problems. By the late 1960s, Oriental Jews represented less than one-third of the party's central committee, not more than 10 percent of the secretariat, and less than 20 percent of the Knesset delegation. Ironically, after Labor's defeat in the 1977 election, Oriental Jewish representation at cabinet level increased, when the new Likud government appointed several Sephardim to top posts.

The Labor party has competed successfully with the religious parties for Orthodox Jewish votes. Even before the influx of Oriental Jews, there were many Orthodox Jews in Mapai. After the large Oriental immigration, a Mapai religious circle was established to make contact with local religious councils in Oriental communities with a high percentage of Orthodox Jews.

Municipal party machines affiliated with the labor movement greatly increased their local power after 1948. Through control of vital economic sectors such as the Haifa dockworkers and municipal employees in Tel Aviv, local labor leaders acquired control over party branches in large cities, giving them blocks of votes in the party convention and central committee. Abba Khoushi, the Mapai leader in Haifa, and the Gush ("bloc") in Tel Aviv became strong components of the national party, playing important roles in selection of national leaders and in national decision making. Other informal groupings represented such distinct interest groups as university professors and former army officers.

Expansion of Mapai's constituency to include diverse interest groups, factions, and circles tended to undermine the original Socialist ideology; increasingly the trend was towards national rather than class interests. Growth of party institutions, both official and unofficial, not only increased the size of the bureaucracy, but ended much of the informality and sense of intimacy prevailing during the prestate era. The party bureaucracy was no longer easily accessible to the average member. As some party leaders became established, they acquired not only influence and prestige but material advantages which created a social distance between many of them and the rank and file.

The Rafi Party

To counteract growing development of special interest groups, bureaucratization, and inbreeding of leadership, Ben-Gurion and a group of Mapai young leaders *(zeirim)* began demanding party reform during the late 1950s. An initial step was election of several *zeirim* to the Knesset on the 1958 Mapai list. Impatient with lack of opportunity for advancement in the party councils, Abba Eban, Shimon Peres, and Moshe Dayan entered the Knesset in 1958 with Ben-Gurion's assistance; later Ben-Gurion became the group's unofficial spokesman. With a national figure as leader, the *zeirim* attempted to shift the focus of party activity from internal partisan matters to questions concerning Israeli society as a whole. The group's theme was loyalty to nation above loyalty to party. Their approach was expressed in the term *mamlachtiut* ("statism"), coined by Ben-Gurion. Initially they focused attention on the trade-union movement and the powerful Histadrut. Challenging a cardinal principle of the trade-union movement, they insisted that management had the right to dismiss inefficient labor in order to lower production costs and increase productivity. Without increased productivity, they argued, the social benefits received by union members would weaken the country's entire economic structure.

Ben-Gurion and the *zeirim* believed it essential to extend the concept of pioneering *(halutziut)* beyond agriculture and the land to include other sectors of society and the economy. Industry based on science and technology, they believed, was equally essential for national development. Expertise and efficiency replaced Mapai's traditional glorification of physical labor.

The *mamlachtiut* ideology polarized growing tensions between the government and the Histadrut. Pinchas Lavon, secretary general of the Histadrut, became a defender of the old land-rooted values. Temporarily discredited by the 1954 "security mishap" (an operation of Israeli intelligence in Egypt which misfired), Lavon rose again to become head of the Histadrut in 1956. Some Mapai old guard even considered him as a candidate for prime minister to replace Ben-Gurion. By 1958, the intensity of ideological division in the party polarized the leadership into factions. The *zeirim* assumed the mantle of reformers in opposition to the party's old guard, the Histadrut, and other powerful interests like the Tel Aviv Gush.

Ideological and organizational differences were intensified by sharp personality clashes, especially between Lavon and Ben-Gurion. These disputes came to a head in 1960, when Lavon demanded that Ben-Gurion clear him of any responsibility for the 1954 "security mishap." Lavon had been cleared by a cabinet committee, but its authority was challenged by Ben-Gurion, who insisted that only an impartial judicial inquiry could make a valid judgment. Ben-Gurion threatened to resign unless the cabinet and party accepted his position. Finance Minister Levi Eshkol, one of the middle-ground Mapai leaders, who was later to succeed Ben-Gurion as prime minister, proposed a compromise involving dropping of Lavon as head of the Histadrut and shelving of any further discussion or inquiry into the affair.

After Eshkol succeeded Ben-Gurion in 1963, he downgraded the *zeirim* and their "statist" approach, returning to the previous pattern of party politics, with the old guard and the Histadrut at the center of power. Moshe Dayan, a new member of the cabinet as minister of agriculture, threatened to resign if he was not taken into the inner cabinet councils.

Threatened by the rapidly rising popularity of Ben-Gurion's reforms, the old guard searched for ways to strengthen its position. The old guard's declining influence was evident in the reduction in Mapai's control of the Histadrut, from 80 percent of the organization during the 1930s to 55.4 percent in the 1960 Histadrut election. With a new election due in 1964, the Mapai leadership thought it had found a solution in an electoral alliance with another strong Labor group.

The most logical choice seemed to be Achdut Ha-Avoda, a Labor group formerly affiliated with Mapai, which had left in 1948 to join Mapam. Achdut Ha-Avoda had broken with Mapam, and was again interested in affiliation with Mapai. Reunion of Mapai and Achdut Ha-Avoda would also be a step toward unity of all the major Labor parties.

Many Achdut Ha-Avoda leaders were traditional Socialists and skeptical of, if not outright opposed to, the statist doctrines of the *zeirim*. Several had worked closely with the Mapai old guard as cabinet ministers in earlier governments. Against this background of shifting alliances and new factions among Labor organizations, Lavon again made a request, this time to Eshkol, that he be cleared. His actions angered Ben-Gurion, who had made the Lavon affair into an issue of personal trust. Ben-Gurion insisted once more that only an impartial judicial inquiry, not a ministerial committee of Lavon's associates, could clear him.

At the tenth Mapai conference in 1964, issues of ideology, party tactics, and personality difference converged to create a crisis in the party. The crucial questions were: who should succeed Ben-Gurion following his resignation; whether Mapai should realign itself with Achdut Ha-Avoda; how to deal with the Lavon affair; and how to resolve the fundamental ideological dispute between the traditionalists and the new statists. When the majority of the conference voted in favor of the old guard, Ben-Gurion announced that he and several of the *zeirim* would leave Mapai to form a new Labor list, Rafi.

The new Labor list commanded substantial support in the 1965 elections to the Sixth Knesset, but far less than had been anticipated, considering that its leader was Ben-Gurion and that it included leaders of the Labor movement like Peres and Dayan. Rafi had no well-defined and comprehensive program. Rather, it played the role of opposition critic. Above all, it was anti-Eshkol, anti-Mapai, and anti-Histadrut. It challenged many basic and widely accepted values and institutions of the old Yishuv without substituting new ones plausible enough to compete with Mapai.

Many supporters and opponents of Rafi perceived it as Ben-Gurion's party, and thus the issue became loyalty to "the old man" versus fidelity to the party. Ben-Gurion's charismatic hold on many voters was evident in the transfer of allegiance by many notably Oriental voters from Mapai to Rafi. Rafi appeared as a separate list only once, in 1965. Even with the charismatic leadership of Ben-Gurion and an array of rising stars, it won only 7.9 percent of the votes and ten seats in the 1965 election. Later it rejoined Mapai and Achdut Ha-Avoda to form the Labor party; a few Rafi members maintained their separate identity as the Mamlachti list, and later this faction joined the right-wing Likud.

The new Labor alignment of Achdut Ha-Avoda and Mapai retained its strength in the 1965 election with 44.6 percent of the votes and forty-five seats. The election demonstrated Mapai's institutional strength through a variety of Labor-affiliated organizations. In the contest between traditional party institutions and an array of colorful personalities, the party won. None of the main branches of Mapai defected, although several leaders left to join Rafi.

Rafi's major weakness as a separate party was its lack of control over local patronage, government jobs, and the Histadrut. It could enlist only about 25,000 members, less than one-tenth of the number in Mapai. Sixty percent of the Rafi members were under thirty-five years old, demonstrating the extent to which the new party represented opposition to the old guard. The fractious tone of its pronouncements, the bitter personal attacks on Mapai leader Levi Eshkol and its great hostility to the Histadrut worried many Labor sympathizers who otherwise might have agreed with criticism of the party's entrenched leadership.

Not all members of Achdut Ha-Avoda were eager to merge with the larger and more powerful Mapai. Many wanted to retain a distinctive identity as left-wing Socialists with a separate federation of *kibbutzim*. Some leaders were apprehensive about Eshkol, who was known for his consensus approach to difficult problems. Both domestic and foreign affairs conspired to weaken the Mapai old guard between 1965 and 1967. On the home front, the country entered a serious economic recession, with nearly 10 percent unemployment. Labor unrest, increasing emigration of professionals, and disappointment in Eshkol were undermining confidence in the government. The situation was characterized by one of the country's well-known satirists, Dosh, in a cartoon showing a queue of people leaving Israel. A sign at the departure point requested: "Will the last one out please turn off the lights!"

Under these difficult circumstances, Israelis feared that a grand alliance of Arab states would start a third war against the Jewish state. Rhetoric from the neighboring capitals became so shrill that many Israelis and their Jewish supporters abroad feared another Holocaust. By June 1967, most were sure that an Arab attack was imminent.

Eshkol's consensus approach to critical problems, his lack of dynamism by comparison with Ben-Gurion, and his lower-key style of crisis management, made him appear indecisive and fumbling. Many Israelis thought the country was adrift without leadership at its most critical moment. Some newspapers and opposition leaders called for Eshkol's resignation. Others demanded that he turn the Ministry of

Defense over to Dayan or Ben-Gurion. Menachem Begin, the Herut leader who had been Ben-Gurion's chief antagonist for fifteen years, proposed that "the old man" assume leadership of the country's military forces.

The Labor Party

A few days before eruption of the June 1967 war, a compromise was worked out in which Dayan was invited to become defense minister and the first coalition of national unity was formed, excluding only the Communists and other minor parties. Herut entered the government for the first time, breaking a long-established Labor principle not to participate in a coalition with Begin.

This demonstration of national unity healed many deep rifts among factions in the Labor bloc and between Labor and other parties. With all Labor groups from Mapam to Rafi once again serving in the same government, hopes of establishing a united Labor party were revived. Preparatory to elections for the Seventh Knesset in 1968, Mapai, Achdut Ha-Avoda and Rafi merged into a new Labor party. Mapam, guarding its independence and distinctive ideology, did not join the new party but became affiliated with it in a single Knesset list, the Labor alignment or Maarach.

It took several more years for the three components of the Labor party, Mapai, Achdut Ha-Avoda, and Rafi, to abandon their separate identities and merge their party machines. After Prime Minister Eshkol's death in 1969 and the succession of Golda Meir, there was a trend toward domination by the Mapai old guard, except in the realms of defense and the occupied areas, which were controlled by Defense Minister Dayan. The old guard was reenforced by Mrs. Meir's frequent consultations with and reliance on old party colleagues in her informal "kitchen cabinet."

The 1973 war created another major shift in the Labor party's internal organization. Following inquiries by a special commission into conduct of the war, Mrs. Meir and several other old-guard figures resigned. A new government was formed under Yitzhak Rabin, Israel's first native-born prime minister and the first who was not intimately identified with the Mapai leadership. Rabin's government was really run by a triumvirate: Prime Minister Rabin, who was not closely identified with any party faction; Shimon Peres, the defense minister representing Rafi; and Foreign Minister and Deputy Prime Minister Yigal Allon, a leader of Achdut Ha-Avoda.

Ben-Gurion never returned to the mainstream; after merger of Mapai, Rafi, and Achdut Ha-Avoda in 1968, he refused to join the new Labor party. Instead, he and a few close personal followers formed their own Mamlachti list for the Knesset, which declined to 3.11 percent of the vote and four seats in the 1969 parliamentary election. Its strength continued to decline after Ben-Gurion's resignation from parliament. The last splinter of Rafi, a one-man faction called the State party, was finally merged into the right-wing Likud block formed before the eighth Knesset election of 1973.

Mapam

Since the establishment of Israel, Mapam ("United Workers Party") has represented the left wing of the Labor bloc. It was established in 1948 by three groups on the far left: Hashomer Hatzair ("the Young Guard"), a revolutionary Socialist group founded in 1927; Achdut Ha-Avoda, which had split from Mapai in 1948; and Poale Zion Smole ("Left Zion Workers"), a small Marxist faction that had remained outside Mapai when it was established in 1927.

Mapam has gone through extensive ideological, tactical, and political change since 1948. In the first Knesset elections of 1949, it was the second-largest party, with nearly 15 percent of the vote and nineteen seats. Since then its fortunes have steadily declined because of internal divisions, loss of support, and the departure of Achdut Ha-Avoda. In the sixth Knesset elections of 1965, it won only 6.6 percent of the vote and eight seats. During 1969, 1973, and 1977 it was aligned with the Labor party, but maintained a separate identity.

Mapam's decline has been caused by failure to adapt to social and political changes in Israel. The Marxist overtones of its ideology, although modified after 1948, were still considered too doctrinaire by the growing middle class. Its moderate positions on foreign policy, and toward Israel's Arab minority, were not nationalistic enough for the Oriental Jewish voters. Long association with the Communist International and early friendship with the Soviet Union made it suspect in the eyes of many Israelis, who regarded Russia as Israel's enemy.

Internal quarrels over Mapam's affiliation with the Communist International and the Soviet Union precipitated party upheaval between 1952 and 1954. During this era, Moscow, Israel's first supporter in the United Nations, turned its Middle East allegiance toward the Arab states. Forced by Soviet policy to choose between Jewish nationalism and socialist solidarity, the party split into supporters of the international revolutionary labor movement and Zionists. The division was so sharp that it divided many Mapam *kibbutzim* into warring factions, separating families and culminating in actual physical division of some *kibbutzim* into pro- and anti- Soviet sectors. The nationalists, those with primary loyalty to Zionism, were mostly from the Achdut Ha-Avoda movement. They separated from Mapam in 1953, again becoming a distinct non-Marxist party. Achdut Ha-Avoda rejoined Mapai to form the Labor alignment in 1965. In 1968, Mapai, Achdut Ha-Avoda, and Rafi formed the Labor party.

Hashomer Hatzair, the core group of Mapam, began as an Eastern European Zionist youth movement with a Marxist orientation and strong devotion to the *kibbutz* or collective ideal. Its members considered themselves an integral part of the world proletariat, striving to replace "the capitalist system with its profits and exploitation of the many for the good of the few" with a new economic and social order where class distinctions would disappear. After its founders settled in Palestine and established Hashomer Hatzair as a political party, leadership came largely from the left wing of the *kibbutz* movement. Its federation of collectives, Kibbutz Artzi, could claim nearly one-half the membership of the *kibbutz* movement, but the party had relatively few urban supporters.

Mapam's many agricultural settlements contributed greatly to development of frontier areas and to continued idealization of the traditional pioneer, or *halutz*, values. Strong ideological commitment to rural development led Mapam to overlook the importance of organizing urban workers and the significance for Israel of large scale industry. (Many Mapam *kibbutzim* did develop small industries.) Because few of its members played leading roles in industry, Mapam was unable to compete with Mapai in placing members as directors of nonagricultural enterprises.

Before the establishment of Israel in 1948, Hashomer Hatzair ideology strongly emphasized compromise with Palestinian Arab nationalism by formation of a binational state rather than one that was exclusively Jewish or Arab. The ideological justification for binationalism was that economic and social differences caused the clash between Jewish and Palestinian nationalism, and that British imperialism exploited these differences. Removing class rivalries and imperialist exploitation would end the struggle between the two national movements.

Hashomer Hatzair's binational program isolated it from the rest of the Yishuv on the most vital political issue of the day. When most Zionists supported the 1942 Biltmore Program calling for establishment in Palestine of a Jewish commonwealth, Hashomer Hatzair continued to support an Arab-Jewish state. Until independence in 1948, the movement continued to oppose partition of Palestine or establishment of a separate Jewish state. Then it totally reversed its position and stated that only in partitioned Israel could Zionism be realized. Now it opposes incorporation into Israel of heavily populated Arab areas acquired during the 1967 war.

Before independence, Hashomer Hatzair was the most vital element in the *kibbutz* movement and a high percentage of collectives are still identified with Kibbutz Artzi. Mapam's Socialist program since 1947 has stressed greater centralization of the economy, more emphasis on planning in the agricultural and industrial sectors, and nationalization of the country's natural resources.

The Radical Left

Many of the dilemmas, trials, and tribulations of the Israeli left were epitomized by the career of Dr. Moshe Sneh. Born in Poland in 1909, Dr. Sneh headed the General Zionist movement there during the 1930s. After immigrating to Palestine in 1940, he headed the Haganah, was a member of the Jewish Agency executive, and director of the Political Department in the agency's European office. When Mapam was formed in 1947, he became a member of its Executive Committee and editor of its daily newspaper, *Al-Hamishmar* ("On Guard"). Although his international political orientation appeared to have become pro-Soviet, he maintained that he was still a Jewish nationalist. He claimed that Israel's future, however, was with the Third World; inevitably the Soviet Union would play a dominant role in the Middle East. These views were consistent with the strong anti-British feeling in the Yishuv during 1947-48. Sneh was shaken by the massive efforts of the United States to rebuild West Germany so soon after World II. Furthermore, the Soviet Union supported the UN plan to partition Palestine, and the delegates of the USSR at the United Nations were the most outspoken for a Jewish state.

After the split in Mapam, Sneh kept faith with the Communist International. He blamed Israel's difficulties with the Eastern bloc on its overzealous attachment to the United States. In protest against Mapam compromises, he left the party in 1953 to form a new faction called Siat Smole ("Left Faction"), and in 1954 he joined Maki, the Israeli Communist party.

Maki was a blend of several radical ideological perspectives, mostly outside, if not opposed to, the Zionist movement. It grew out of the Palestinian Communist party formed in 1924. Only a few of its leaders, like Sneh, considered themselves Jewish nationalists. Communist encouragement of Yiddish rather than Hebrew symbolized the opposition to Zionism. According to the Soviet line, Zionism was a bourgeois movement closely identified with Western imperialism. Despite the fact that most members of the pre-1948 Palestinian Communist party were Jewish, it could never obtain more than 3 percent of the Yishuv's votes. In 1943 the party split into three factions: the Arab League of National Liberation, which supported Palestinian Arab aspirations; a Jewish non-Zionist group; and a few individuals who called themselves the Communist Education Association, which later joined the militant Lehi underground movement. The Jewish and Arab factions were reunited as Maki in 1948, pledging loyalty to the new state, but opposed to Zionism.

Maki was in an untenable position in the Jewish community because it followed the Soviet line unfailingly. With the shift from Soviet support for Israel to unswerving backing for Arab nationalism, Maki attracted a large Arab vote. The strain of reconciling anti-Zionism with support for Jewish nationalism, and loyalty to the state of Israel with Soviet guidance on foreign policy, was too great for the party. In 1965 it again split into two groups: the parent organization, and Rakkah (the New Communist List), most, but not all, of whose followers were Israeli Arabs.

After 1948, the Communist party in Israel was identified by many Arabs as a nationalist or liberation movement rather than a Marxist movement. It was quick to defend the interests of Israel's Arab citizens and to criticize government intrusions on civil rights, the sequestering of Arab land, and the imposition of military government. The Arab community, most directly affected by these measures, perceived the Communist party as a legitimate expression of nationalist sentiment and dissatisfaction with government.

After bifurcation of Maki in 1965, Moshe Sneh continued to lead the parent organization, which was left with fewer members than the breakaway Rakkah party. Sneh attempted to maintain a neutral position in the Arab-Israeli dispute, as Arab nationalism became more militant and the Soviet Union intensified its hostility to Israel. Moscow maintained its associations with both Maki and Rakkah for two years, until the 1967 war. Sneh blamed both Jewish and Arab "reactionary chauvinist" leaders for the conflict, rejecting the Soviet interpretation of the war. Following an independent line, he attacked Arab terrorism and opposed Israel's evacuation of the occupied territories prior to a peace settlement. Soviet support for Arab aggression was, said Sneh, a "tactical blunder." Even though he continued to regard Moscow as the leader in the struggle against imperialism, he asserted that it should have remained neutral in the Arab-Israeli conflict.

As Sneh became increasingly critical of the Arab states, his ideology shifted back toward Mapam. His ideas differed from those of the Jewish new left movements formed after 1967 in his recognition of the Jewish nation as a cohesive international community with its own distinct aspirations. Before his death in 1972, Sneh reaffirmed a commitment to Zionism and requested a traditional Jewish burial. The funeral was an occasion for his reinstatement as a leader of the Yishuv; it was attended by David Ben-Gurion, Golda Meir, Pinchas Sapir, Moshe Dayan, and representatives of the Labor community from Rafi through Mapam and Maki. Sneh's death removed the conflicts caused by his political positions and again raised him to the status of an Israeli patriot and an international Jewish figure.

The few Jewish Communists who remained in Maki after Sneh's death were so splintered that the party finally disappeared altogether. One faction was absorbed into the peace group, Moked ("Focus"), formed on the eve of the 1973 election. It also embraced other defectors from Mapam dissatisfied with their party's membership in the Labor alignment. Moked's greatest asset was its popular leader, Meir Pail, a retired army colonel known for his innovative military strategy and outspoken original political views. In the 1977 election Pail joined Arie Eliav and a few other independent radicals to form still another party, Shelli, which obtained two Knesset seats.

Rakkah continued to gather strength among Israeli Arabs. It obtained 23.6 percent of their votes in 1956, 37 percent in 1973, and nearly 50 percent in 1977. Its greatest coup was winning the mayoralty of Nazareth, Israel's largest Arab community, in 1973. Although Jewish Rakkah members still served in the party's highest offices and in its Knesset delegation, it continued to represent Arab nationalism and was a respectable voice of dissent for leftists.

Israel also has its Maoists and Guevarists, a cluster of neo-Marxist revolutionary factions that have split from the Communist movement. The Israeli Socialist movement or Matzpen ("Compass") is small and outside the circle of political acceptability. The revolutionary Socialists in Matzpen divide into at least five tiny factions. They often quarrel over tactics, their relationship with the Palestinians, whether to continue association with Rakkah, and how to deal with the issue of Jewish nationalism. The Israeli revolutionary Socialists were the first political groups in the country to enter into a dialogue with the militant radicals of the Palestinian nationalist movement.

During 1967, several peace groups gained attention, more for their colorful personalities and rhetoric than for their political attractions. After the 1973 war, they again gained attention when many Israelis became disillusioned with both establishment and opposition parties. Although they received about 5 percent of the vote in the 1973 election, they were so divided that they could not win even one Knesset seat. If they had combined forces with Moked in a single Knesset list the left could have obtained enough votes for a small but influential Knesset delegation.

Typical of the divisiveness among small parties were internal clashes in the Israeli Black Panther movement and in the Koah Ha-Hadash ("New Force") and Ha-Olam Ha-Zeh ("This World"). Ha-Olam Ha-zeh has its base in a popular weekly magazine of the same name, whose editor and founder, Uri Avnery, specialized in sensational political revelations, scandal, expert photography, and appeal to sex. His publication is one of the most widely circulated weeklies in Israel. Avnery, a political maverick, is left of center but anti-Communist. In 1965 he ran as an independent, winning a seat in the Sixth Knesset. By 1969 Ha-Olam Ha-Zeh won two Knesset seats with 1.23 percent of the vote, on a platform of peace initiatives with the Arab states and internal political reforms to include welfare services for all. Personality clashes between Avnery and his fellow Knesset member from Ha-Olam Ha-zeh, Shalom Cohen, divided them into two factions, neither of which won a place in the 1973 elections. In 1977 Avnery was third on the Shelli list, but failed to win enough votes to place him in the Knesset.

The Israeli Black Panther movement was formed by Oriental Jewish youth in 1968 to protest social and economic conditions and discrimination against non-Western Jews. Initially, the movement was not political, but as it gained visibility and support among many Orientals, it became a political movement. By the eve of the 1973 elections, the Black Panthers were so divided that one group split off to establish the Blue and White Panthers (based on the colors of the Israeli flag), assuming a more patriotic stance than the original organization. Neither group was elected. In 1977 the former Panthers were divided among four parties: Zionist Panthers, Hofesh ("Freedom"), Shelli, and the Democratic Front for Peace and Equality (the Rakkah-organized list). Only the candidate on the Rakkah list obtained a Knesset seat, thanks to the many Arab Communist party votes.

THE CENTER-NATIONALIST BLOC

General Zionism

After the religious and the Labor Zionists had organized into separate groups within the Zionist movement, the mainstream was called General Zionism. The General Zionists perceived themselves as the core of the movement, following the direction of Herzl and the movement's founders. During Herzl's time, Zionism was not a movement of political parties. Weizmann, Herzl's heir as a world Zionist leader, saw General Zionism as the bridge between right and left.

General Zionism became a counterforce to the Labor and religious groups, rallying to its ranks those who opposed particularist ideologies. During the 1920s and 1930s, when Jewish workers in Europe and America were becoming more class conscious, middle-class Zionists rallied to General Zionism. Increasingly, General Zionism also represented middle-class or entrepreneurial interests in Palestine, as a counterforce to the Labor faction. Owners of small shops in Tel Aviv and Haifa, citrus growers, operators of the country's new industries and businesses, tended to identify with the General Zionists. In Palestine, they were a minority, unable to compete with the strong institutional base which the Labor parties had in the Histadrut. Abroad, where Jewish institutional life in Western Europe and America was dominated by an upper-middle-class leadership, General Zionism was stronger.

The stresses and strains of ideological diversity soon produced right and left wings within the General Zionist movement. By the 1930s, the movement was divided between those who insisted that General Zionism should be nonideological and those who believed that the movement needed a social program to attract the Jewish working class. At a 1935 world conference of General Zionists in Cracow, Poland, a major division ensued between liberals, who formed General Zionist group A, or the World Confederation of General Zionists, and conservatives, group B, who formed the World Union.

Chaim Weizmann, president of the World Zionist Organization for many years before World War II and the movement's most prominent international personality, identified with the liberals. Most support for General Zionism then came from American Jewish leaders such as U.S. Supreme Court Justices Louis D. Brandeis, Benjamin Cardozo, and Felix Frankfurter, and Rabbis Stephen Wise and Abba Hillel Silver. Ideological disputes in the Yishuv between right and left, or capital and labor, were of less interest to them than the larger Jewish national interest. Furthermore they were Social Democrats, non-Marxists who distrusted Labor Zionism's class-consciousness. In the United States, General Zionism was identified with the Zionist Organization of America and Hadassah, the Women's Zionist movement, which directed its efforts toward assisting development of "good works" in the Yishuv.

The liberals in group A were more aware of the problems of organized labor. They urged the General Zionist Workers organization to join the Histadrut; in contrast, the conservative group B opposed labor unions.

German Jewish professionals and other middle-class immigrants who came to Palestine after 1933 formed another middle-of-the-road liberal party, Aliya Hadasha ("New Immigrants"). It was moderate in domestic and foreign affairs, advocating policies like Weizmann's. Its leaders had a philosophy similar to that of the General Zionist A movement: non-Marxist, prolabor, and favoring compromise with Great Britain and the country's Arabs in attaining Zionist goals. In disputes between militant nationalists and moderates, Aliya Hadasha became the Progressive party, representing the liberal wing of General Zionism in the new state of Israel after 1948.

Before joining Mapam, Moshe Sneh was identified with the liberal General Zionists. His unsuccessful efforts to merge groups A and B may have pushed him toward Mapam in 1948.

In the first Knesset elections, seven General Zionist factions were represented: Progressives, General Zionists, the Women's International Zionist Organization (WIZO), Yemenites, Sephardim, the pro-Jerusalem list, and Yitzhak Gruenbaum (an independent General Zionist). The first five collectively won eighteen seats, the General Zionists leading with seven. The smaller groups disappeared or merged with the General Zionists, making it the second-largest party, with twenty-three Knesset seats. The Progressives kept their separate identity, although they fell from five to four Knesset seats in the second election.

The General Zionists were gradually replaced as Israel's major opposition party by the more nationalistic Herut party, led by Menachem Begin. As the Labor party broadened its appeal and constituency, absorbing many professionals, artisans, and other middle-class voters, the General Zionists lost support. Unlike Mapai, with Ben-Gurion, or Herut, with Begin, there were no colorful political figures among the General Zionists. The party had no patronage to offer the average voter. Like the Liberal party in England, it seemed too middle of the road, too moderate, and too "general."

Recognition that their respective constituencies were rapidly declining led to remerger of the Progressives and General Zionists into the Liberal party during 1961. Its leaders hoped that combined strength and a new label would create sufficient appeal to compete with Herut, now the largest opposition party. The new Liberal party won about the same number of votes as Herut in 1961, encouraging leaders of these groups to consider amalgamation. Among the serious questions to be resolved were who would lead the combined Knesset list, and how to reconcile differences between liberals at one end of the spectrum and militant nationalists and conservatives at the other end.

The dilemma was lessened when the leaders of the Liberal party who had been Progressive decided to leave the party and retain their separate identity. Unable to compromise with

Herut over their positions in favor of women's rights, separation of state and religion, and compromise in a peace settlement with the Arab states, they formed the Independent Liberal party.

The Independent Liberals were minority members of government coalitions advocating middle-of-the-road positions in both domestic and foreign policy. Their foreign policy followed the moderate line of the Labor doves. In domestic affairs, they advocated nonstatist social welfare programs and policies to improve working-class conditions.

The larger component of the Liberal party is a lineal descendent of the former General Zionists. After joining Herut during 1965 in the Gahal bloc, it was overshadowed by Begin's leadership, although both parties in Gahal had about equal strength in 1965.

Herut; Gahal; Likud

Herut was established as a new party in 1948, but its doctrinal roots were in the Zionist Revisionist movement established by Vladimir Zeev Jabotinsky during the 1920s. He, like his follower, Begin, was a militant nationalist and firm believer in Jewish activism. Weizmann's policies during the mandate seemed to Jabotinsky like appeasement of Great Britain; he believed that the Zionist mainstream was not reacting strongly enough to "anti-Jewish" attitudes and policies of the Colonial Office in Palestine. Zionism, Jabotinsky's followers asserted, was a political movement, not a society to colonize Palestine. "Buy acres, build houses, but never forget policy!," they admonished.

When Great Britain unilaterally decided in 1922 that the Jewish national home concept was applicable only in Palestine west of the Jordan River, Jabotinsky and his followers vehemently protested. A fundamental Revisionist tenant has always been that the 1922 partition was illegal and that both banks of the Jordan River (Palestine and Jordan) are integral parts of the Jewish home.

The Revisionist movement opposed all partition schemes, insisting on immediate establishment of all Palestine as a Jewish state, in contrast to other Zionist parties, which were willing to accept compromise solutions. Revisionists also opposed mandatory regulations limiting Jewish immigration to Palestine, basing their argument on economic grounds. They have consistently opposed the social policies of the Labor bloc, advocating larger middle-class colonization and more private investment to encourage national development. Their ideological hostility to Marxism was once expressed in proposals to outlaw class struggle and to insist on compulsory arbitration of labor disputes. During the Mandate, they formed a separate Revisionist labor federation, but, without an extensive network of social and welfare services and economic enterprises, they were unable to compete in any real sense with the much larger Histadrut.

Jabotinsky formed the World Union of Zionist Revisionists in 1925. Its organizations, intended to compete with the labor movement, included movements for students, Jewish war veterans, Orthodox Jews, sportsmen, laborers, and women. An independent political action called the World Petition movement was started during 1934, appealing to all governments for free Jewish immigration to Palestine. As a result, the Revisionists were suspended from the World Zionist Organization. They responded by forming the New Zionist Organization, with Jabotinsky as president. In defiance of mainstream Zionist compliance with British restrictions, Revisionists organized illegal immigration to Palestine, bringing 30,000 Jews to the country between 1935 and 1942. (After the 1939 White Paper, the official Zionist organization also organized illegal immigration.)

The best-known component of the Revisionist network was the IZL, or Irgun Zvai Leumi ("National Military Organization"), formed in 1937 to challenge the official Zionist policy of *havlaga* ("restraint") in reaction to Arab guerrilla activity. Irgun policy was to organize "preventive strikes" against Arab attacks on the Yishuv, in contrast to Haganah's policy of limited retaliatory attacks. By "taking the action to the Arabs," the Irgun believed that it could intimidate them and keep them from supporting the guerrillas.

During World War II, the IZL announced that it would suspend military activity in Palestine. Instead, Jabotinsky and his followers turned their attention to organization of a Jewish army which would give the Jewish people belligerent rights alongside other Allied groups "in exile." After Jabotinsky died in 1940, the United States became the principal center of the Revisionist movement. Its leaders demanded immediate recognition of the Jewish people as members of the United Nations and replacement of the Mandate by the Jewish state. The conflict between Jews and Arabs in Palestine, they argued, could be resolved by population transfers—"Palestine for the Jews—Iraq for the Arabs!"

World events and the traumatic recent experiences of European Jewry brought the Revisionists back to the official Zionist movement at the Twenty-second World Zionist Congress in 1946. Both mainstream and Revisionist Zionists joined forces to support illegal immigration, a Jewish army, the anti-Nazi war effort, and the Biltmore Program calling for a Jewish commonwealth.

After the war, Revisionists again opposed mainstream Zionism. In Palestine, the Irgun renewed its fight against Great Britain and Arab guerrilla forces. When the Jewish Agency and Haganah devised a program of peaceful resistance to British immigration restrictions, the Irgun renewed its military activities. Retaliating against arrests, trials, and death sentences imposed by British authorities on Jewish guerrillas, the IZL blew up British military installations, and carried out their own executions of British soldiers captured in retaliatory raids. When civil war broke out between the Palestinians and the Yishuv during 1947, the IZL conducted actions against the Arab community.

The Irgun was transformed into the Herut political party by Menachem Begin when Ben-Gurion outlawed all military groups not part of the Haganah or Israeli Defense Forces. There was also a small Revisionist party in Israel during 1948, but it received so few votes in the first election that it disbanded and most members gave their support to the new Herut party. At the international level, the Revisionists remained intact, with their affiliates represented in various national associations and in the World Zionist movement. It was understood that Herut would represent the movement in Israel.

After 1948, Herut deemphasized, but did not abandon, claims to Jordan. When the West Bank and Gaza were captured in 1967, the party urged their incorporation into Israel, with civil rights for the indigenous Arab population. Those Arabs who desired would be given Israeli citizenship; others would be permitted to remain as nonvoting residents. Herut leaders maintained a "flexible" position on the future of the Syrian Golan Heights and the Egyptian Sinai, offering "meaningful" concessions in these territories in order to obtain a full peace settlement with the Arab states.

In domestic affairs, Herut and other non-Socialist groups advocate a national health service and insurance system to replace the Histadrut-controlled Kupat Holim ("Sick Fund"). Herut adamantly insisted that the complex of Histadrut organizations and economic enterprises be separated from trade unions. Fusion of unions with management and their ownership of a substantial part of the economy, Herut leaders believe, foster corruption, inefficiency, and expanding bureaucracy. Herut also favors compulsory arbitration of labor disputes, especially in essential industries and services, to avoid the annual round of strikes which has become customary in Israel. In contrast to their counterparts in many Western countries, Israeli conservatives have urged nationalization of major industries and public services as the only way of wresting them from Histadrut control.

Special circumstances have forced the opponents of Labor into positions not usually associated with conservativism. In many respects, the ideology of the non-Labor bloc resembles classical European liberalism. For example, Herut supported legislation to terminate the military government in Arab-populated areas of Israel during 1966, and has advocated laws to protect civil liberties.

Formation of the Gahal bloc in 1965 greatly helped to legitimize Herut. Fusion of General Zionism, the Liberals, and Herut, moderated some of the vehement Herut rhetoric and made the new bloc more acceptable as a partner in a Labor-dominated cabinet. When the comprehensive coalition cabinet of national unity was formed during 1967, Begin became minister without portfolio and temporarily abandoned his characterization of the political struggle as one between Socialists and patriots.

Like the Labor party, Gahal has moved toward internal democratization. Although Herut's leadership is unchanged after thirty years, the party's national conference did change the method of selecting members for its 1977 Knesset list. Instead of giving the power of selection to the 15-member Appointments Committee of party leaders, the 400-member party convention was authorized to choose the Knesset delegation. Acceptance of the party was furthered when Labor-party leader Moshe Dayan and Israel's President Ephraim Katzir attended its 1976 annual convention.

Growing dissatisfaction with Herut's traditional leaders was demonstrated when part of the Herut young guard formed a separate Knesset list called the Free Center, led by an independent-minded lawyer, Shmuel Tamir. He rallied enough strength to win two Knesset seats in the 1969 election and sustained his political following through 1977, when he joined the DMC.

Several nationalist and right-of-center political groups formed an even larger coalition, the Likud ("Unity") list, during the eighth Knesset election of 1973. Headed by Begin and dominated by his Gahal bloc, the Likud also included the Free Center, the State party (a last remnant of Rafi, which was more nationalist than Socialist), and the Land of Israel movement. The bond holding Likud together was adoption of the Land of Israel or Greater Israel movement's program for incorporating into Israel all territories acquired in the 1967 war. The movement was headed by a group of ideologically diverse personalities, including Ariel Sharon, a general who became a hero of the 1973 war; and former members of Mapam, Mapai, Achdut Ha-Avoda, and the non-Labor parties. Differences on other issues and growing disagreement on foreign policy undermined the unity of Likud so that by 1977 it was still a very loose alliance.

RELIGIOUS PARTIES

The religious bloc maintains consistent strength at between

12 and 15 percent of the electorate. Most Orthodox Jews, however, are not affiliated with any religious parties, and a high percentage do not even vote for them. Both the Labor party and Herut have affiliations with Orthodox Jews, and they collect more of the Orthodox votes than the religious parties.

Religious Zionism began as a separate faction in 1902, when a group of rabbis opposed plans for a secular school system in the Jewish state. They decided to remain in the Zionist movement as a faction called Mizrachi, from the Hebrew letters for "spiritual center" (*mercaz ruchani*). On issues other than religion, Mizrachi's program has been general enough to collaborate with the Labor party in most cabinet coalitions since 1948. It takes strong positions on fostering Jewish education, against any violations of the Sabbath, on enforcement of Orthodox dietary laws in public life, and in preservation of legislation which gives the Orthodox rabbinate control over Jewish marriages, divorce, inheritance, adoption, and the like. The Orthodox bloc adamantly opposes secular marriage in Israel, and insists that in all matters pertaining to Jewish law, the country's Rabbinical Council will have the final say.

In 1922, younger members of Mizrachi close to the working class formed Hapoel Hamizrachi ("The Mizrachi Workers"), intended to win the support of Orthodox laborers in Palestine and to foster development of religious *kibbutzim*. Recently, the labor wing has become the strongest component of the Orthodox political movement. It has developed a network of *kibbutzim* and agricultural villages and is affiliated with the Histadrut.

The religious bloc believes that the separation of Jewish religion from the state distorts the essence of Judaism. Proponents believe that only through the Torah has Israel become a national entity and only the Torah can preserve Jewish identity and traditional culture. Like Ben-Gurion, Mizrachi maintains that the Jewish people has an ethical mission which cannot be fulfilled except in Israel. Therefore, the Orthodox parties have placed strong emphasis on education, insisting on maintainence of their own school system. One of the first cabinet crises was caused by disagreement between the Orthodox parties and the rest of the government over education of new immigrants. The Labor leaders wanted to establish a secular system; the Orthodox insisted that they be given control over educating immigrants from religious families.

The Orthodox parties maintain their influence despite small numbers through the Rabbinical Council and the chief rabbinate. Both Ashkenazic and Sephardic chief rabbis are colorful figures. Shlomo Goren, the Ashkenazic chief rabbi, was formerly chaplain of the armed services and a national hero who led the advance to the Wailing Wall in Jerusalem under fire during the 1967 war.

Both Mizrachi and Poaeli Mizrachi have important affiliates abroad in the world Zionist movement to assist in fund raising and in developing the network of religious schools, *yeshivot,* and other institutions.

Religious Zionists abroad perceive the Orthodox parties as a bulwark against secular trends in Israel, as the link with traditional Judaism, which preserves the Jewish character of the state. After 1967, when disputes arose in the cabinet over establishment of Jewish settlements on the West Bank, the Mizrachi parties leaned toward affiliation with Likud. Ultimately, fear of liberal secular trends in Likud brought about the decision to maintain a separate identity. While generally in accord with the Labor party on socio-economic and foreign policies, the Mizrachi parties found Labor's ambivalence about the future of the West Bank difficult to accept, causing serious strains in the coalition. The Mizrachi parties, with strong support from the chief rabbinate, opposed surrender of the West Bank, which they regard as an integral part of historical Eretz Israel.

In Israel, Mizrachi and the Mizrachi Workers have been amalgamated in most elections as the National Religious party (Mafdal—from the Hebrew first letters). In the first election, they joined in the United Religious Front with the two ultra-Orthodox groups, Aguda Israel ("Community of Israel") and Poaeli Aguda Israel ("Workers of the Community of Israel").

The Aguda movement was formed at Frankfurt am Main, Germany, in 1911, as a world organization of Orthodox Jews with a constitution based on the Torah. The purpose of the organization was "solution of the common ideals and social tasks of the Jewish community." Every member had to accept unconditionally the supreme authority of the Torah and affirm that Jewish law rather than the Jewish nation was the heart of the Jewish people.

The movement was formed when most Orthodox Jews regarded nationalism as a threat. Throughout the mandatory period, members of Aguda Israel refused to formally associate with the Yishuv and they were considered anti-Zionist. Israel's role, they believed, was to be "the territorial tool of providence for the realization of the Divine planning for Israel and for the whole of mankind." Their strong belief that all Jewish problems can be solved by the Torah makes them indifferent if not actively hostile to other movements, including Zionism.

After the establishment of Israel in 1948, Aguda Israel recognized the country as the Jewish homeland and joined the first coalition cabinet. Like other political groups, the Agudaists have youth and women's groups and overseas affiliates. The labor wing of the movement was formed during the Mandate as a way of obtaining land for settlement from the Jewish National Fund. Aguda Israel and Poaeli Aguda Israel combined forces during several elections to form a united list, the Torah Religious Front. Although the Agudaists have their own separate rabbinical organization, the Council of Sages, they maintain contact with the mainstream of the Yishuv through the National Religious party, with whom they frequently vote on matters of Jewish law.

Neturei Karta ("Guardians of the Gate"), at the most Orthodox end of the religious spectrum, has yet to recognize Israel. This sect maintains that the Jewish state can be established only by God, not through the will of man. During the war of independence in 1948, its leaders attempted to remain in Jordanian-controlled Jerusalem. The group still refuses to acknowledge the authority and government of the state of Israel; it will not submit to any secular authority which claims to speak for or govern on behalf of Jews. (See "Politics of Religion," chapter 6.)

DEMOCRATIC MOVEMENT FOR CHANGE

A few months before the 1977 Knesset election, a new political party, the Democratic Movement for Change (DMC), was established by former general Yigal Yadin. The DMC evaded traditional Israeli political classifications. It was neither left nor right, Labor or anti-Labor, nationalist nor anti-nationalist. Its leaders and membership came from the spectrum of nonreligious Zionist parties, from Labor to Herut. One issue distinguished DMC from the other parties—its insistence on electoral reform as the key to revitalizing the country's political system. The common theme uniting this coalition of hawks and doves, conservatives and liberals, zealous and moderate nationalists was their demand for change in the political environment. They focused their campaign on the Labor party's mismanagement of the country, protesting against corruption, nepotism, and cronyism under the previous Labor-led coalitions.

Yadin, one of Israel's first army chiefs of staff, had been "nonpolitical" for nearly a quarter of a century, during which he had acquired international fame as an archaelogist and professor. He was joined by law professor Amnon Rubinstein, a liberal with "dovish" views, who was leader of the Shinui ("Change") movement established after the 1973 war in protest against government ineptitude in a series of war mishaps. Other leaders included an ex-general who had headed one of large industrial complexes of the Histadrut; a former advisor to Labor prime ministers on Arab affairs; an ex-general who had directed the Israeli land authority; and members of the Free Center movement, which broke away from Menachem Begin's Herut party in 1967. This coalition of diverse and often contradictory political and social perspectives had become disenchanted with the old guard in Israeli politics, whether it was on the right, left, or center.

The DMC's primary emphasis on electoral reform gave it fewer votes than had been anticipated. This issue was not rated as a high national priority in public opinion polls before the election. However, DMC leaders believed that the power of the governing establishment could be broken if the existing system of at-large candidates was replaced by one with candidates from separate electoral districts. In each district, the party winning plurality, or the largest number of votes even if less than one-half, would obtain a Knesset seat. Knesset members elected in this fashion would be less dependent on their party organizations, and more responsive to their constituents, thus diminishing the throttlehold on political power of the traditional leaders and their parties. Members of the DMC argue that this system would bring new blood into government and stimulate fresh ideas to deal with the country's pressing domestic and foreign problems. The proposed reforms, they say, would facilitate formation of a stable two- or three-party system, in which it would no longer be necessary to assemble coalitions of diverse, even conflicting programs, leading to compromises which thwart effective government. The DMC have demanded that electoral reform be adopted by the Knesset within two years, an unlikely possibility since most parties in Israel thrive on the existing system.

On other issues, there were few major differences between DMC and the large nonreligious Zionist parties. Its stance on a peace settlement and on the occupied territories resembled the Labor party's—return of some territory in exchange for a conclusive peace settlement. Because of the diverse background of its leaders, DMC had no clear-cut domestic platform, although it was sharply critical of the Histadrut and other Labor-run agencies.

In the 1977 election, DMC won less than 12 percent of the votes and only fifteen Knesset seats, not enough to bring about the changes it advocated within the next two years. Its major impact was to diminish the strength of the Labor alignment in the Knesset, forcing it into the opposition. The election results indicate that voters were speaking out against Labor rather than for anything in particular. One in five Labor votes was lost to DMC in collective settlements, usually considered the mainstay of Labor. Most support for DMC came from middle-class professionals, such as professors and government employees, who shifted their allegiance from Labor. It received little support from the working class, Oriental Jews, or Arabs.

It was largely a middle-class Jewish protest against Labor.

After the election, DMC was invited to join Menachem Begin's coalition government. It took several months for the DMC leaders to make up their minds, as many believed that cooptation into government would vitiate the principles for which they stood. In the end, DMC joined the coalition with permission to vote independently of Begin's leadership on certain questions such as those pertaining to religion or to Israel's continued presence in the occupied territories. Yigal Yadin became deputy prime minister, and three other leaders accepted cabinet posts under Begin.

The Likud government has made no commitment to DMC about its principal goal of electoral reform. The major dilemma facing DMC after the election was whether it would fragment into the diverse trends it represented once the mood of protest had passed. While DMC had thrown the traditional party system askew because of public disenchantment with Labor, its own future was very much in doubt. Perhaps by making possible Likud's accession to power with only one-third of the vote, DMC had accomplished something significant in Israeli politics. The party system was now in a state of transition, because no party had more than one-third of the votes. Initially, after his election, Begin had the advantage of a popular image created by an appearance of decisiveness and authority. But a year after his election, the country was still plagued by internal economic problems and a constant threat of war, despite Egyptian President Sadat's peace initiative. Whether the future lay with the old Labor-dominated system, a Likud coalition, or yet another balance of power remained to be seen.

CHAPTER FOUR

Interest Groups

So many aspects of political, economic, social, cultural, and religious life in Israel are organized through political parties that interest groups express themselves mainly through the party system. Nearly every significant interest group is represented through one or more of the political parties.

Orthodox Jews are not only represented by the religious parties. They are also organized into interest groups within the Labor party. Retired military officers have their own lobbying groups in both the Labor party and Likud. Private farmers and industrialists represented by the Israeli Citrus Growers Association and the Israeli Manufacturers Association have input through the liberal wing of the Gahal bloc in Likud. Associations of new immigrants, veterans, educators, and the like are represented in more than one party.

LABOR INTEREST GROUPS

By far the largest and most influential interest group is the General Federation of Labor in Israel, or the Histadrut. Until defeat of Labor in the 1977 election, the Histadrut had a quasi-official status because of its intimate relationship with the governing party. There was frequent interchange between Histadrut leadership, the Labor party, and the government. Several secretaries general of the Histadrut had also headed the Labor party as prime ministers or cabinet members. The broad social programs of Labor, as well as specific social welfare legislation, were Histadrut inspired. These laws included fundamental legislation assuring workers the right to strike, the National Insurance Law of 1954, the Hours of Work and Rest Law, the Annual Holidays Law, the Youth Employment Law, the Employment of Women Law, the Pay Severance Law, and the Labor Exchange Law.

With defeat of Labor and accession of Likud to power in 1977, the Histadrut lost its quasi-official status and became part of the opposition, a nongovernmental interest group with much the same status as labor unions in Western countries where labor is not part of the government. As the Likud's economic and social program gathered momentum, the Histadrut developed a new role as an interest group outside government. It exerted great pressure on those in power, becoming more relevant as a separate interest group than it had been before. When the Likud government announced, in October 1977, that it would lift many economic and fiscal controls and terminate the government subsidies which the Labor government had adopted during the previous three decades, the Histadrut confronted the new government with threats of strikes sanctioned by its leaders. The Histadrut argued that abolition of tight currency controls, devaluation of the Israeli pound, and reduction of subsidies on bread, oil, margarine, eggs, milk, poultry, and public transportation would raise the cost of living between 10 and 25 percent without substantially reducing the inflation rate, which reached 38 percent in 1976. Consequences of this turnabout in social policy seemed to the union leadership to call for concerted and decisive action by interest groups outside government, a difficult accomplishment considering how low the Labor party fell in public esteem in 1977.

The Histadrut is not only important as a labor federation. It is also the country's largest social organization, its largest single economic entrepreneur and employer, and a major influence on cultural and educational life. In 1977, more than one-half of all Israelis were members of, and participated with their families in, the Histadrut. Ninety percent of the country's organized workers belonged to one or another of the Histadrut trade unions. More than two-thirds of the population was insured by the federation's health fund (Kupat Holim). Nearly a quarter of the total labor force was employed by one of the Histadrut enterprises.

Hevrat Ovdim, the holding company of Histadrut-owned industrial enterprises, also organized the cooperative sector of the economy, including the largest *kibbutzim* and *moshavim*. Hevrat Ovdim owned the two major transportation companies and the largest supermarket chain. The country's largest construction firm, Solel Boneh, and Koor, an industrial network, were part of the Histadrut. Histadrut holdings included the large Worker's Bank, several local savings and credit banks, and Israel's largest insurance company. Tanuva, Histadrut's agricultural marketing cooperative, handled more than two-thirds of the country's farm produce and was active in agricultural exporting. The Histadrut published one of the major daily newspapers, *Davar*, controlled large publishing houses, organized some of the major cultural organizations such as the Habima theatrical group, and was involved in immigrant absorption, social welfare, and rehabilitation.

The large number of Israelis affiliated with the Histadrut and its vast range of activities made it the most influential Israeli organization, more important than any single political party. With Labor out of government, the Histadrut is likely to become even more influential, because its trade unions will be in a better position to directly influence the new administration than is the Labor opposition in parliament.

Even under Labor, there were occasions when Histadrut unions defied their leadership, staging walkouts, strikes, or other actions in opposition to policies of the government. With the possibility of industrial action in mind, the Likud program has included proposals to nationalize sectors of the Histadrut economic empire such as public transportation, Kupat Holim, and several strategic industries. Likud fears that the Histadrut will use its vast economic power to further "collective ideologies" threatening private enterprise. There have been instances when large Histadrut companies such as Solel Boneh controlled a commodity to the extent that it could freeze out private builders. Solel Boneh has been able to gain a near monopoly on all public works contracts because it controlled building supplies. When the Labor government was attempting to attract foreign capital, it was not unusual for it to grant special concessions in the form of currency allocations or import licenses to investors who sold 51 percent of the shares in a new company to the Histadrut.

Although the Histadrut was established by the country's two largest Labor parties and was dominated by Mapai until the 1960s, the strength of other parties has been rising sharply, as demonstrated by recent elections to the governing body, the National Convention. All Histadrut members can vote for delegates to the convention. The various parties form lists for the Histadrut Convention as they do for the Knesset, with the goal of attaining as much influence as possible within the organization. Between the seventh convention election in 1949, when Labor parties won more than 90 percent of the vote and the thirteenth election in 1977, their representation fell by 35 percent to just over 55 percent of the vote. It was ironic that Likud, the chief critic of Labor hegemony in Israel, won 28.2 percent of the votes in the 1977 convention. Many voters who participated in both Knesset and Histadrut elections split their votes, supporting Likud in the Knesset and Labor in the Histadrut, to demonstrate their dissatisfaction with the government.

Increasingly Israeli trade unionists and leaders of local labor councils have become independent and resentful of the central leadership, which remained unchanged for nearly two generations. Several national unions that belonged to the central federation frequently ignored directives of the Histadrut executive and the secretary general. Physicians, teachers, airline pilots, and port workers have struck without authorization of Histadrut leaders in opposition to wage guidelines established by the Labor government in collaboration with the Histadrut.

In addition to its growing influence in the Histadrut, Likud is also associated with another labor organization, the National Labor Federation. This small group, with fewer than 100,000 members, is not officially affiliated with any party, but is an outgrowth of the Revisionist movement. The National Labor

Federation was formed in 1934 in opposition to the Socialist policies of the Histadrut. It advocated compulsory national arbitration in all labor disputes, establishment of nonparty labor exchanges, and a shift in labor ideology, with emphasis on unity in the national struggle rather than on class conflict. In contrast to the red flag used by Histadrut, the National Labor Federation used the blue and white Zionist colors; its anthem was the Zionist "Ha-Tikva" ("The Hope") rather than the "Internationale"; its annual workers' holiday was the anniversary of Herzl's death rather than May 1.

Like Likud, the National Labor Federation strongly objected to labor ownership of industrial or commercial enterprises, insisting that the functions of employer cannot be combined with those of a trade union. It also objected to intervention by political parties in labor disputes, demanding that they be settled by a national institution for compulsory arbitration.

The National Federation has its own insurance and pension funds for unemployment, disability, labor disputes, mutual loans, and members' credit. Its housing company has constructed thousands of apartments and shopping centers, synagogues, and public buildings for veterans and new immigrants. If the Likud continues to gain influence in Histadrut elections, the future of the National Federation will be in doubt, unless Likud, through its position in government, decides to encourage and support the NLF as a competitive institution to the Histadrut.

THE PRESS

Israel's daily press represents a broad array of views from radical to conservative. Israelis are avid readers of daily newspapers and other publications ranging from sports and fashion periodicals to highly technical scientific and philosophic journals. Israel's approximately 3.5 million inhabitants have one of the highest rates of newspaper and book readership per capita in the world. The leading morning newspapers sell between 40,000 and 50,000 copies on a weekday. Weekend editions, published on Friday, reach 70,000. (No newspapers are published on Saturdays.) The more sensational mass-circulation afternoon and evening papers sell between 130,000 and 160,000 copies daily; their weekend editions reach 300,000 copies.

The number of newspapers and other publications is high. There are some two dozen dailies, about one-half published in Hebrew, the others in more than half a dozen European languages and Arabic. The European-language dailies cater to the large immigrant populations; the Arabic press is mostly read by the country's Arab minorities. An English language daily, *The Jerusalem Post,* is read by the diplomatic and foreign community, as well as by English-speaking immigrants. It has a substantial clientele abroad, especially in Great Britain and the United States. During the years when the government was controlled by the Labor party, *The Jerusalem Post* usually presented an official perspective on events in Israel.

Most dailies were established by political parties, and nearly every party had its own newspaper. The daily *Ha'Aretz* is an exception. An independent newspaper that began to appear in 1919, *Ha'Aretz* acquired an international reputation for its high journalistic standards, its extensive coverage, its large staff of excellent writers and editors, and its reliability. Many observers regarded *Ha'Aretz* as "the *New York Times* of Israel." *Davar,* the Histadrut's newspaper, was first published in 1925 and traditionally reflected a labor viewpoint. Until the Labor party was defeated in 1977, it also expressed the government viewpoint on most issues. *Davar* has had a large circulation because it has a captive audience—Histadrut members who receive the paper in exchange for dues. *Al-Hamishmar,* Mapam's daily, has a much smaller circulation. It has frequently criticized the government, even though Mapam was part of the Labor coalition. Its rather doctrinaire approach to problems and the predictability of its editorial positions have prevented it from attracting a large readership. The daily press of the religious parties, led by *Ha-Tzofeh,* also has a limited appeal, having failed to reach audiences beyond the Orthodox Jewish community. In 1977, many parties on the right and the left no longer published their own dailies, although the views and perspectives of Likud were frequently articulated in the mass-circulation evening papers, *Ma'Ariv* and *Yediot Aharonot*. The Communist party's *Kol Ha'Am* ceased publication as a daily in 1970 to become a weekly.

Although the two mass-circulation dailies, *Ma'Ariv* and *Yediot Aharonot*, are independent, their founders and chief editors have tended to support conservative domestic, and hawkish foreign policies. However, both papers, as well as the independent *Ha'Aretz*, have frequently opened their columns, letters to the editor, and pages of commentary to opposite views. Thus, several of Israel's most dovish writers, political dissidents, and satirists could be found in the pages of its most conservative newspapers. In recent years, as the span of political views within some parties broadened, party organs like *Davar* also opened their pages to diverse views on the nation's pressing problems.

One of the most persistent critics of the political and social scene has been the weekly magazine *Ha'Olam Ha-Zeh* ("This World"), published independently by Uri Avnery. Combining sex, sensationalism, and political muckraking, the magazine appeals to the younger generation; it has one of the largest readerships in Israel. Revelations of scandal and malfeasance in high places have frequently made it the target of official pressures. Yet *Ha'Olam Ha-Zeh* has successfully weathered government censorship, physical attacks on its editor, and bombings of its offices, to remain one of Israel's most popular and outspoken critics.

The Arabic press in Israel also persistently criticizes the government for its policies in the occupied territories and toward the Arab minority in Israel. Three of the four Arabic dailies published in Jerusalem were established by journalists from the West Bank or East Jerusalem. They became advocates of various nationalist viewpoints, giving voice to widespread dissatisfaction with the occupation of the West Bank and Gaza. Along with the Arabic publications of Rakkah, they have frequently publicized violations by the government of the rights of Israeli-Arab citizens and the inhabitants of the occupied territories.

Domestic publications and the dispatches of foreign

correspondents are subject to military censorship, officially confined to security matters. The army censor's ruling can be appealed before a three-man committee representing the military, the association of newspaper editors, and the public. A majority of the committee can override the military censor. On occasion journalists have protested that army censors interpret "security" too broadly, excising politically sensitive items that should not, in the opinion of the press, fall within jurisdiction of the military censors. An attempt at political censorship occurred shortly after the new Likud government took office in 1977. The new prime minister's advisor on overseas information called on the press to adopt a set of "semantic corrections" in terminology related to the occupied territories. He requested that the West Bank be referred to as "Judea and Samaria," and annexation be called "incorporation." Local journalists as well as government radio and television editors treated the proposed "corrections" disdainfully and most disregarded them.

Because the press is so widely read, Israel's political leaders follow its diverse currents closely. Even though a large part is controlled by political parties, it is considered a fairly accurate gauge of public opinion. Its revelations of administrative and bureaucratic inefficiency, mismanagement, or corruption put government officials and politicians on their guard. Along with the court system and the ombudsman, the press is a vital defender of the public interest and of the rights of the individual citizen.

In addition to the daily newspapers there are over 500 other periodical publications, including 70 published by the government. Sixty-five are weeklies and about 150 biweeklies or monthlies. More than one-half are in Hebrew, about 50 in English, and the rest in a dozen other languages. They range from technical trade journals to periodicals representing the most militant leftist or the most Orthodox religious critiques of the government, the society, and even the existence of the state of Israel.

THE MILITARY

There is no entrenched bureaucracy in the Israeli army,

thanks to the nature of recruitment into the officers corps, policies of rapid promotion for gifted officers, and a relatively short tenure in senior ranks before retirement at an early age. There are no elite service academics of the West Point or Annapolis type. Recruitment at the top grades of the army is from a cross-section of the Ashkenazi or *sabra* group of young men. Until the 1970s, no general staff officers came from the Afro-Asian Jewish community. An exceptionally high percentage of officers, between one-fourth and one-third, came from *kibbutzim* and *moshavim*, although the population of these settlements was less than 8 percent of Israel's total. The policy of rapid turnover in the military produced, over the years, a relatively large number of young retired high-ranking officers available for civilian posts.

A survey of seventy-five senior officers (colonel and above) who retired between 1950 and 1973 showed that about one-third became senior officials in industrial and economic institutions, one-fourth worked for the Defense Ministry and defense-related institutions, over 10 percent became senior officials in government or in public institutions, 10 percent worked for political parties, and the rest were involved in university teaching, research, administration, or work in the diplomatic or foreign service.

Five retired generals were in the twenty-one-member cabinet of Prime Minister Meir in 1973, constituting the largest number in any single government up to that time. The political affiliations of retired officers are diverse; they range from Likud to peace groups such as Shelli and Moked. The leader of Shelli, the only peace party to win a place in the 1977 elections, was retired Colonel Meir Pa'il. Most retired officers active in politics belong to the Labor party, a not unusual development considering the very high percent who came from the Labor-oriented *kibbutzim* or youth movements. Among officers who became generals, there has been a tendency toward political neutrality as they acquired a bureaucratic rather than an ideological outlook after decades of army service. This is evident in cases where generals about to retire have conducted negotiations for future political careers with more than one party. General Lahat, who ran for mayor of Tel Aviv on the Likud list in 1973, acknowledged that he also discussed his candidature with the Labor alignment.

Despite efforts of army officers to influence foreign or security policies, either individually or through organized groups like the Etgar circle in the Labor party, civilian control of the military has remained firm. Although army officers have ascended to top political positions including the Prime Ministry, civilian political influence has always outweighed that of the military in formation and implementation of national policies. During the years of Ben-Gurion's leadership, there were few occasions for serious disagreements between military and civilian leaders, because Ben-Gurion combined the posts of prime minister and minister of defense. As defense minister, he commanded full loyalty of his generals, and he was able to bridge any gap between the army and the cabinet through his role as prime minister. Security has been the central factor in foreign-policy formulation; Ben-Gurion used to say that the defense ministry should direct foreign policy and the foreign ministry explain it. However, control of security and foreign policy has remained under civilian direction.

After ex-Chief of Staff Yitzhak Rabin became prime minister in 1974, a triumvirate closely associated with the military ruled. It consisted of Rabin; Yigal Allon, a former Palmach general; and Shimon Peres, closely identified with the military establishment. However, civilian influence still dominated. In effect, the former generals became demilitarized in their civilian posts and responsibilities, weighing the claims of the army and security establishment against a wide range of nonmilitary considerations.

When Menachem Begin, a former commander of the Irgun, became prime minister in 1977, he appointed two former generals to the cabinet posts next in importance to his own. Ex-Chief of Staff Moshe Dayan was invited to join the cabinet as foreign minister, and Ezer Weizman, former Israeli Air Force commander, became minister of defense. Ex-General Ariel Sharon became minister of agriculture. Later, when the DMC joined Begin's coalition, former Chief of Staff Yigal Yadin became deputy prime minister and another ex-general from the DMC also joined the cabinet. Begin left no doubts about his control of policy and the extent to which the former generals served the prime minister. Although he was once a military commander, Begin's role as prime minister was definitely that of a civilian.

The only officer who ran independently in his role as war leader was ex-General Ariel Sharon, hero of the 1973 war. Soon after winning two seats in the 1977 national election, he abandoned his separate identity and joined Likud. After becoming a member of Begin's cabinet, he too acknowledged the leadership of the prime minister, although from time to time he issued flamboyant proclamations and hinted at grandiose new policies that his ministry would undertake. Generally, army officers who became politicians lost their military identities, adapted to the civilian modus operandi of the party system, and acknowledged supremacy of the party's civilian leadership.

Surveys of Israeli army officers have indicated that their political attitudes and orientations are as diverse as those of the population at large. They do not constitute a distinct or separate ideological bloc. More than one-half voted for the Labor alignment in 1965. Nearly two-thirds were either liberal or moderate in attitudes related to nationalism, economics, state and religion, and democracy. In a survey conducted in 1972, retired senior officers expressed a greater willingness to make territorial concessions for peace than did the civilian population. Some 57 percent were ready for concessions on the West Bank and 52 percent were willing to grant self-determination to the Palestinians. Their relatively liberal attitudes were also expressed on questions of religion and state, civil marriage, and economics. The diversity of views is reflected in the hawk/dove spectrum of views on foreign and security policies. In 1977, former generals Dayan, Weizman, and Sharon, members of the Likud government, opposed withdrawals from the occupied territories. In the Labor party and the Democratic Movement for Change, ex-generals Rabin, Allon, Bar-Lev, Yadin, Amit, and Yariv advocated territorial compromises on all fronts in return for peace. On the left, former General Peled and ex-Colonel Pail advocated dialogue with the Palestine Liberation Organization.

As increasing numbers of senior officers leave the army at

relatively early ages with extensive administrative and bureaucratic experience, they are likely to enter the upper ranks of
Israel's political parties and public institutions. Their
experience as army commanders may lead them to replace
traditional party ideologies with the perspective of technocrats,
emphasizing efficiency, orderly administration, and rapid
technological development.

DIASPORA JEWRY

In an address to the Twenty-fifth World Zionist Congress
during 1960, Prime Minister Ben-Gurion stated: "The State of
Israel was not established for its citizens alone. It is the foremost
bulwark for the survival of the Jewish people in our
generation." The interest of world Jewry in Israel received
international recognition in the League of Nations Mandate
for Palestine and in the United Nations Partitions Resolution.
It was officially sanctioned by the government of Israel through
its Declaration of Independence and in subsequent legislation,
especially in the 1952 law giving special status to the Jewish
Agency and World Zionist Organization.

Although only about one in five Jews lives in or is a citizen of
the Jewish state, all Jews, in many ways, constitute interest
groups within the country's political system. The nearly 6-
million-strong American Jewish community is the largest,
most affluent, and most influential in the diaspora. It is the
most visible interest group, although other diaspora communities are also represented in the institutions which relate world
Jewry to Israel. The most important are the World Zionist
Organization and Jewish Agency, whose executive members
are located both in Israel and in the United States.

Representatives to the periodic congresses of the World
Zionist Organization are elected by members of Zionist groups
in many different countries. Most are chosen as members of
groups affiliated with political parties in Israel. Between
congresses, the executive carries on organizational business
with the government of Israel through departments headed by
the executive members. They include Torah Education and
Culture in the Diaspora, Information, Youth Aliya (Immigra-

tion), Aliya and Absorption, and External Relations. Through these contacts, the Israeli government makes known its needs to world Jewry; funds are raised, educational and informational themes propagated, and political support rallied. While Zionists in the diaspora can influence the Israeli political system, in practice the Israeli government usually determines the nature of the contact. The dominant role of Israel in this relationship is facilitated by the large number of Israelis on the Executive and in the administrative apparatus of the World Zionist Organization. In most non-Communist or non-Arab countries outside Israel with large Jewish populations, Israeli embassies or consulates are active in rallying support for Israel, in assisting or guiding local Zionists and other Jewish organizations, and in maintaining ties between the Jewish communities and the Jewish state.

Because of its size and extensive organizational apparatus, American Jewry has a unique relationship with Israel. Dozens of Jewish organizations in the United States have special ties with Israel, from those emphasizing religious or cultural ties to general fund-raising institutions. Many ties are informal; others have been institutionalized in written agreements. Groups like the American Jewish Committee and American Jewish Congress play a role in diffusing information about Israel and in helping to explain its policies to the American public. Members of these groups are in frequent contact with Israel's representatives in the United States and have direct access to the country's political leaders.

Because of the prestige and wealth of its members, the American Jewish Committee has been especially cultivated by Israel's leaders. It is the only private organization with which the Israeli government has reached a quasi-official agreement defining a "proper" relationship with diaspora Jewry. In an agreement in 1950 between Prime Minister Ben-Gurion and the AJC President Jacob Blaustein, the Israelis agreed that American Jews "have only one political attachment and that is to the United States of America. They owe no political allegiance to Israel. . . . The State of Israel represents and speaks only on behalf of its own citizens, and in no way presumes to represent or speak in the name of the Jews who are citizens of any other country." In accord with AJC support for the Law of Return and its opposition to automatic Israeli citizenship for Jews, the agreement stipulated that immigration of American Jews to Israel "rests with the free discretion of each American Jew himself. It is entirely a matter of his own volition."

The American Jewish leader called on Israel to "recognize that the matter of goodwill between its citizens and those of other countries is a two-way street: that Israel also has a responsibility in this situation—a responsibility . . . of not affecting adversely the sensibilities of Jews who are citizens of other states by what it says or does." He rejected Ben-Gurion's thesis about diaspora Jews by emphasizing that: "American Jews vigorously repudiate any suggestion or implication that they are in exile. American Jews—young and old alike, Zionists and non-Zionists alike—are profoundly attached to America. . . . To American Jews, America is home."

American Zionist interests are consolidated through the American Zionist Federation, which coordinates the efforts of fourteen Zionist organizations and ten Zionist youth movements, most affiliated with political parties in Israel. They include Herut-affiliated Zionist Revisionists of America, associated with the Likud; Americans for Progressive Israel, affiliated with Mapam; the Zionist Organization of America, associated with the Liberal wing of Likud; the Religious Zionists of America, affiliated with the National Religious party; the Labor Zionist movement, related to the Israeli Labor party, and others.

The American Israel Public Affairs Committee (AIPAC), known as the "Israeli lobby," is financed and supported by diverse American Jewish groups. It is one of the most effective lobbies in Washington, D.C., where it has access to and frequently influences members of the U.S. Senate and House of Representatives on matters related to Israel. AIPAC originated in the American Zionist Council and acquired its present name in 1954, when it became autonomous. Through its close contacts with American Zionist and other Jewish organizations and with the diplomatic representatives of Israel, it makes known to American legislators and officials the views and desires of the Israeli government on important American legislation affecting the Jewish state.

The highest level of American Jewish organization reflecting the interests of Israel in the United States is the Conference of Presidents of Major American Jewish Organizations, representing thirty-two American Jewish groups. The conference, or Presidents' Club, was organized in 1955 by Dr. Nahum Goldman, then president of the World Zionist Organization and the World Jewish Congress, and other Jewish leaders. It supposedly represents the collective will of American Jewry on matters related to their relations with Israel.

Many of the differences within American Jewry in its relations with Israel, such as the distinction between Zionists and non-Zionists, have been obscured since 1967. The trauma of the 1967 and 1973 wars led to consolidation of efforts by most American Jewish organizations, emergence of unanimity in policy, and a common perspective toward their relationships with Israel. To most Jews in the diaspora as well as to many of their non-Jewish friends, the wars evoked memories of the Nazi Holocaust during World War II. To many it seemed that not only was the existence of Israel imperilled, but the future of diaspora Jewry threatened as well. As the international Jewish community was galvanized in massive efforts to support Israel, both materially and politically, there was a tendency to evoke the slogan of one former non-Zionist, the editor of AJC's monthly magazine, *Commentary*, who wrote, "We are all Zionist now."

While the existence of Israel is seen to be threatened, lesser problems that the diaspora has had with the Jewish state, such as dispute over the monopoly of the Orthodox rabbinate over personal-status matters or the exclusion of Reform and Conservative rabbis from official recognition in Israel, have been relegated to second place. Rather than representing the interests of diaspora Jewry, Israel has called on diaspora Jewry to represent its interests in their various homes abroad.

The question of Soviet Jewry is somewhat different. After 1967, many Jews in the Soviet Union, like those elsewhere in the diaspora, were stimulated by a new self-awareness expressed in revival of interest in Israel, study of Hebrew, and demands by Jews to practice traditional religious customs and observances. Thousands of Soviet Jews requested permission to emigrate to Israel.

At first, the position of the Israeli government was ambiguous, but increasingly it urged support for Soviet Jewish dissidents, especially for those who wanted to emigrate to Israel. Although one of the fundamental credos of Zionism was that the Jewish state was established to provide a home for just such Jews, the government of Israel was hardly in a position to intervene in the internal affairs of the USSR. Instead of direct intervention by the government of Israel on behalf of Soviet Jews, efforts were organized in Western countries to assist them. In the United States, the National Conference on Soviet Jewry became an effective lobbying group. It persuaded American legislators to pressure the Soviet government into authorizing Jewish emigration. Many of these efforts were taken in consultation with Israeli government officials, whose role was not given great visibility.

ETHNIC GROUPS

Interest groups organized along ethnic lines outside the country's major political parties have been largely ineffective in Israel's political system. As we have seen, attempts to organize ethnic groups into separate parties have not been successful. Instead, major parties have coopted the more influential ethnic leaders, and their supporters have followed them into various political groups.

After 1970, when poverty among Israeli Jews of Afro-Asian origin (Sephardic or Oriental Jews) became a salient national issue, a group of young men from Morocco and Iraq organized the Israeli Black Panthers as a protest movement seeking greater opportunity and fairer treatment for Orientals. During the first years of its existence, the Black Panthers attracted attention to the plight of the Oriental Jewish community, especially to its youth. Black Panther leaders were invited to testify before parliamentary committees, were written up in the press, and received audiences with cabinet ministers and Prime Minister Golda Meir. As the Panthers evolved from a protest movement into an organized political group, they began to splinter into factions divided more by personality differences and jealousies than by ideology. By 1977, the movement was no longer cohesive. Its former leadership was scattered during the 1977 election among three or four competing groups. Panther or former Panther leaders appeared on lists including Hofesh and a new group called the Zionist Panthers. Rakkah, the former New Communist list, now called the Democratic Front for Peace and Equality, gave its number-three "safe" position to a former Panther leader. Shelli gave its fourth highest position to an ex-Panther.

A small group of Yemenites have continued their unsuccessful attempt to create an ethnic pressure group. As in every election up to 1977, they attempted to foster ethnic separatism with their own Knesset list. Only in the First Knesset was the Yemenite list able to win a single seat. Since then it has failed to obtain even the 1 percent of the votes required to win a place in parliament.

The Sephardim identified with the Sephardic elite of the old Yishuv and with some of the Ladino-speaking Jews from the Balkans and Asia Minor have maintained their own interest group since mandatory times. In the first Knesset election in 1949, they ran a separate Sephardic list, but it was absorbed into the General Zionist party, predecessor of the Liberals. The Sephardic Community Council in Jerusalem was active up to 1977, but its vitality and viability have depended on a handful of individuals. Through its close association with the Sephardi chief rabbi, it has kept a degree of visibility and is treated respectfully by political leaders. However, it has lost most of its following to the major parties. During Israel's first thirty years, the Jerusalem Sephardi Council has supported efforts to encourage Jewish immigration from Muslim countries; it demanded compensation for Jewish property left in Arab countries, and favored diplomatic relations with Spain.

In the 1970s, when the social and economic conditions of Afro-Asian Jews became a major public issue, some Sephardi leaders supported the youthful Black Panthers. "We are all Panthers now," a senior Jerusalem Sephardi Council leader once exclaimed in a burst of enthusiasm.

After the 1967 war, a few Jerusalem Sephardi Council leaders became identified with "dovish" views on political compromise with the Arab states. In the council's bimonthly publication, the government was urged to seek a final peace settlement with the Palestinian Arabs and to recognize their national rights. The author also opposed Jewish settlement in the occupied territories and negotiation of a Palestinian entity on the occupied West Bank.

HAWKS AND DOVES

The future of territories seized from Egypt, Syria, and Jordan during the 1967 war became a focus of national debate and the basis on which several new groups were formed, some affiliated with established political parties, others independent citizens' organizations. The spectrum of views ranged from advocates of return of all territory acquired in 1967 to advocates of incorporation of all the occupied areas into Israel. In the middle were those who supported gradual return of areas in exchange for peace on a step-by-step basis.

The Land of Israel or Greater Israel movement was formed shortly after the 1967 war and included prominent members of all Zionist parties from Mapam to Herut. The movement opposed return of any territory, stating that no Israeli government was "entitled to surrender any part of this territorial integrity, which represents the inherent and inalienable right of our people from the beginning of its history." The new boundaries would guarantee peace and security and "open up unprecedented vistas of national, material and spiritual consolidation," according to the movement's spokesmen.

The Greater Israel movement became an influential pressure group because a wide variety of prominent personalities joined it, including many from the governing Labor establishment, the nationalist opposition, and the religious bloc. Its activities in arousing public opinion against return of territories helped prevent the Labor government from taking a clear-cut and unambiguous position on the question.

The movement lost political neutrality when its members joined the Likud bloc before the eighth Knesset election in

1973. By the 1977 Knesset elections, the Greater Israel movement had been totally absorbed into Likud. Its original objectives were modified considerably after Likud came to power, and especially following Egyptian President Anwar Sadat's visit to Jerusalem and the beginning of direct peace talks with Egypt.

Gush Emunim ("Bloc of the Faithful") was established inside the National Religious party during 1968 with objectives parallel to those of the Greater Israel movement. Its leaders represented a young, militantly nationalist group within the religious bloc opposed to the cautious outlook and policies of the older leaders. Whereas the Land of Israel movement was emphasizing the historic connection of the Jewish people with the land, Gush Emunim began as a religious revival looking toward a messianic redemption of the Jewish people through its ties with Eretz Israel. The leaders concentrated on Judea and Samaria (the West Bank) as the territorial focus of their aspirations, with little attention to Gaza, Sinai, or the Golan Heights. The territories taken in 1967 from Egypt and Syria, although significant for strategic reasons, did not have the deep emotional or spiritual connotations associated with Judea and Samaria.

Gush Emunim concentrated not only on discussion but also on action. A major thrust of its activity was establishment of Jewish settlements on the West Bank, frequently without government sanction. The precipitous and unannounced establishment of Gush Emunim settlements on the occupied West Bank helped to revive a pioneering ethos among many young people, including many who were not religious, and the movement quickly expanded beyond the National Religious party. Many of the new Gush Emunim settlements included both Orthodox and non-Orthodox settlers, who worked together and lived side by side.

The movement created a serious dilemma for the Israeli government. On the one hand, the unauthorized settlements, often established in heavily populated Arab regions beyond the areas regarded as Israel's by the Labor party, aroused fears and apprehensions among the indigenous Arab population. Many officials believed that these settlements would undermine peace negotiations. Indeed, one of Gush Emunim's objectives was to preempt Judea and Samaria, to prevent or make more difficult the return of the region to Arab control. The consensus of the Gush Emunim settlers was that areas where they established their new homes would not be surrendered and would remain part of Eretz Israel. Gush Emunim was an effective pressure group, which made it difficult for the government to formulate definitive policies about the future of the occupied West Bank.

After Menachem Begin became prime minister in 1977, his sympathy and support for Gush Emunim cooled considerably. When its leaders threatened to continue establishing new settlements without approval of the Likud government, it seemed that a rift was imminent. Some leaders of Herut and the National Religious party, once in power, began to regard the unauthorized actions of Gush Emunim as a threat to democracy and to orderly government.

The influence of "dovish" interest groups has been less apparent. Their public following is much smaller, and their allies in government less outspoken. Groups like the Movement for Peace and Security, established in 1968 to oppose Israel's annexation of the territories, and the Israel Council for Israeli-Palestinian Peace, which advocated recognition of and negotiations with the PLO, have included members from across the political spectrum, among them former high-ranking army officers capable of appraising Israel's security position and requirements.

Generally identified as the non-Communist peace movement, they have been closely associated with *New Outlook,* a magazine established in 1957, shortly after the second Arab-Israeli war, to further rapprochement between Jews and Arabs. Originally, *New Outlook* received much of its support from Mapam, but it attracted an increasingly broader constituency eventually representing the whole Israeli political spectrum. As Mapam become more closely integrated into the Labor alignment its leaders were increasingly ambivalent about supporting a publication with such independent views.

New Outlook's major contribution to improvement of Arab-Israeli relations is that it makes known to non-Israelis, especially to readers in Arab countries, the diversity of Israeli views on a peace settlement. It is noteworthy that President Sadat sent the magazine a congratulatory cable at the opening of a symposium in Tel Aviv to commemorate its twentieth anniversary in 1977, and that he requested to meet with a delegation from the conference during his historic visit to Jerusalem.

A major shortcoming of the peace forces in Israel is that they have been divided by personality differences and disagreements over tactics and strategy. Peace groups have supported one or another of the small peace parties such as Moked and Shelli in Knesset elections. But disagreements over whether to accept Communist support, whether to recognize the PLO, and whether to combine forces during elections have prevented any of the peace parties from winning more than one or two Knesset seats. Because of their close personal ties with the Labor establishment and the Labor party, these leaders' dovish views have at least been given exposure in important Israeli political circles.

ACADEMICS

The university community in Israel is an important unorganized interest group. Israeli academicians represent the whole spectrum of political parties from right to left. Because Israel is such a small community, it is not difficult for academicians to make themselves known to those in influential positions. Israel's Middle East scholars are frequently at the service of their government in appraising and evaluating trends and developments in the region. There are close ties between academic organizations like the Shiloh Institute of Tel Aviv University, devoted to research on the Middle East, and the government. And, of course, scientific institutions affiliated with the various universities have close links with the government, many providing research facilities for former government officials, or sending their own researchers to assist in government work. Many of Israel's retired generals have gone into academic life as scholars or administrators. Academic economists frequently work as official or unofficial consultants, through their writings in scholarly publications or through personal associations with colleagues in government.

On several occasions after the 1967 and 1973 wars, groups of professors met with the prime minister and other cabinet officers to exchange views on trends and possible government policy. Many professors have also been selected by cabinet members to participate in investigations, study groups, or other high-level groups organized to formulate policy. In Israel, academicians are frequent contributors to the popular media, the press, TV, and the lecture circuit, and thus their views on public issues of the day receive extensive exposure and frequently become the focus of discussion both in and out of government.

CHAPTER FIVE

How the Government Works

Israel's government institutions and constitutional system have developed within a structure established formally through parliamentary legislation and government regulations and informally through practices and procedures that have become constitutional law. The Declaration of Independence called for a constitution to be adopted by an elected Constituent Assembly. But fundamental ideological differences over the purposes and content of the constitution blocked its adoption. The Constituent Assembly became the First Knesset. It deferred the task of drafting a formal document. Instead, at its first session in 1949, the Knesset passed the Transition Law, also called the "small constitution." It provided the foundations for government, defining the powers of and interrelationships between the president, parliament, and cabinet. Periodically, the Transition Law has been amended to adjust to requirements of the system.

The task of drafting a formal constitution was given to the Knesset's Constitution, Legislation, and Judicial Committee. It constructed a series of articles, each of which became a fundamental Basic Law. By the 1970s, the Knesset had adopted four Basic Laws, pertaining to the Knesset, Israeli lands, the president, and the government.

Among the obstacles to a full-fledged constitution were fundamental differences between religious and secular parties. The Orthodox religious parties insisted on including traditional Jewish law; the secularists were adamantly opposed. Liberals and leftists wanted the constitution to include a formal and specific Bill of Rights. Other interest groups also fought to include provisions they considered vital. Experience soon showed that government could operate without a formal constitution, working under legislation passed by the Knesset. Israel's first prime minister, David Ben-Gurion, found that he had a freer hand without a formal document, and he discouraged hasty drafting of a constitution. The British, he argued, took centuries to evolve their system. Thus in Israel customary procedures evolved to carry on day-to-day work of government, as in the British system.

THE TRANSITION LAW

Before election of the First Knesset in January 1949, the Provisional Council of State adopted Palestinian legislation in existence during the Mandate. Its Law and Administration Ordinance of May 19, 1948, defined the composition and function of the Provisional Council and the provisional government. It also declared that local government would continue, and that all laws in force in Palestine on May 14, 1948, the final day of the Mandate, would continue unless they conflicted with legislation enacted by the new provisional government. Courts were to continue their operations under existing mandatory legislation.

During the months of the provisional government, mandatory legislation conflicting with the Zionist goals and objectives of the new state, such as those limiting Jewish immigration and land sales, were amended or abolished. However, emergency legislation passed by the mandatory government to deal with civil unrest was maintained and became the basis of the military government in the Arab sections of the country.

Elections for the Constituent Assembly were held in January 1949, and it convened in February. The first law passed was the Transition Law establishing the principal organs and offices of government, and defining their powers, prerogatives and duties. As in most constitutional systems, practice did not always conform with provisions of the basic documents, and constitutional custom frequently deviated from the original document.

The Transition Law requires all acts of the legislature to be signed by the prime minister, the minister or ministers responsible for their implementation, and the president of the state. They must be published in the *Official Gazette* within ten days after approval by the Knesset.

The president of the state is elected by the Knesset for a five-year term, and may be reelected for one additional successive term. He signs all laws except those concerning presidential powers; in forming new governments, he consults with leaders of the various parties, then calls on a member of the Knesset to head a new regime; he accepts the accreditation of foreign ambassadors and ministers; he appoints Israel's ambassadors, ministers, judges, and state comptroller; and he has the right to pardon or commute prison sentences.

The president of Israel is legally its highest official. Drafters of the Transition Law tried to find a compromise between efforts to place an internationally recognized Zionist at the head of the new state and the realities of political power. In practice, the role soon became symbolic, with the presidency becoming an honorary position rather than one with political power. Since 1949 the post has been given to men of stature who have served the nation in an unusual capacity and are above political controversy. The most important political function of the president, designating the head of government or prime minister when a new cabinet is formed, is so circumscribed by constitutional convention that it has become a mere symbolic act resembling the appointment of a prime minister by a British monarch.

Personality differences between Ben-Gurion, the first prime minister, and Weizmann, the first president, helped to shape these developments. When the state was formed, the presidential role could have developed in one of four ways. Under initial legislation, the president could have shared broad executive powers with the cabinet; he might have been elected, like the American president; he might have assumed supreme power, like de Gaulle in France, with a prime minister who served him; or, as actually happened, he could have been a symbol of national sovereignty with ceremonial functions only.

Ben-Gurion, already head of the strongest political party in the Yishuv, automatically became head of the provisional government. As leader of the Mapai party, he headed the most influential group in the National Council, and was also a leading figure in the world Zionist movement. Consequently he was the logical choice to head the new government. His job began even before the state was established.

The office of president was not set up until the provisional government was formed, and Weizmann was chosen to fill the post. At the time, Weizmann was abroad, and Ben-Gurion quickly assumed real power. When Weizmann arrived to take up his duties, relations between the president and prime minister were already established. Weizmann, ill and aging, was in no position to assume a vigorous role in day-to-day affairs. In contrast to Ben-Gurion, who dominated the political apparatus of Mapai and the Histadrut, Weizmann had no strong political base in Israel. His strength was in the World Zionist Organization, which he headed for many years; the influence of its non-Israeli leaders was small in the new state.

CONSTITUTIONAL PRECEDENTS ESTABLISHED BY BEN-GURION

Ben-Gurion extended his influence by assuming the post of defense minister as well as prime minister. He also assumed leadership in foreign affairs, immigration, and development. During his tenure, the prime minister became the keystone of government, overshadowing the rest of the cabinet, the president, and parliament, although he was still responsible to the Knesset.

Many constitutional precedents were established by the forceful Ben-Gurion and the directions in which he led the state during its first precarious years. In time, the state itself rose above the interests of parochial ideologies and groups, and became the object of loyalty for most citizens.

The centrality of state authority was determined within a few weeks of the government's establishment, when Ben-Gurion took control over the several Jewish military factions which had fought the 1948 war. During the latter days of the Mandate, at least three Jewish military groups coexisted in the Yishuv. Haganah, the Yishuv's official military arm, operated under the Jewish Agency and National Council. Two dissident factions split from the Haganah because of political disagreements and differences over tactics. The Irgun Zvi Leumi (IZL) was associated with the Revisionists and favored more militant tactics against British and Arabs. Its offshoot, the Lohemei Herut Israel or Lehi ("Fighters for the Freedom of Israel"), also called the Stern Gang after one of its founders, refused to halt action against the British during World War II. After World War II, it continued, resorting to even more militant measures than IZL. When Israel was established, Haganah became its official army, but initially the other two groups refused to give up independent action, including terrorist attacks on Arab and British civilians and importation of private military supplies.

A showdown between the government and the separate military factions occurred only a month after independence, when a shipment of arms destined for IZL arrived from Europe on the ship *Altalena* at an embarrassing moment for the provisional government. Ten days earlier it had signed a UN truce halting military activity, including arms imports. When IZL leaders insisted on unloading the arms against orders of the cabinet majority, Ben-Gurion, as defense and prime minister, responded by ordering the army to prevent the landing of the cargo. During the struggle between army and crew, the ship was shelled and sunk, and several of its crew killed or wounded. Most of the arms were destroyed. Two cabinet members representing the Orthodox Mizrachi party resigned in protest. Ben-Gurion responded by ordering the army to take command of all military groups. Thereafter, no independent or autonomous armed factions would be permitted. Only the state would be responsible for military security.

During the encounter, many Israelis feared that a civil war would erupt, and rumors circulated that the IZL intended to set up a separate Jewish state. Instead, IZL leader Menachem Begin gave orders not to fire on fellow Jews in the army contingents and agreed to dissolve his military organization.

Later he converted it into the country's principal opposition party, Herut. The much smaller Lehi also dissolved its military forces and the leader, Nathan Friedman Yellin-Mor, established the Lohamim ("Fighters") party, with a one-man delegation in parliament. The party ceased to exist after the First Knesset.

After the *Altalena* incident, Ben-Gurion also decided to absorb the Haganah's elite striking force, Palmach, into the army, against the wishes of its leaders. Although not an independent military organization, it was created by members of the left wing of the *kibbutz* movement, maintaining a distinctively leftist political orientation and an elite membership. Eight of the Palmach's thirteen commanders were from the leftist Achdut Ha-Avoda and Mapam parties.

Through these acts, Ben-Gurion established supreme authority over all military factions, concentrating armed power and the use of force in government hands. But he also antagonized some of the country's political and military leaders. The *Altalena* incident created such bad blood between Begin and Ben-Gurion that the two men broke all contact, establishing a precedent in which Mapai, later the Labor party, refused to form a coalition with Herut for nearly twenty years.

During Ben-Gurion's tenure, highest priority was given to development of the country's military machine, with the understanding that the military was always subordinate to the civil administration. To avoid ambiguity, Ben-Gurion also became defense minister. He personally selected leaders of the armed forces, and guided their military strategy and political orientation. A close personal bond was forged between the young commanders and the chief of state, in which he became an intermediary and spokesman for their interests in the cabinet.

Ben-Gurion saw to it that the armed forces received not only the lion's share of the national budget but the cream of the country's youth. Universal conscription of men and women was adopted with little controversy, despite Orthodox opposition to drafting women. Those who completed service remained on reserve duty until their fifties. The objections of Orthodox Jews were honored, and women requesting exemption for religious reasons were not required to serve. Ben-Gurion envisaged the military forces as a socializing agent, where class distinctions would be obliterated and new immigrants integrated. The educational activities of the army became one of its significant features.

The army was one of the few institutions in the new state to remain free of party politics. Promotions in the forces and positions in the Defense Ministry were based on merit rather than on party dealings. The military became one of the few state institutions respected by all factions.

Ben-Gurion was not a doctrinaire Socialist. In keeping with his principle of state above party, he frequently compromised in economic and social policy. Unable to win a majority in any national election, Labor was forced to rely on coalition partners to obtain Knesset support for its policies. Coalitions always included non-Socialist parties such as the General Zionists, Liberals, and the Orthodox, who were opposed to Socialist doctrines. Because large amounts of foreign capital were required to fuel its rapid economic growth, Israel established close ties with capitalist countries and capitalist Jewish communities in the diaspora. Although welfarism was an accepted credo, other Socialist policies such as central economic planning and income redistribution were diluted in deference to non-Socialist domestic and foreign alliances formed by the Labor-led coalitions. Emphasis was on a mixed economy, with many sectors under government control. Many institutions were quasi-public, like the Histadrut and the Jewish National Fund. The public sector coexisted with private enterprise. Such compromises, required to develop a mixed economy and to overcome the sharp ideological differences between Socialists and non-Socialists, would probably have been more difficult without Ben-Gurion's leadership.

A sharp ideological split between Orthodox Jews and secularists also threatened unity in the early years. Ben-Gurion was intimately associated with traditional Jewish values and consciousness, but he never hesitated to deliver heretical views on Old Testament exegesis, nor did he shun contact with other creeds and dogmas. He epitomized the learned secular Jew with

traditional roots, whose mind grasped for broader knowledge
of the world. He realized that feelings in Israel were deep
enough to precipitate a *Kulturkampf*, or religious war. A
compromise was necessary to protect both Orthodox Jews and
secularists. The result was that many aspects of Orthodox
Jewish observance were maintained but circumvented when
required by national emergency. Strict Sabbath observance and
kosher cuisine were maintained in public institutions, but
there was enough private leeway to avoid discomfort to
secularists. Personal status matters such as marriage and
divorce remained under the control of the clerics, but
individuals, including Ben-Gurion's son, could go abroad to
intermarry. Rather than imposing either a secular or religious
educational system on the country, both types of schools were
supported with government aid. Pig raising was banned in
Jewish sectors, but leftist *kibbutzim* raised the animals and
called them giraffes. Many secularists objected to these
evasions, or deceptions, as they called them, yet such
compromises avoided serious constitutional crisis. In effect,
Ben-Gurion achieved a constitutional dualism, in which the
state was secular and Jewish at the same time.

The relationship between Israeli Arabs and the government
was determined in large measure by Ben-Gurion's early
policies. During the Mandate, he attempted to make personal
contact with Palestinian Arab leaders, at one time proposing
establishment of a binational federation where the two
communities would share sovereignty in separate cantons.
Before the Mandate ended, however, he concluded that what
the Arabs were willing to accept the Jews could not give, and
what the Jews were willing to give the Arabs would not accept.
He retained the negative view of Arab personality and character
derived from stereotypes existing not only in the Yishuv but in
the West as a whole. Although widely read in the classics of
several non-Jewish cultures, he never regarded Islamic
philosophy or literature as of major significance. He learned
Greek and Spanish, but never thought it worthwhile to master
Arabic. His attitudes toward Middle Eastern culture were
revealed in his evaluation of Oriental Jewish culture and in his
policies toward Israeli Arabs. They could not really join the

mainstream of life in the Jewish state. Throughout Ben-Gurion's tenure, policies toward Israeli Arabs were improvised by a special office in the Prime Ministry headed by an advisor on Arab affairs.

His closest associates in government were not the Labor party old guard but young members of the movement who agreed with him on supremacy of the state over partisan ideologies. Many younger advisors and followers, such as Moshe Dayan and Shimon Peres, came from the military sector, either as officers or high-level technocrats. They broadened many of the prestate Zionist themes or dogmas, introducing concepts that had never occurred to the leadership before 1948. The idea of *halutziut,* or pioneering, which focused on Jewish settlement on Jewish land, was extended to nonagricultural sectors. National security required integration of Israel's economy with the non-Socialist Western world. Development of technology would meet defense needs through national industrial expansion. Therefore scientists and technicians were also considered pioneers, or *halutzim,* whose contributions were sometimes more valuable than those of *kibbutz* members or farmers.

Ben-Gurion set a personal example in pioneering when he established residence at one of the newer *kibbutzim,* Sade Boker, in the undeveloped Negev area of southern Israel. The government continued to encourage youth and new immigrants to set up settlements in sparsely populated rural areas, although as time went on the relative importance of the collective settlements declined along with the overall contribution of agriculture to national development.

Zionist, security, and humanitarian factors influenced Ben-Gurion's decision to expand immigration rapidly and to develop national policies directed toward its stimulation. Political and social rather than economic considerations received priority in early decisions to double the country's Jewish population within a decade. In Eastern Europe, Jewish communal life was so disrupted and the number of displaced Jews so great immediately after World War II that the moment was ripe for "ingathering," before new Communist regimes in Rumania, Poland, Bulgaria, Hungary, and Czechoslovakia adopted restrictive emigration policies.

In the Arab world, clashes between Israeli and Arab nationalism exacerbated local prejudices against indigenous Jewish communities, making life insecure if not untenable. In Israel, social and political conditions were sufficiently fluid to facilitate rapid improvisation of new policies. The Yishuv was still euphoric over its newly won independence. A spirit of sacrifice and ideals of egalitarianism were strong enough to overcome second thoughts about the economic wisdom of bringing in such large numbers of immigrants in so short a time. The unanticipated flight of Arab refugees left a windfall which could help provide for the new immigrants. Tens of thousands of acres of agricultural land, large blocks of urban property, and whole towns and villages left by the departing Palestinians were available for Jewish settlement. These diverse circumstances stimulated the early decision to bring in as many Jews as possible. In 1950, the Law of Return was passed, guaranteeing every Jew (with minor exceptions) the right to immigrate; in 1952 the Nationality Law came into effect, conferring automatic citizenship on those who entered the country under the Law of Return.

Without Ben-Gurion's urging, it is quite possible that those who placed more emphasis on economic absorptive capacity might have had a greater influence on policy. If immigration had been geared to the pace of economic growth, the rapid rate of Jewish movement into the new state would have slowed. Many who immigrated between 1948 and 1953 might have come later or not at all.

Efforts to speed up immigration required sacrifices by the Yishuv, by the immigrants, and by the world Jewish community. During their early years, many immigrants lived in *maabarot* ("transition camps"), which were often little better than the displaced-person's camps they had left in Europe. Oriental Jews usually remained in the *maabarot* much longer than European immigrants, becoming the source of social unrest.

Doubling the population in so short a time was costly to the state. Its narrow economic base and lack of preliminary planning for such large-scale immigration caused serious economic repercussions, leading the country into its first recession during the early 1950s. This was the first era of major financial contributions from diaspora Jewry. (Later periods, including the 1967 and 1973 wars, required even greater efforts in overseas fund raising.)

Israel's first prime minister also played an influential role in establishing the general direction of Israeli foreign policy, despite fundamental divisions within the cabinet. In the early days of the cold war, Israel required and received the support of both the United States and the Soviet Union. Without support from both the Eastern and Western blocs, the UN Partition Resolution could not have passed the General Assembly. Economic assistance from the United States was as essential as military supplies from the Soviet bloc during the 1948 war for independence.

Initially, Israel attempted to follow a nonaligned or neutral foreign policy. Political opinion was divided between advocates of closer ties with the Soviet Union and those who favored a Western orientation. Soviet policy and Ben-Gurion's own analysis of the situation soon compelled a major reorientation from neutrality to identification with the West, especially the United States. Once Israel had brought about diminished British influence in the Middle East, Soviet support shifted rapidly to the Arab states. Within a year or two of Israel's foundation, the USSR perceived the new state as another tool of imperialism and an ally of Western forces in the region. In time, changes in Soviet policy undermined the once extensive support Russia had enjoyed among significant groups in the Israeli labor movement.

Relations with the United States were also difficult, because of broader American interests in the Middle East. However, the two countries remained cordial and developed increasing intimacy. The United States was the home of the world's largest and most affluent Jewish community, providing extensive political and economic support to steer the country through its perilous first years. Under Ben-Gurion's guidance, foreign policy moved toward closer identity with the West while avoiding another area of possible internal political warfare.

Not all of Ben-Gurion's policy objectives were realized.

Despite major efforts, there were two significant failures. Ben-Gurion's inability to integrate Oriental Jews was a keen disappointment to him. He personally attempted to raise funds to facilitate their integration. He went out of his way to encourage affirmative action in promotion of army officers, in admissions to higher educational institutions, and in advancement of government careers. But his personal efforts could not overcome the broad cultural chasm between the Oriental and Western Jew. The problem is still one of the most serious confronting Israel.

Ben-Gurion's other unrealized aspiration was to populate the Negev and other regions sparsely settled by Jews. Few individuals followed Ben-Gurion's personal example by moving to the underpopulated regions, and visions of Negev reforestation remained a dream. Internal population movement continued toward urban areas and urban pursuits. Water shortage contributed to limiting settlement of these areas. Perhaps Ben-Gurion's vision of 1 million Jews in the Negev was a reason why he showed little enthusiasm for plans to establish large numbers of Jewish settlements in the territories occupied during 1967.

Ben-Gurion's strong leadership was decisive in shaping the role of prime minister as the most powerful office. His energy and dynamism, the network of political lines he controlled, and the initiatives he seized were so great that he overshadowed all other officials including the president. Weizmann was soon relegated to a purely honorific position. His successors as president have also been statesmen chosen for past contributions to development of the Zionist movement or to the state. Weizmann's immediate successor in 1953, Izhak Ben-Zvi, a Zionist leader of lesser stature, was restricted by illness, as was Weizmann. He attempted to make the presidency a center for scholarly discussion of subjects which interested him, including religion and Israel's minority communities. The third president, Zalman Shazar, was also a scholar. He formalized scholarly discussion, founding the Bible Study Circle and the Circle for the Study of the Diaspora. Ephraim Katzir, the fourth president, who assumed office in 1973, was a scholar who headed scientific research projects at the Weizmann Institute of

Science and in the Israeli Defense Forces. Younger than his predecessors, more vigorous in health, and more assertive in his own political views, he aroused speculation that the presidency might become a more assertive post. However, events in Israel overshadowed any such aspirations, and by the end of his term in 1978 Katzir was ready to go back to his academic pursuits. After one term, he was succeeded in 1978 by Yitzhak Navon, Israel's first native-born, or *sabra*, president and the first Oriental Jew to attain the position. His election by the Knesset to the country's highest post, even though largely honorific, was regarded as a prestigious achievement of the Sephardic community. The honor was even greater since Navon, a former Labor party MK and ex-aide to Ben-Gurion, ran unopposed and was chosen during the reign of a Likud government, when Navon's own Labor party was in the opposition.

Despite Ben-Gurion's dominant role, the coalition basis of his cabinets and the constitutional stipulation of collective responsibility required him to consult frequently with government colleagues. The extent of consultation between prime minister and cabinet depends on interpersonal relationships and on the government leader's force of personality. Ben-Gurion frequently took decisive action without consulting the cabinet; often he merely informed it, pro forma, of some policy he was about to implement. A threat to resign was usually sufficient to win over dissenting members.

The political styles and powers of his successors have varied. Moshe Sharett, who served for the brief period of Ben-Gurion's "retirement" between December 1953 and February 1955, concentrated on foreign affairs, and turned over to his cabinet colleagues other policy decisions. During this era for the first time, the prime minister lost control of the Defense Ministry. Sharett complained that Defense Minister Pinchas Lavon failed to consult him over reprisals against neighboring Arab states for raids into Israel. The lack of centralized control became even more of an issue when it was revealed that an espionage and sabotage operation had been conducted in Egypt without the knowledge of the defense minister. This episode later became a cause célèbre leading to quarrels in the cabinet, deep personal animosity between Ben-Gurion and his colleagues, and factional strife within Labor. When Ben-Gurion returned to power in 1955, he again imposed his strong personality on the government and raised the prime minister to the government's paramount officer.

BEN-GURION'S SUCCESSORS

Levi Eshkol, Ben-Gurion's successor, did not command his prestige or extensive influence in the party. He functioned on the basis of cabinet consensus. During the most critical period of his tenure, on the eve of the 1967 October War, public opinion and pressure from his colleagues forced him to give the Defense Ministry to former General Moshe Dayan, a leading competitor for the post of prime minister. During and after the war, Dayan seized the initiative in matters concerning defense and administration of the occupied territories. He operated with little influence or intervention from the prime minister or the cabinet. In matters related to defense and the territories, his power was equal to if not greater than Eshkol's.

Golda Meir, one of the first women in the world to head a government, was chosen by the Labor party as a stopgap following Eshkol's death in 1969. She remained in power until the political turmoil following the 1973 war. A long-time party leader who had been foreign minister and minister of labor under Ben-Gurion, she demonstrated a strength of personality and forcefulness which placed her in a commanding cabinet position, although not as strong as Ben-Gurion's. She relied heavily on a small group of advisors in the cabinet, often called "Golda's Kitchen." Because this closed circle did not include all cabinet members, several, including Dayan, felt excluded from vital decisions of the day. Several times during Mrs. Meir's tenure, Dayan threatened to resign in protest.

Israel's first native-born prime minister, Yitzhak Rabin, had never been part of the Labor party's inner circle. His only high office outside the army, where he was chief of staff during the 1967 war, was ambassador to the United States. In the 1973 election, before becoming prime minister, he was not even among the party leaders heading the Labor ballot. His appointment was an unexpected compromise resulting from the party's desire to select a leader not identified with the 1973 war reverses. Throughout his tenure, it often appeared that the government was run by a triumvirate: Prime Minister Rabin, Defense Minister Shimon Peres, and Foreign Minister and Deputy Prime Minister Yigal Allon. Each represented a different Labor party faction. Peres had been leader of the party's right wing, Rafi; Allon was a leader of the leftist Achdut Ha-Avoda; Rabin was the compromise candidate of the old-guard Mapai politicians. He had never before been active in party affairs, although as a young Palmach officer he had been close to Achdut Ha-Avoda. Throughout his tenure, Rabin's administration suffered from factionalism, not only among different parties in the coalition but within his own party.

The Labor alignment, theoretically headed by Rabin, was divided over policy for the occupied territories and terms of a peace settlement with the Arab states. In addition, there were disputes between supporters of a strong labor movement and those who wanted to curb the Histadrut's power during the country's increasing economic difficulty. Perhaps Rabin's most decisive action was the act which toppled the government; he demanded that members of the religious party in his coalition resign, because they failed to support him in a Knesset vote. Consequently, elections scheduled for the end of 1977 were advanced to May. This supposedly gave the incumbent Labor party an advantage. Instead, the party was turned out of government and the opposition Likud party came to power for the first time in Israel's twenty-nine years.

The first non-Labor prime minister, Menachem Begin, took full charge of the government after he assumed power in 1977. To many observers, his style at first seemed like Ben-Gurion's—assertive, innovative, and personal. Once again there was no doubt that the prime minister was in the driver's seat. During his first months in office, Begin made few significant changes in the upper levels of the bureaucracy, retaining most directors of ministries, department heads, and diplomats, including Israel's ambassadors. Nevertheless, appointees from the Labor era were left with no doubts about where authority lay and who was to make significant policy decisions.

Begin's appointment of Moshe Dayan as his foreign minister underscored the emphasis on national rather than party considerations. The appointment was such a deviation from traditional political behavior that it shook the Labor party and sent tremors through Begin's own coalition. It was unheard of to give such a post to a leader of the opposition. The Labor opposition itself considered it unacceptable for Dayan to accept the post of foreign minister under Begin.

Begin's personal style illustrated the political orientations of his government. He was Israel's most conservatively dressed prime minister to date, seldom appearing in public without a suit and tie. He was always courtly in manner and firm and unambiguous in his policy statements. He removed many of the ambiguities and uncertainties which had surrounded Israel's foreign policy since 1967 by stating clearly his party's opposition to surrender of any territory in Palestine and its refusal to recognize the Palestinians as a partner in peace negotiations. Despite these positions, he did not preclude the possibility of concessions by Israel in order to gain peace with Egypt, Syria, and other Arab states. After Egyptian President Anwar Sadat's visit to Jerusalem in November 1977 and his attempts to open direct peace negotiations with Israel, many of Begin's Israeli critics believed that he was not forthcoming enough in his response to Sadat; that he was too much of a nationalist ideologue to make the concessions required for a settlement.

On the domestic front, Likud made efforts to reverse the Socialist measures of the Labor governments that had preceded Begin's takeover. Appointment of the American economist Milton Friedman, of the University of Chicago, as an advisor to the government was symptomatic of the new government's conservative domestic orientation. By the end of Likud's first year in power, there were few, if any, improvements in the economy.

THE PRIME MINISTER AND HIS CABINET

The powers of the prime minister are not defined and his relationships with other cabinet ministers are only loosely presented in the Basic Law which establishes him as "head of the government." Real power depends on his conduct in office and on his strength of personality.

The cabinet has both policymaking and administrative functions. Cabinet members supposedly serve with, rather than under, the prime minister in making crucial decisions. As heads of their respective ministries, they are responsible for implementing government policy. Neither the composition nor the powers of cabinet ministers are strictly defined in the Transition Law or the 1968 Basic Law laying out the structure of the government. There is no fixed number of cabinet posts; the number depends on coalition requirements. In 1949 there were twelve. They increased to twenty-four in 1969, and decreased later. The prime minister cannot discharge cabinet members. They leave only if they resign of their own accord, or if the prime minister resigns, in which case the whole cabinet must also resign and the government falls.

Ministries are divided among parties of the government coalition in proportion to their influence. Frequently ministers without portfolio are appointed if more cabinet appointments are required than there are ministries. In smaller coalitions, cabinet members may hold more than one ministry. Although cabinet members have traditionally belonged to the Knesset, only the prime minister is required to do so. Between 1965 and 1970, six out of eighteen cabinet members were not in the Knesset. Deputy ministers, however, must be Knesset members.

Usually cabinet posts are political appointments given to leaders of Knesset factions represented in government. Certain ministries, such as Foreign Affairs, Finance, and Defense, are always assigned to knowledgeable and experienced individuals. Because of its dominant position in all government coalitions until 1977, the Labor party, and, before it was formed, Mapai, always held the Prime Ministry, Defense, Foreign Affairs, and Finance. Certain other ministries are customarily assigned to specific parties if and when they join the coalition. Thus the Ministry of Justice was often assigned to the Independent Liberals and Social Welfare to the religious bloc.

From the first cabinet in 1949 until the 1977 elections, there were eighteen governments, a record which shows a remarkable stability. Until 1973, many of the same faces appeared in every cabinet, because all governments were led by the Labor party or Mapai, and the National Religious party also served in most of these cabinets. Government coalitions are based on elaborate and detailed agreements, which set out the principal lines of government policy, major items for legislative and administrative action, and the division of cabinet posts.

The prime minister can neither appoint nor discharge individual cabinet members. Parties in the coalition designate which of their leaders will participate in government and they receive posts on the basis of the agreement among coalition members. When the coalition agrees on a cabinet, its members must be confirmed by the Knesset. If there is a cabinet disagreement, the only way a prime minister can get rid of a colleague is to resign, bringing down the whole government.

When a prime minister resigns, because of dissatisfaction with the government or because the government fails to receive a vote of confidence in parliament, the president calls on another Knesset member to form a new government. The president may go through the formality of consulting several Knesset members from various parties, but the person finally selected is usually leader of the party with the largest number of Knesset seats. The procedure of choosing a prime minister occurs after every parliamentary election and between elections when a prime minister resigns.

When he resigns because his government failed to receive a majority vote in parliament, a prime minister is asked by the president to form an interim government until the results of the next election determine who will form a new government. An interim or caretaker government may serve for several months between the prime minister's resignation and a new election. The precedent for this was established in 1951, when Ben-Gurion's government received a no-confidence vote on an educational issue. The religious bloc members of the coalition refused to support government legislation permitting immigrant parents free choice in selection of schools. They insisted that all children of religious immigrant parents be sent to religious schools. Failing to receive Knesset support for his government-proposed legislation, Ben-Gurion resigned, but continued as prime minister for eight months until the next election. During this interval, the religious bloc left the cabinet and Mapai governed without a parliamentary majority.

The cabinet usually meets once a week, on Sunday—the first business weekday in Israel—to discuss major policy issues, new legislation, and other government affairs. Decisions, supposedly secret, are by majority vote and are covered by collective responsibility; i.e., all members of the cabinet must support them in parliament. The day-to-day business of government is managed by the ministries or by committees of relevant cabinet members. There are many cabinet committees dealing with a variety of issues, from security and foreign policy to agriculture and social welfare.

The Government Secretariat, within the Prime Ministry, provides clerical services to cabinet committees; it also prepares agendas, takes minutes, circulates decisions, and informs the press of cabinet actions. Despite the secrecy rule, discussions in cabinet meetings and in the committees have frequently been leaked to the press. At one time the government considered introducing legislation making leaks a criminal offense.

Collective responsibility requires that all members of the cabinet and the parties they represent support the government in parliament or resign from the government. The fall of the Labor government in 1976 was precipitated when two of the three National Religious party members refused to support the government against a motion of censure introduced by the Aguda Israel party. The motion charged that the Sabbath had been desecrated when a ceremony was held on a Friday afternoon to celebrate the arrival of fighter planes from the United States. Prime Minister Rabin demanded resignations from members of the government who abstained on the censure vote. Resignation of the National Religious party members left the government with a minority in the Knesset, although it continued to govern until after its defeat in the May 1977 elections.

The crisis leading to the June 1967 war set new precedents in coalition formation. On the eve of the war, three opposition

leaders, including Herut leader Menachem Begin, were invited
to join the cabinet. Sharp ideological differences and a strong
Labor animus against Begin going back to the 1948 *Altalena*
incident had been obstacles to cooperation between Labor and
Herut. These were overcome in the national crisis, and Begin
was invited to become a minister without portfolio. (He was
then leader of Gahal, a Knesset bloc formed by Herut and the
Liberal party.) A national united government coalition
included all Zionist parties; only the Communists, the Labor
party's Arab members, and a one-man party called Ha-Olam
Ha-Zeh were excluded from the coalition.

After Levi Eshkol's death in 1969, Golda Meir also formed a
national unity government with two categories of cabinet
members. Full membership required support for the coalition
and full collective responsibility. Accession to the broader National Union required support for security matters and foreign
affairs only. The national unity government collapsed in 1970,
when Gahal withdrew because it opposed Israel's acceptance of
a cease-fire agreement with Egypt. (See chapter 6.)

KNESSET SUPREMACY

While the prime minister and cabinet dominate the political
system in Israel, their authority is more circumscribed than that
of a British cabinet or an American presidential administration. Unlike the British system, which was a model for Israel,
neither the prime minister, the president, nor any other
authority can dissolve the parliament. Even if the government
falls, only the Knesset can dissolve itself and only it can set a
date for new elections. Until the Basic Law of 1958 was passed,
there was no fixed term or tenure for the Knesset. Each session
determined its own longevity. Since 1958, a Knesset term has
been fixed by the Basic Law at four years, unless the Knesset
itself decides to advance elections to an earlier date. Unlike
the American system, no one can veto legislation passed by the
Knesset. All its laws are supreme.

The Knesset is a single-chamber parliament and, according
to constitutional theory, the supreme authority in Israel.
Neither the executive nor the judiciary can alter its legislation.

Its laws cannot be declared unconstitutional by any authority. Like the British Parliament, it can pass any law it desires. In reality, however, both the Knesset and the British Parliament are controlled by whatever government is in power. It, is in turn, dominated by a prime minister, as long as he can command a majority of votes in parliament.

The name Knesset ("assembly") was taken from the ancient Jewish Knesset ha-Gedola ("Great Assembly") of the early Second Temple era, which had 70 members. The modern Knesset was increased to 120 to provide for broader representation. The first Knesset was opened in Jerusalem during 1949, but, because of the city's insecure location and its division between Israel and Jordan, it first met in a cinema building in Tel Aviv. After the government move to Jerusalem in 1949, the Knesset was established there. Until 1966, it was accommodated in a converted bank building; then a new parliament was constructed in Jerusalem which had been officially declared Israel's capital.

Knesset members are not chosen individually, but from lists compiled by leaders of the diverse political parties. Nor do they represent specific geographic constituencies or districts. Representation is on a national basis. All Israelis participating in national elections vote for one of several lists of candidates. Thus the power of Knesset members is not derived from votes they receive as individuals but as members of a national ticket.

The smaller the party, the greater a Knesset member's influence as an individual. If there are only one or two representatives of a party in the Knesset, they carry more weight or influence as individuals than do most members of parties with several dozen Knesset representatives. In the larger parties a Knesset member's influence depends on his position in the party. Party leaders are leaders in the Knesset, while Knesset members at the bottom of a large party list are often unknown to the general public.

By virtue of their freedom to be outspoken, individual members of small parties are often better known nationally than lower-ranking Knesset members in the large parties. They are also allocated more time in parliamentary debates than ordinary members of coalition parties. Uri Avnery, member of a one- or two-man Knesset faction for several years, became well known because he was given frequent opportunity to debate. Members of the small Communist party are also better known than most members of the Knesset because of their frequent participation in debates.

The Knesset's major function is to pass legislation, which becomes Israeli law. Most legislation is originated by the government and is presented by the cabinet to parliament for discussion and approval. Members of government who are also usually Knesset members, lead legislation through the parliamentary process, explaining and defending it. Occasionally, individual Knesset members can introduce private bills, although these bills rarely succeed in passing the required gauntlet of committees and other formal procedures.

Knesset members can modify, amend, improve, and discuss government legislation, and, when they feel strongly about it, bring it to public attention. Most MKs (members of the Knesset) who belong to the government parties usually do not attack legislation introduced by the cabinet. Government leaders can take reprisals against dissidents by removing them from the party list in the next election. Criticism of government-introduced legislation comes from the major opposition parties and small parties not represented in the government.

Knesset candidates must be Israeli citizens and at least twenty-one years of age. Disqualified are active civil servants above a certain grade, anyone who has been a permanent officer in the defense forces within a hundred days of the election, the president of the state, the Ashkenazi and Sephardi chief rabbis, judges in the civil and religious courts, the state comptroller, and rabbis and priests receiving government remuneration for their services.

The Knesset passes an average of seventy to a hundred laws a year. A large part of its work has been to update, modify, in effect to Israelize, legislation from the mandatory and Ottoman eras in force when the state was established. During the nearly three decades of the Mandate, much Ottoman legislation remained on the books. Until the 1970s, much of Israeli law, like that pertaining to landholding and ownership, came from Ottoman legislation derived from a variety of sources: traditional Islamic law based primarily on the Koran; French law adapted by the Ottoman empire during the nineteenth century and personal status law drawn from various non-Muslim countries. Mandatory law was based on acts of parliament and on English common law. Thus the Knesset spent much time during its first decade updating the laws in effect in Palestine on May 14, 1948.

The legislative process is long and complicated, as in most parliamentary democracies. Formal disposition of a bill introduced by the government is the following: (1) it is introduced by the responsible cabinet minister who "puts it on the table," where it stays for at least forty-eight hours before being debated; (2) at the "first reading," the responsible minister introduces it with an explanatory speech, after which debate is opened by an opposition member (the length of debate having been fixed by the Knesset Committee); (3) the bill is voted on and either "returned to the government," i.e., defeated, or "sent to committee," meaning it has passed the first reading; (4) in committee, the bill is discussed in detail and amendments are proposed for adoption or rejection; (5) the bill is returned to a plenary session for a "second reading" by the responsible committee chairman or his deputy, with amendments adopted in committee; members whose amendments were defeated in committee may reintroduce them with a short speech; (6) after an interval of at least a week, the bill with all approved amendments is voted on by the Knesset in a "third reading." If approved, it becomes law after being signed by the prime minister, the responsible minister, and the president; it is then published in the *Official Gazette (Reshumot)*.

Most of the legislative work of the Knesset occurs in its nine permanent committees. Each committee is like a small parliament of nineteen MKs appointed in approximately the same ratio as that of the parties in the Knesset. The committees are constructed around legislative issues; they are (1) the Knesset or Procedure Committee; (2) Constitution, Law, and Justice; (3) Finance; (4) Economic Affairs; (5) Foreign Affairs and Security; (6) Education and Culture; (7) Labor; (8) Internal Affairs; and (9) Public Services.

In the minute examination of bills, Knesset committees can

conduct inquiries, and summon for questioning senior civil servants, ambassadors, army officers, and ministers (with permission). In addition to legislative duties, the committees can monitor the operations of the government and conduct administrative inquiries. Membership in some committees is more prestigious than in others, and preference is given to certain parties. For example, Communist MKs are traditionally excluded from the Foreign Affairs and Security Committee.

After being sworn into a newly elected Knesset, its members elect a speaker and deputies, who represent the main parties. They constitute the Knesset presidium. The speaker is usually a respected and uncontroversial member of the party leading the coalition. In 1972, Israel Yeshayahu, of the Labor party, was the first Oriental Jew selected as speaker in an effort to broaden ethnic representation. An Arab from one of the Labor-affiliated minority parties was chosen as a deputy speaker with the same intent.

Plenary sessions of the Knesset are held three days a week, leaving three days for committee meetings, which occupy the largest amount of time. Plenary sessions are not held on Fridays, Saturdays, or Sundays because these are the Sabbath days of Muslim, Jewish, and Christian members.

During their work, MKs acquire public visibility and take initiatives through several parliamentary devices. Any member may submit a question to a minister, who is obliged to reply in the Knesset within twenty-one days. The MK who asked the question may ask one supplementary question after the minister's reply to the original inquiry. In a ten-minute speech, a member may propose a motion requesting debate on any subject which the government has not placed on the agenda, to which the minister concerned replies. Following the minister's reply, a motion may be offered to refer the matter to committee for consideration and a report, or a motion may be made for further debate.

Members may submit motions requesting permission to introduce a bill on any subject. After the member introduces the bill, a minister replies, and the Knesset then votes on whether to reject the bill or sent it to committee for further consideration. Before using any of these devices, a Knesset member usually obtains approval from his party. One session a week is reserved for introducing private members' motions and bills. These sessions give smaller parties the opportunity to raise controversial issues or embarrassing questions and deal with matters which the government is likely to avoid in management of day-to-day business, such as treatment of the Arab minority, civil rights, or misuse of authority by a government official.

Rights of MKs representing minority, opposition, or dissident views are protected by a law passed in the First Knesset during 1951. It protects all MKs from prosecution for any vote cast, opinion expressed, or act done in or out of the Knesset in fulfillment of duties as a member of parliament. This immunity continues even after a member is no longer in the Knesset. Members are immune from searches of their property and persons; their mail, including postal packets, may not be opened or confiscated; nor may MKs be arrested, unless caught in the act of committing a crime involving use of force, treason, or disturbance of the peace. In these cases, arresting authorities must notify the speaker of the Knesset about the arrest within ten days. No Knesset member may be brought to trial for any offense committed while a member or before he became a member unless the Knesset itself withdraws this immunity. Members are not required to obtain permits to travel abroad, except during wartime. When traveling abroad they receive special service passports. These immunities and privileges may be withdrawn only by a majority vote of the Knesset, after the member has been given the opportunity to state his case. The privileges have been especially helpful to Communist members, exempting them from the restrictions and interference by security authorities to which other Communists have been subjected.

Other fringe benefits received by Knesset members include free public transportation; a home telephone installed free of charge with priority over others waiting for service; free calls and priority in long-distance calls; franking mail privileges from the Knesset building; and free receipt of all government publications.

Knesset privileges and immunities add to the aura of prestige attached to being an MK and guarantee an open forum for debate, where members will not be penalized for exercizing their right to criticize government. When MKs break with their party to form a new faction or parliamentary group they cannot be removed until the next election, although they are likely to be removed from their party's electoral list at that time. Several new parties or factions have been formed by MKs who broke party discipline. A few such independents became influential enough to run their own separate list, becoming a new political party with a new and distinctive identity.

THE CITIZEN AND ELECTIONS

The average Israeli participates in the formal process of government through elections. Although he may have little or no voice in actual decision making, he has a wider range of choices in selecting his government than in most Western democracies. The large number of parties and the system of at-large elections are features inherited from the Zionist movement. They make it possible for the Israeli voter to find a broad and diverse spectrum of political views from which to choose. Supporters of the system argue that proportional representation and many parties are advantageous because they emphasize national ideological and policy concerns rather than narrow local interests and personalities. Critics perceive the system as unstable and precarious in times of crisis. They believe it reenforces dogmatic ideological positions and undermines the compromises necessary to attain a consensus.

There is no constitutional obstacle to changing the system, and efforts have been made to eliminate smaller parties through legislation requiring a minimum number of votes for representation in parliament or through other constitutional devices.

All Israeli citizens, male and female, Jewish and non-Jewish, over eighteen years old may vote in elections for the Knesset. Elections for local government councils and municipalities are usually held at the same time. Voters in local elections are not required to be Israeli citizens, but they must be legal residents. When East Jerusalem was incorporated into Israel after the 1967 war, its residents were entitled to vote in the municipal, but not in national, elections, an option that only a small percentage took up.

Each party list is assigned a Hebrew letter or letters as its ballot symbol. A voter may not cross off names, but must vote for the whole list by selecting a paper with the appropriate party symbol on it, which he places in the ballot box.

Seats received are in approximate proportion to the percentage of votes a party receives. If a party obtains 10 percent of the vote, it will have twelve Knesset seats. The number of votes required for a Knesset seat is determined by dividing the total number of valid votes cast by the 120 Knesset places. Lists which fail to obtain a minimum of 1 percent are disqualified. Their votes are redistributed among lists with the largest number of excess votes short of the number required for a Knesset seat.

Election lists are submitted by the parties represented in the Knesset and by other groups, some of them factions which have split from Knesset parties. Elections are supervised by the Central Election Committee, made up of representatives from several parties, presided over by a Supreme Court justice as impartial chairman.

The lists are usually formed by the party leaders, by the party's central committee or by some other party organ. The largest parties, such as the Labor alignment and Likud, submit lists with a full complement of 120 names. Since fewer than one-half will become Knesset members, the choice spots are on the upper quarter or third of the list. The top dozen or so positions are reserved for party leaders, who will become cabinet members if the party is in the government. The person heading the list is the party's leader and its candidate for prime minister. Smaller parties often do not submit an electoral list of 120 names.

List formation often involves internal bargaining in which political debts are paid by placing recipients in "safe" positions, assuring them a Knesset seat. Parties attempt to place their most colorful or charismatic figures at the head of the list. Ben-Gurion headed the Mapai list until he formed his own separate Rafi party. People like Moshe Dayan, Golda Meir, and Pinchas Sapir, who are known to party members and to the

larger public, have headed Labor lists. Menachem Begin has
always headed Herut, later Gahal, and then Likud. Names of
military heroes attract voters who are more influenced by
personalities than by issues. Parties such as Rakkah or Moked
attract voters who wish to express opposition to government
policies; thus the percentage of Arab votes for Rakkah has
steadily increased during recent elections.

Groups forming alliances or parliamentary blocs, like the
Labor alignment, a combination of Mapam and the Labor
party, or Gahal, a combination of Herut and the Liberals, have
to bargain over which leaders from each faction will be in safe
positions at the head of the list. If an influential political
leader feels that he is not high enough on the list, he may leave
the bloc and form his own separate list, thus weakening the
larger group.

Election campaigns are much shorter than in the United
States. They are strictly monitored by law. Campaign devices
such as illuminated signs, aircraft or watercraft, entertainment
programs, torchlight parades, awarding prizes, serving food
and drink, posting public notices, and the like are either
prohibited or regulated by the 1959 Elections Law. Because
radio and TV are owned and operated by the Israeli government, they are neutral during elections, although during the
campaign each party is allocated a small amount of airtime
according to its size. Candidates and parties campaign through
personal appearances and the press. Few voters actually read
party platforms, but party members still haggle over them to
the point of severe strain. Even small parties have difficulties
with their platforms, and several have split into tiny factions
over obscure ideological points.

Despite elaborate controls on Israel's election campaigns,
they have become very costly. Before the 1969 election, an effort
was made to control campaign spending by allocating each
party represented in the Knesset a specific amount from the
state budget for every seat it held. Thus the largest parties
received the most money. Each party was limited to spending
from its own funds an amount equal to one-third of the
Treasury allocation. The law was later amended to provide
government subsidies for parties unrepresented in the previous

Knesset, if they won seats in the next election.

Surveys of Israeli voters have shown that changes in population and social structure since 1948 have not generally been reflected in election returns or in Knesset membership. One survey, taken before the 1977 electoral upset, demonstrated that most voters cast ballots to the left of their general ideological orientation; i.e., they were more likely to vote Labor than their political values would indicate. As in most countries, there is frequently a wide gap between the policies of a party in power and its election platform. When voters become accustomed to identifying with a specific party in election after election, the party's ideological orientation and its leaders' charisma become less significant. This tendency was established in the 1965 election, when Ben-Gurion and Dayan, two of Mapai's most colorful figures, joined the new Rafi faction. Their defection did not have the impact on Mapai that many observers anticipated. Despite Ben-Gurion's leadership of Rafi, it obtained only 7.9 percent of the vote and ten seats, weakening but not demolishing the Labor alignment. A survey taken in 1961, based on 20,000 voters in seventeen towns and cities, showed "ecological correlations," i.e., a relationship between country of birth and party voted for. Cities with a high proportion of Iraqi-born immigrants cast more votes for Herut and the religious parties. North African and Rumanian urban inhabitants supported Mapai. These "ecological correlations" persisted through the 1977 elections, when voters of Afro-Asian descent and recent Jewish settlers gave more support to Likud than to other parties. Older immigrants of European background tended to support the Labor alignment and the new Democratic Movement for Change, the party established shortly before the 1977 election in protest against the established parties.

CHAPTER SIX

Government Administration
and Policy

Day-to-day administration in Israel is carried out by ministries, whose number has varied since the state was established in 1948. There have at times been over twenty ministries and special agencies, but the number can decrease due to amalgamations and shifts of party alignments. After the 1977 election, the Ministry of Police was absorbed by the Ministry of the Interior. At an earlier period, Commerce and Industry absorbed Tourism. The Begin government combined the Ministry of Health and the Ministry of Social Welfare into a new Ministry of Social Betterment. The number of civilian employees in government, excluding teachers and those in organizations such as the state employment service or the broadcasting authority, has been about 1.8 percent of the total population. In 1972 the total number, excluding the 13,500-member police force, was 57,014 (see Table 2).

When Israel was established, there were only four ministries with an organized civil service. They were Foreign Affairs, a continuation of the Jewish Agency's Political Department; the Ministry of Defense, which descended from the Haganah; the Ministry of Social Welfare, developed from the Welfare Department of the Yishuv's National Council; and the Ministry of Education and Culture, which had been the National Council's Educational Department. An early precedent was established in which members of the coalition government assigned posts to colleagues of their own parties;

Table 2.   State Employees, according to Ministries

	1952	1959	1972
PRESIDENT'S OFFICE, KNESSET, STATE COMPTROLLER	328	535	677
PRIME MINISTER'S OFFICE, INTERIOR, JUSTICE, POLICE	2,452	3,242	3,769
FOREIGN AFFAIRS, DEFENCE	1,427	1,844	2,819
FINANCE, LANDS AUTHORITY, AGRICULTURE, COMMERCE AND INDUSTRY, TOURISM	7,754	9,013	12,150
DEVELOPMENT, HOUSING, IMMIGRANT ABSORPTION	–	279	1,440
HEALTH, SOCIAL WELFARE, EDUCATION AND CULTURE, RELIGIOUS AFFAIRS	4,469	8,261	14,622
COMMUNICATIONS, TRANSPORT, LABOUR	10,418	14,001	21,537
Total	26,848	37,145	57,014

From **FACTS ABOUT ISRAEL, 1975**

thus a newly formed ministry often reflected the party origin of its minister. Most ministries were new, but several carried on from the mandatory government or the Jewish Agency. Although many mandatory government files were destroyed or removed to England, several agencies left their records and facilities intact. Thus the new government of Israel took over the railroad stock of the former government, many of its police facilities, the telephone and telegraph services, landholding records, and broadcasting services.

Under Labor, the Israeli government vastly extended the functions for which the British mandatory authorities had been responsible. Although Labor governments formally had a socialist orientation, in reality a mixed economy developed which included a very large public sector. The number of government ministries and their subsidiary agencies involved in business, trade, commerce, and financial activity increased many times. For example, the Ministry of Development became one of the country's largest entrepreneurs, with control over a wide network of government-owned industries. They include the Electricity Corporation, which has a monopoly on the country's supply of power and light. Service to its more than 1 million customers has been extended beyond Israel's 1967 frontiers into the occupied territories. Israel Chemicals is a Ministry of Development conglomerate that holds shares in several enterprises including Chemicals and Phosphates, Negev Phosphates, the Dead Sea Works, Dead Sea Bromine, Bromine Compounds, Arad Chemical Industries, Dead Sea Periclase, and other subsidiaries. The ministry also operates Timna Copper Mines, one of Israel's largest companies with over 1,000 employees, a transport company, a geological institute, and several research institutes. These companies are among the major contributors to the country's export earnings.

Initially there was suspicion of former senior officials, who were given technical tasks rather than policymaking positions. Most high policymakers and many middle-level officials came from the Jewish national organizations such as the Jewish Agency, National Council, or Histadrut; some were former military officers and others who had worked with immigration; others were from the staffs of the Yishuv's political parties.

At first, the prime minister was in charge of the civil service. Later it was shifted to the Ministry of Finance as in Great Britain. By the mid-1950s, an independent Civil Service Commission was established; it was headed by a commissioner appointed by the cabinet, but was still responsible to the finance minister. The commission has attempted to depoliticize government service through competitive examinations, civil service training and education, and more efficient organization of government services. However, party politics has remained an influential factor in appointments to high-level posts in the ministries and agencies that have remained

under the jurisdiction of a single party. After Likud's defeat of
the Labor party in 1977, Prime Minister Begin, head of Israel's
first non-Labor government, made surprisingly few changes at
top ministerial levels. He retained several directors-general,
ambassadors, and other high officials who had served in the
previous Labor governments.

When the new Likud government assumed office in 1977,
extensive changes in the country's economic, social, welfare,
and planning policies were anticipated. During the election,
the Likud had promised to reduce inflation by one-half, to 15
percent, within a year, and then to 10 percent. Likud had also
promised to boost Israel's GNP by at least 40 percent within
five years through encouragement of investment, reduction of
the trade deficit, and curtailment of bureaucratic interference
in economic processes. Promises were made to transfer the
numerous state corporations and those of the Histadrut to the
private sector. Public lands would be sold to raise funds. To
advise the government on implementation of these policies,
conservative economist Milton Friedman of the University of
Chicago was invited to Israel.

It soon became evident that accomplishment of Likud's
conservative economic program would take several years,
perhaps more time than the Likud would be in power. There
were serious questions about Friedman's recommendation to
privately finance education, about abolition of foreign
currency controls, and about the sale of government corporations. The sale of even profitable institutions such as banks and
some industries would be complicated by problems of
valuation and future ownership. There was argument over
whether it would be in the country's strategic interest to give up
control of companies involved in aircraft and arms manufacturing. Some companies, such as Israel Chemicals, were so
large that it would be difficult to find private capital sufficient
to purchase them. In attempting to carry out its promise to
lower inflation rates, the government was stymied by the
necessity to keep printing the huge amounts of new currency
required to redeem government bonds. The new government
was locked into a series of creeping devaluations of Israel's
currency begun by the Labor government. One area where it

appeared that the Likud was having some success was in cutting government expenditures, even in the Ministry of Defense, whose programs and policies were usually not tampered with.

POLICY CENTRALIZATION

Although the Prime Ministry is at the apex of the administrative pyramid (see Figure 2), there are many occasions when ministries headed by members of other parties carry out policies seemingly uncoordinated with those of the ruling party. Since each ministry and special office carries out a wide array of functions, their coordination into a single broad-based program has often been difficult if not impossible. Under a strong prime minister, prospects of coordinating these diverse programs are much greater.

The most important ministries, such as Defense, Foreign Affairs, and Finance, have always been controlled by the party which heads the government coalition. Less strategic ministries, such as Health, Commerce and Industry, or Housing, are allocated to other parties in the government. Thus programs and policies of some ministries often change after an election if a cabinet post is shifted to a new party in the coalition.

Management of a single ministry with far-flung activities can be difficult when both the minister and the director-general are new to government. For some political figures, a cabinet post is less an opportunity for shaping administrative policies and programs than for extending political influence. There have been instances of cabinet ministers who took little interest in jobs such as running the postal system, the railroads, agriculture, or industry, preferring to leave these operational functions to civil servants while they were involved in higher politics. In such cases it is difficult not only to integrate the work of a ministry into the larger framework of government but to coordinate the various activities of even a single ministry. To get around this problem, formal and informal committees of ministers or their deputies have frequently been assigned to deal with problems or plans which cut across departmental boundaries.

Figure 2.   State Institutions

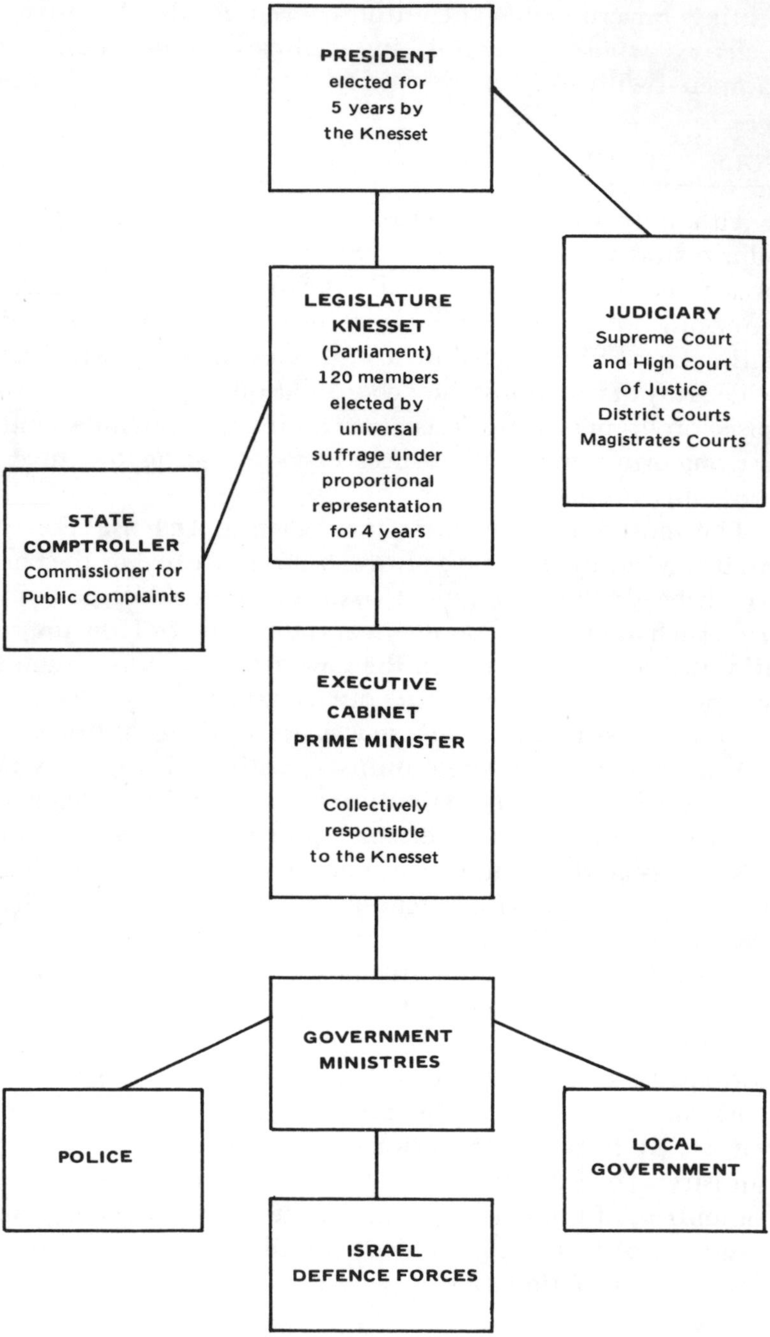

PRESIDENT
elected for
5 years by
the Knesset

LEGISLATURE
KNESSET
(Parliament)
120 members
elected by
universal
suffrage under
proportional
representation
for 4 years

JUDICIARY
Supreme Court
and High Court
of Justice
District Courts
Magistrates Courts

STATE
COMPTROLLER
Commissioner for
Public Complaints

EXECUTIVE
CABINET
PRIME MINISTER

Collectively
responsible
to the Knesset

GOVERNMENT
MINISTRIES

POLICE

LOCAL
GOVERNMENT

ISRAEL
DEFENCE FORCES

Adapted from FACTS ABOUT ISRAEL 1975

The minister of finance is one of the most influential cabinet members because his department, the Treasury, raises the funds and pays the bills of government. A strong finance minister such as Pinchas Sapir, who was also one of the most powerful men in the Labor party, has a large input into the direction of government policy. While major policy decisions are theoretically collective, with all cabinet members participating, a strong prime minister in collaboration with a powerful minister of finance can use the power of the purse to determine priorities. All cabinet members must consult with the finance minister in preparing their budgets, even though they may not necessarily have to consult each other in setting policy. Departments which can make the most convincing cases to the finance minister and the prime minister have an advantage over those less skillful in presenting their plans. National security has always been given top priority and receives as much as 40 percent of the budget with relative ease; other ministries have had to struggle for the remaining 60 percent.

Even within the Prime Ministry, the range of activities is extensive. A Government Secretariat is charged with coordinating interministerial interests, keeping the prime minister in touch with government activity, and maintaining contact between the cabinet and parliament. The Government Secretariat is also responsible for the Government Press Office, one of Israel's most strategic points of contact with the outside world, because it is the principal agency providing information and services to foreign journalists. The prime minister's advisor on Arab affairs determines policies relating to Israel's minorities, including Christians, Muslims, and Druze Arabs who are Israeli citizens. (Arabs in the occupied territories are under jurisdiction of the military government in the Ministry of Defense.)

Another important agency in the Prime Ministry is the Central Bureau of Statistics, which collects, processes, and publishes economic and social statistics. Its impressive array of publications including the *Annual Statistical Abstract* is among the most extensive and scientific of any government, and by far the most reliable in the Middle East. The National Council for Research and Development attempts to rationalize allocation of funds for science and technology. Since Israel is one of the few states spending more than 2 percent of its GNP on research and technology, the council's functions are of major importance. Similarly, the Atomic Energy Commission is vital. It advises the government on everything connected with atomic research and development. Other diverse branches of the Prime Ministry include the National Parks Authority, the State Archives, the Place Names Committee, and the Government Coins and Medals Corporation.

DEFENSE MINISTRY

Because of Israel's precarious security situation, its Defense Ministry has become one of the largest government agencies, responsible not only for organizing and maintaining the defense forces but for coordinating a large military industry. In recent years, the ministry has absorbed as much as 40 percent of the state budget and 20 percent of the gross national product. It thus plays one of the most influential roles in the national economy, in developing industry, science, and technology. Military equipment exported by the Defense Ministry has become one of Israel's major sources of foreign exchange. Military industries under the jurisdiction of the Defense Ministry have also become some of the country's largest employers. Its Israel Aircraft Industry produces both military and civilian planes, which are sold on the world market. Although an independent company, IAI is owned by the Defense Ministry, and its board of directors consists of representatives from defense establishment and other interested government and public organizations.

Since 1967, the Ministry of Defense, acting through the Israeli army, has governed more than 1 million Arabs in the areas occupied during the Six-Day War—Gaza, the West Bank, the Golan Heights, and Israeli-held Sinai. Regional military commanders in each area are designated as its legislators and chief executives. They appoint all local officials, including judges, and are responsible for the system of military justice established under emergency regulations in the occupied areas. The military commanders are assisted by Israeli civilians representing various ministries such as Agriculture, Education, Social Welfare, and Commerce and Industry.

An Israeli Committee for Coordination of Economic Activities in the Occupied Territories was organized in 1967 to plan and direct civilian activities, but in practice the military directs operational decisions in economic/civilian affairs as well as in military/security matters. The chief executive of the Directors-General Committee for Economic Affairs, subordinate to the ministerial committee mentioned above, is a senior army officer. When Prime Minister Levi Eshkol attempted to increase the policymaking role of the cabinet in the occupied territories during 1968, he was unsuccessful. The most important day-to-day decisions at all levels in the territories remained in the hands of Defense Minister Moshe Dayan. Links with the six regional military governors were maintained at the Defense Ministry through a major general *(aluf)* designated as coordinator of government operations in the administered areas and head of the general staff's Military Government Department.

Policy under the Labor government was to enforce security in the areas while maintaining normal civilian life. Legal systems existing before occupation were continued, subject to amendment by the military authorities for security reasons. The existing tax and judicial systems remained in force; taxes were paid to the military government, and military courts were set up to deal with security offenses.

After the 1967 war, many public services were not only reactivated but were reorganized and expanded. Postal and telephone services were linked with the Israeli system and placed under supervision of Israeli officers. Israeli technicians and engineers improved the water-supply system and conducted hydrological surveys to expand the service. Health, social welfare, and educational services were continued under Israeli supervision. Israeli regulations were introduced to license radios, to regularize weights and measures, to certify Arab tour guides, and to implement Israeli road safety standards and Israeli automobile registration.

A number of Israeli businesses and commercial operations were permitted to operate in the West Bank and Gaza, and local

Arabs were employed as their representatives. These included certain Israeli banks and transportation services that were extended into the territories.

Local government was maintained in the West Bank and Gaza. At first the military government appointed mayors or heads of local councils, but by 1976 local elections were permitted in the towns of the West Bank. Under Jordanian government, the larger West Bank towns had had twelve-man councils elected by taxpaying males. Regulations for these elections were modified in 1976, extending suffrage to women and broadening the categories of voters. The 1976 West Bank elections were remarkable in that widespread criticism of Israel was permitted and several candidates were elected on platforms supporting the Palestine Liberation Organization.

Dayan implemented a double-edged policy. He forcefully repressed overt manifestations of political opposition and tried to thwart organization of Arab movements other than purely local ones. On the other hand he attempted not only to normalize but to improve day-to-day civilian life in the occupied territories. One of the most innovative aspects of this policy was to open the bridges across the Jordan River, linking the occupied West Bank with the Jordanian East Bank. This facilitated the movement of hundreds of thousands of Arabs and other visitors between Israeli-held territory and the Arab world. The vast majority of those who had fled the territories during the war and before were not permitted to return. However, family visits were exchanged, West Bank students in Arab countries were permitted to visit their homes during vacations, and an extensive trade was developed between the West Bank and the rest of the Arab world. The policy also made it possible for Israelis to have direct contact with the Arab world through visitors from across the Jordan River.

Israel has rejected the view of the United States and of the United Nations that provisions of the Fourth Geneva Convention concerning protection of civilian populations under military occupation apply to its governance of the occupied territories, although it claims voluntary compliance with most of the convention's stipulations. In Israel's view, the West Bank and Gaza are not occupied territories belonging to some recognized foreign nation but areas whose legal status is uncertain; therefore, they argue, the territories are not subject to the Geneva Convention.

A major issue of controversy is the establishment of some seventy nonmilitary Jewish settlements, with a population of about 8,000, in the occupied areas. There have also been frequent allegations of torture by Israeli officials during interrogation of Arab security suspects. A 1978 report by the U.S. Department of State to the U.S. Congress on human rights in the Middle East concluded that: "We know of no evidence to support allegations that Israel follows a consistent practice or policy of using torture during interrogations. However, there are documented reports of the use of extreme physical and psychological pressures during interrogation, and instances of brutality by individual interrogators cannot be ruled out."

The report also observed that there were instances of excessive use of force to quell demonstrations and to restore order, although "these actions did not reflect government policy." The selective expulsion of West Bank and Gaza residents suspected of terrorism or anti-Israel political agitation was viewed by the report as contravention of the Geneva Convention. By the beginning of 1978, there were more than 3,000 Arabs from the occupied territories in prison, of whom an estimated 75 percent were being held for security offenses.

Most Western observers considered the Israeli occupation to be benign, but there was general agreement that inhabitants of these areas were becoming increasingly restive and disenchanted with more than a decade of military rule. As evidenced by the 1976 local elections on the West Bank, the trend toward identification with Palestinian Arab nationalism was intensifying.

INTERIOR MINISTRY

Local government in Israel is supervised by the Interior Ministry. Its responsibilities are divided among the country's six administrative districts, each with its own administrative center: Jerusalem (centered in Jerusalem); Northern (Nazareth); Haifa (Haifa); Central (Ramla); Tel Aviv (Tel Aviv); and

Southern (Beersheba). The ministry drafts legislation regulating local activities, and approves local tax rates, budgets, and bylaws. Local governments oversee municipalities, and local regional councils help to provide education, health and sanitation, social welfare, water, road maintenance, parks, and fire departments. Funds for such activities at the local level are raised through taxes or levies on the inhabitants, with extra aid for Jewish settlements provided by the Jewish Agency. Because Jewish settlements have the advantage of receiving allocations from the Jewish Agency, Arab local authorities have often charged that they are being discriminated against when they receive lesser matching funds for services such as roads, water supplies, or schools.

Elections for local and municipal councils are usually held simultaneously with Knesset elections. All voters qualified to participate in the national polls as well as residents who are not Israeli citizens may cast ballots in local elections. Thus, in elections for the Jerusalem municipality since 1967, there have been many Arab voters from East Jerusalem who were not eligible to participate in the Knesset balloting because they had not acquired Israeli citizenship. Until the 1970s, mayors and heads of local councils were chosen by the councils. Two attempts to provide for direct elections of mayors and council heads have been defeated by the Knesset, in 1969 and 1973. However, voters in recent elections have tended to support the party with the most popular local following, regardless of how they vote in the Knesset elections. In 1973 several municipalities and towns split their votes, electing Knesset candidates from one party and local government officials from another. Another recent phenomenon has been the ascent of Oriental Jews to positions of prominence in local government as a result of their leadership role in various political parties at the local level.

As in the Knesset, parties at the local level usually govern in coalitions, because a single list rarely gains a majority. Candidates for local office, who usually represent the same parties as those in the Knesset, must bargain and make concessions with members of other parties in the council. Smaller parties often hold the balance and thus are influential in local policy. Sometimes national party headquarters instruct their local candidates or agree among themselves that one party will obtain a mayoralty in exchange for another. Such complicated maneuvers have even affected negotiations for national coalitions.

Forty-nine regional councils have been formed, representing some 700 villages, to help provide services to thinly populated areas. *Kibbutzim,* cooperatives, small farms, agricultural schools, and similar institutions are represented in the regional councils. The smaller village committees must submit their annual budgets to the regional councils for approval. The councils are also authorized to levy approved taxes and to pass bylaws, a privilege that has rarely been used.

In instances of adjoining municipal boundaries, where services cross town or city borders, towns may form municipal unions to provide hospitals, schools, slaughterhouses, sewers, or other services. Since the first such municipal union in 1955, between Tel Aviv and some of its suburbs, the number has increased to over thirty.

The minister of the interior supervises activities of the local authorities through commissioners in each of the six districts and district officers in fourteen subdistricts. The minister has authority to remove local authorities because of inefficiency or serious dissention among the councilors. In such cases he may appoint a local committee of officials to replace the council until the next elections. Proposals have been made to establish a local-government court with jurisdiction over disputes between citizens and local authorities. Judges would be members of the public with magisterial qualifications and would have the status of other members of the Israeli judiciary.

The Ministry of the Interior has developed several country-wide master plans to unify and coordinate a variety of national services. They include master plans for a national highways system, power stations, and electricity grid, flood water storage and dispersal systems, national parks and nature reserves, recreational and tourist facilities, mining, and preservation of farmsteads.

In 1977 the Ministry of Police was incorporated into the Interior Ministry, adding to its responsibilities the frontier guard and national prisons systems. The police system in Israel is not local but is organized and administered at the national level, with headquarters in Jerusalem. The more than 13,000-member force includes women and members of Israeli minority groups.

MINISTRY OF RELIGION AND THE POLITICS OF RELIGION

The nature of Israel's political system, in which coalition governments usually include cabinet members from the religious bloc, has given the Orthodox establishment an important role in government administration through its control of the Ministry of Religious Affairs. The ministry has been at the center of several controversial issues affecting the lives of all Israelis, both religious and secular. These issues have included marriage and divorce, the status of immigrant Jews under the Law of Return, Sabbath observance, supervision of dietary laws, and questions of citizenship. Knesset law pertaining to these questions and administrative decisions of the Ministry of Religious Affairs concerning them are often influenced by the chief rabbinate and the Supreme Rabbinical Council. The rabbinate often examines such controversial issues, pronouncing judgments based on traditional Jewish law or *halacha*. Decisions or judgments of the chief rabbis feed back into the political system through their followers in the religious parties who, by virtue of their important positions in the coalition, can influence cabinet policy or Knesset legislation.

The organizational structure of the religious hierarchy is a relic of the Ottoman era, when Palestine's religious communities were known as *millets* ("nations"). Various Christian *millets* of the Ottoman Empire were led by patriarchs who served as high priests or religious functionaries and as ethnarchs or national leaders. The Jewish *millet* was headed by the *hacham bashi* ("chief rabbi") of Jerusalem, also called *rishon le-Zion* ("first in Zion"). The tradition of separate Sephardic and Ashkenazic chief rabbis was established during this period, and each community conducted its own rabbinical courts.

Ottoman practice was continued during the British Mandate, which recommended that a board of electors consisting of officiating rabbis and laymen elect a Supreme Rabbinical Council headed by both Sephardic and Ashkenazic chief rabbis. The rabbinical council's two joint presidents were assisted by three Sephardic and three Ashkenazic rabbis who were members of the Council and three laymen who acted as advisors.

The mandatory government gave the rabbinical courts exclusive jurisdiction in matters of marriage, divorce, alimony, confirmation of wills, and other personal-status matters and religious endowments. The Supreme Rabbinical Council was authorized to decide on interpretations of Jewish law in matters not within the jurisdiction of the rabbinical courts.

Since the Mandate, the Supreme Rabbinical Council has been enlarged to include twelve rabbis, among them the chief rabbis of Jerusalem and Tel Aviv as well as the country's Sephardi and Ashkenazi chief rabbis.

There are eight regional rabbinical courts with sixty-five Jewish religious judges *(dayanim)* and a rabbinical court of appeals headed by the two chief rabbis. Members of the Supreme Rabbinical Council are self-appointed; thus only Orthodox rabbis become members and only Orthodox jurisdiction is officially recognized in Jewish ritual or legal matters. Attempts by Conservative and Reform Jewish leaders in the United States to obtain recognition for their rabbis in Israel have been unsuccessful because of the Orthodox monopoly.

In addition to operating the Jewish religious courts and administering *halacha,* the chief rabbinate supervises *kashrut,* or ritual purity of imported food and of food in kosher restaurants. Its staff of rabbis, ritual slaughterers, examiners, and inspectors travels as far as Argentina, Brazil, Uruguay, Yugoslavia, Bulgaria, Rumania, Hungary, and Ethiopia to supervise ritual slaughter of cattle imported into Israel.

The Ministry of Religion is responsible for nearly 200 religious councils and over 300 religious committees in smaller communities, which are provided with assistance in religious matters by the Supreme Rabbinical Council. The country's

6,000 synagogues and nearly 400 officially appointed rabbis are also supervised by the council.

Muslim, Druze, and Christian religious courts operating within the Ministry of Religious Affairs have exclusive jurisdiction in personal-status matters affecting their community members. Up to now, the directors of offices for Muslim, Druze, and Christian affairs have been Jewish. In matters of personal status involving persons of different religious communities, the president of the Israeli Supreme Court decides which religious court will have jurisdiction.

If there is a question about whether or not a personal-status case is within the exclusive jurisdiction of a religious court, the matter is referred to a special tribunal of two judges from the Supreme Court and the president of the highest religious court of the community concerned. Judgments of the religious courts are executed through the civil courts, although the civil courts may refuse to execute such judgment if they exceed the jurisdiction of the religious authorities or are contrary to "natural justice."

Although less than 15 percent of the Jewish population supports the Orthodox parties in national elections and less than one-third are considered consistent observers of Orthodox Jewish traditions and practices, decisions of the chief rabbinate affect the total population, especially in matters pertaining to personal status, immigration, and citizenship. Secularists have at times sought to challenge or circumvent religious authority in personal status or citizenship matters, resulting in intervention by the civil judiciary or secular authorities.

Controversies in Israel between religious authorities and secular nationalists derive from ambiguities in defining who is a Jew. They also revolve around the fact that Israel and the Zionist movement which gave birth to Israel are explicitly Jewish. The Balfour Declaration, the League of Nations Mandate, and the United Nations partition resolution, the documents on which Israel bases its claims to international recognition, all refer to the "Jewish" homeland or "Jewish" state, yet the term "Jewish" has not been defined by the international community itself.

Only the Orthodox minority has a clear-cut, unambiguous

definition of who is a Jew, based on traditional Jewish law. This definition states that any person whose mother was Jewish or who was converted according to *halacha* is Jewish. When administering laws or regulations in which the question of Jewish identity is relevant, such as those pertaining to marriage and divorce, immigration, or citizenship, the Orthodox use their own narrow definition of who is a Jew, frequently leading to political controversy with secularists, who dispute both their definition and their authority. When he was prime minister, David Ben-Gurion, supported by other nonreligious Zionists, attempted to broaden the definition to include any individual who considered himself Jewish, who conducted himself as a Jew, and who was willing to accept the responsibilities of Jewish identification. Israel's chief rabbinate and the Orthodox parties strongly objected to this broad definition, insisting on the more narrow *halachic* one. The Orthodox community feared that acceptance of the broader definition would dilute Israel's Jewishness, allowing large numbers of "unauthentic" Jews into the Yishuv. They were also concerned that their exclusive authority in religious affairs would be undermined.

One of the first conflicts between Orthodox and secular viewpoints occurred in 1958 over the use of "Jew" on the identity cards which all Israeli citizens are required to carry and in the National Population Register maintained by the Ministry of Interior. The cards and the register listed people's citizenship, religion, and nationality. Controversy arose over the category of *le'um* ("nationality"). Israel's interior minister at the time gave instructions to list any people as Jews under nationality if they declared that they were Jewish, without further proof. The rabbinate and Orthodox members of the government protested that under the existing procedures it would have been possible for an individual to be a Christian by religion and to claim to be Jewish by nationality. The crux of the dispute was Orthodox insistence that there could not be a Jewish nationality separate from the Jewish religion, and that only Orthodox religious authorities had the power to define membership in the Jewish nation. Secular Israelis and secular Zionists abroad opposed granting the Orthodox rabbinate this exclusive jurisdiction. Prime Minister Ben-Gurion stated that his government did not intend to lay down religious law and had no authority to do so. It was concerned only with the civil question of who is a Jew by nationality, not by religion.

The question was complicated by ambiguities in defining Israeli citizenship and Jewish nationality. Jews, Christians, Muslims, and others could be Israeli citizens. But according to Zionist and Orthodox Jewish doctrine, Jews are not only a religion but a nation as well. Secular Zionists therefore insisted that it was the prerogative of the state to determine Jewish nationality, whereas the Orthodox rabbinate claimed that such a determination was a part of religious law under their jurisdiction.

To help resolve the dilemma, a cabinet committee was charged with seeking "the opinion of Jewish sages in Israel and abroad . . . and [formulating] registration rules, which will be in keeping both with the accepted tradition in all circles of Jewry, including all trends, both Orthodox and non-Orthodox, and with the special conditions prevailing in Israel as a sovereign Jewish state in which freedom of conscience and religion are assured, and as a center for the ingathering of the exiles." In accord with this mandate, Ben-Gurion wrote to several dozen prominent Jewish scholars, religious leaders, and legal philosophers around the world requesting their opinions.

After receiving diverse and at times contradictory answers, Ben-Gurion shelved the question. In the meantime, faced with national elections, the Labor government found that it required the support of the religious parties. A compromise was reached in which registration of nationality would continue within the bounds of religious law but no entries would be made for religion and nationality of children from mixed marriages.

During the next twenty years the question of how to define who is a Jew continued to plague the coalition in a variety of contexts. A near crisis arose when a leader of the Independent Liberal party introduced a bill in the Knesset during 1972 allowing civil marriage in Israel for four groups of Jews unable to marry under Orthodox religious law. The groups were

"Cohens," members of priestly families, who could not marry divorcees; offspring of adulterous unions; widows not freed by the childless brothers of their dead husband to marry someone else (*chalitza*); and those unable to have children because of impairment of sexual organs. Orthodox opponents of the bill argued that it would create a separate class of Jews and would undermine the authority of the rabbinate in matters of marriage and divorce. The crisis was resolved when a relatively liberal rabbi, the former chief of army chaplains, was elected chief rabbi. He persuaded the Independent Liberals to withdraw the bill and successfully warded off further introduction of civil marriage laws by making several decisions which were seen as providing a remedy for cases where the strict Orthodox rabbinate had previously prevented marital unions.

An earlier case, arousing international attention in 1962, was that of Brother Daniel. Born Oswald Rufeisen of Jewish parents, he was separated from his family during World War II. After helping hundreds of Jewish and non-Jewish anti-Nazis, he was betrayed to the Germans. He escaped from the Nazis and was sheltered for eighteen months in a convent, disguised as a nun. In 1942 he converted to Catholicism and became a Carmelite monk in 1945, although he still considered himself a member of the Jewish nation. He immigrated to Israel in 1958, where he entered a monastery. With Vatican permission, he requested that he be registered in Israel as of Christian religion and Jewish nationality, and that he receive Israeli citizenship automatically under the Law of Return and the Nationality Law. When the minister of the interior informed Brother Daniel that this classification could not be authorized, he took his case to the Israeli courts, rejecting the suggestion that he become a citizen through established naturalization procedures.

Brother Daniel petitioned the Supreme Court in 1962 to reverse the decision of the minister of the interior and to order that he be granted an immigrant's certificate under the Law of Return. The court was expected to answer the question of whether a person could have Jewish nationality without being Jewish by religion. In his appearance before the court, Brother Daniel argued that if an atheist could receive automatic citizenship under the Law of Return and Nationality Law, it would be illogical to refuse him citizenship. Although his religion was Catholic, his only nationality, he argued, was Jewish.

In a four-to-one decision, the Supreme Court ruled that a Jew who voluntarily converted to Christianity could not be considered Jewish under the Law of Return. The verdict noted: "Once more the question must be asked, what is the ordinary Jewish meaning of the term 'Jew,' and does it include a Jew who has become a Christian?" The reply was "sharp and clear—a Jew who has become a Christian is *not* deemed a 'Jew.'" The court refuted Brother Daniel's charge that refusing his request meant turning Israel into a theocratic state; "if the *religious* categories of Jewish law applied, the petitioner would indeed be regarded as a Jew." According to the traditional Jewish definition of a Jew, Father Daniel was a member of *Am Yisrael* ("the Jewish people"), but not a member of the "Jewish nation." However, "the healthy instinct of the people and its will to survive are also responsible for this general axiomatic belief; experience has taught us that converts eventually become wholly deracinated, simply because their children intermarry with other people." While Brother Daniel's love for Israel could not be denied, he lacked the "absolute inner identification" with Jews and Judaism. Both simple people and scholars clearly admitted, the court concluded, that Jew and Christian were "contradictory terms."

The court's main point was that even though a person was born of a Jewish mother, circumcised, confirmed, and married according to Orthodox tradition, if he severed himself from the Jewish "historic past" by conversion to another religion, he could not be considered a Jew under Israeli civil law, even though he could claim to be a Jew under Orthodox religious law. The court asserted that it had decided who was a Jew in the ordinary sense and under the civil law as it applied to the Law of Return. Since the Law of Return was a secular law, the court asserted that its decision was a civil one, limited to secular law, and that it did not define a Jew according to religious law, which was under jurisdiction of the rabbinate. Although both religious and secular Jews had expected the Supreme Court to give a legally binding definition of who is a Jew, it had circumvented this thorny issue. Instead, it defined who is not a Jew, leaving the question before the public as one which would continue to stimulate political controversy.

Failure to resolve this issue and the ambiguities surrounding it has raised problems for the government in its relations with the large, non-Orthodox Jewish communities who support Israel in the United States. While Reform and Conservative Jewish rabbis and their congregations may hold religious services in Israel, the Orthodox rabbinate has a monopoly over performance of personal-status rites such as marriage. Because of the large financial and political support Israel receives from non-Orthodox American Jews, complaints from Reform and Conservative rabbis about their exclusion have strained relations between the Jewish state and the diaspora. The Orthodox rabbinate in Israel and its coreligionists abroad adamantly refuse to allow non-Orthodox rabbis to break the monopoly they hold on personal-status matters, on overseeing *kashrut,* and on supervision of Jewish cemeteries in Israel.

Orthodox refusal to recognize conversions to Judaism unless carried out by Orthodox rabbis has created opposition among non-Orthodox American Jews as well as among the many Russian Jewish immigrants whose spouses were not Jewish or who were converted by non-Orthodox rabbis. The issue was politicized in 1974, when the Supreme Rabbinical Council ordered the National Religious party not to join any new government coalition unless it pledged to amend the Law of Return to exclude non-Orthodox conversions to Judaism. In March 1974, the Supreme Court of Israel ordered the Supreme Rabbinical Council to show cause why it should not revoke its instructions to the NRP. It also issued a temporary injunction barring the rabbinical authorities from enforcing the ban pending a final decision by the Supreme Court.

In the meantime, a compromise was reached when the NRP agreed to join the coalition government if the cabinet accepted the principle that conversions would be according to Orthodox religious law and if a cabinet committee settled the conversion issue within a year. The agreement also provided that the minister of the interior would officially state that to the best of his knowledge no non-Jew had been registered as a Jew during the previous four years.

With the fall of the government in April 1974, the ministerial committee was dissolved, and the NRP again refused to join the coalition unless the Law of Return was amended according to their demand. In September 1974, the NRP offered a compromise in which it agreed to join the government if registration of immigrants converted to Judaism abroad were suspended for a year and a new ministerial committee appointed to examine the issue of conversion and seek a settlement acceptable to all parties. On these terms, the NRP joined the government in October 1974, causing the resignation from the cabinet of Mrs. Shulamit Aloni, head of the secularist Citizens Rights party. The loss of three Citizens Rights party votes in the Knesset was more than balanced by a net gain of seven NRP Knesset votes.

With defeat of the Labor government in the May 1977 elections, the religious issue again came to the fore. When the leader of the new Likud government, Menachem Begin, approached the NRP to join his coalition, it again imposed as one of its conditions amendment of the Law of Return so that only Orthodox conversions to Judaism "according to *halacha*" would be recognized in registering Israeli residents and in granting citizenship. This again opened the dispute between the Israeli government and its non-Orthodox Jewish supporters in the diaspora.

JUSTICE ADMINISTRATION AND THE JUDICIAL SYSTEM

Under the 1948 Law and Administration Ordinance, the mandatory court system was continued in the new Jewish state. Thus most of Israel's laws and the courts that administer justice are based on the British tradition. The system includes local and district courts headed by appointed judges who follow the British legal code. Under this system, there is a presumption of innocence until guilt is proven, and bail is provided in criminal cases. In addition to the civil courts there are the religious and military courts described above. From 1948 until 1956, when military government was abolished, Israel's Arab citizens were those most affected by the military legal system. Since 1967, Arabs living in the occupied areas of the West Bank and Gaza have lived under jurisdiction of the emergency regulations used by the British mandatory authorities, which make them subject to the military courts.

A major difference between the British and Israeli civil courts is that there are no provisions for trial by jury in Israel. As in Great Britain, the courts are subsidiary to parliament and may not invalidate any law passed by it. Since there is no written constitution or Bill of Rights the Knesset, rather than the courts, has the final word. The courts have the reputation for being scrupulously fair, frequently going out of their way to protect rights of the citizen under law in the face of attempted intrusions by administrative authorities. Because of their record of fairness and defense of individual rights, the civil courts in Israel are among the few areas of government that have remained untainted by scandal, rumors of corruption, or political bias.

During its first decade, the Israeli court system frequently called into question administrative acts of civil and military authorities toward Arabs. In several instances, it charged administrative authorities with abuse of law or arrogating excessive authority. In one case, the High Court of Justice noted that administrative regulations authorizing the government to seize Arab property "gave the authorities broader power than is warranted in these emergency times. The broad right granted by the legislator to any authority places great responsibility in the hands of those who must often decide on the elementary rights of the interested parties. It makes it essential for them to act only after long and fair consideration and understanding of the results of their acts. Even the broadest authority does not justify arbitrary action and reliance on one's own judgment, which may be prompted by heartlessness or obstinacy."

In another case during 1948, the High Court of Justice reminded the military authorities that they too "are subordinate to the law as is any citizen of the State." The court emphatically reminded the military that one of Israel's basic principles was the rule of law and that the interests of both the public and the state would be endangered if the limitations placed upon the use of emergency regulations by the legislature were ignored. The court held that the need to preserve civil rights was no less important than national security. In several of its judgments, the court called attention to English common law, which guarantees individual freedom of movement. The principles of English law were applicable in Israel, the court insisted, and were in keeping with the spirit motivating establishment of the state and with Israel's proclamation of independence. In the court's opinion, the most important aspect of individual rights was not their declaration but their implementation. The court called attention to English judicial remedies, which enable the courts to examine on behalf of imprisoned individuals the legality of their arrest. If the court believed such arrests to be illegal, it was obliged to order the prisoners' discharge.

A major difference between relations of British courts to administrative bodies and those in Israel is that in England such relations have been worked out over 300 years. Today it is an accepted part of the unwritten British constitution that no administrative body will deliberately flout a court order. In Israel relations of the courts and administrative tribunals to authorities such as the army are still evolving. Although the spirit of English law pervades the courts and their decisions, it has not been accepted by many administrative authorities who come from different traditions. Frequently administrative authority has flouted or ignored legal decisions in the name of national security or some higher national interest. Because there is no automatic constitutional authority to implement writs of the High Court of Justice other than writs of habeas corpus, they are not legally enforceable and are therefore largely declaratory. Since the first decade of Israel's independence, the courts have become more cautious about intervening in such disputes lest their authority be undermined by frequent evasion of court decisions by the administrative authorities.

The court system is organized in the following hierarchy. In each of the major cities, there are municipal courts with jurisdiction over offenses committed within the municipal area. They are authorized to impose small fines and short terms of imprisonment. Magistrates courts are established in each district and subdistrict, also with limited jurisdiction in both criminal and civil cases. They may try contraventions or misdemeanors, offenses punishable with no more than three years in prison. Appeals from the magistrates courts are tried by one of the five district courts, located in Jerusalem, Tel Aviv, Haifa, Beersheba, and Nazareth. In addition to hearing appeals from lower courts the district courts also have unlimited jurisdiction as courts of first instance in all civil and criminal cases not within the jurisdiction of magistrates courts. Usually one judge presides at district court. In capital cases, those in which the maximum punishment is ten years imprisonment or more, and in certain other matters, three judges serve in the district courts, with a justice of the Supreme Court presiding.

The Supreme Court is the highest judicial body and has jurisdiction throughout Israel. It can hear civil and criminal appeals from lower courts, and serves as the High Court of Justice to hear charges of arbitrary or illegal acts by public authorities. At times it serves as a special tribunal or maritime court. Although the court has ten members, cases are normally heard by three, five, seven, or nine justices. At the discretion of the president, cases decided by three judges may be reheard by five or more. When constituted as the High Court of Justice, it can consider petitions presented by individuals seeking redress against administrative decisions or cases that are not within the jurisdiction of any other court or tribunal.

The High Court of Justice can issue an order nisi, which requires a public official to show cause why a government action should not be rescinded as illegal. While the Supreme Court may not invalidate parliamentary legislation, it can interpret the law to determine whether an official has exceeded the authority granted him by the legislature, or whether the standards, procedures, and policies laid down by the Knesset have been followed. In this capacity, the court can order the release of persons detained or imprisoned unlawfully; it can issue orders to state and local authorities requiring them to undertake or to refrain from performing certain functions according to the law; if an official has been unlawfully elected or appointed, the court can order him to refrain from acting at all; it can order courts, tribunals, or quasi-judicial bodies to adjudicate any matter and set aside any previous unlawful proceeding or decision; and it can order the religious courts to deal with matters under their jurisdiction or to refrain from dealing with matters not under their jurisdiction.

Although the court system is administered by the Ministry of Justice under a director of courts, an independent judiciary is maintained through the 1953 Judges Law. It states that: "A Judge, in judicial matters, is subject to no authority other than that of the law." Under this law, all civil-court judges and magistrates are appointed by the president of Israel on recommendation of a nine-member nominations committee. In addition to the minister of justice, who is chairman of the committee, it includes the president of the Supreme Court and two of its judges, a second minister chosen by the cabinet, two Knesset members elected by secret ballot, and two lawyers representing the Chamber of Advocates, or Israeli Bar. Judges may be removed only for misbehavior and serve to the mandatory retirement age of seventy. The 1953 law also established qualifications for appointment to the Supreme Court. The most important are experience as a judge in a district court, as a lawyer, or as a legal scholar. A special provision of the law permits eminent jurists of international reputation interested in settling in Israel, especially Jews who have held high judicial posts abroad, to serve as Supreme Court judges.

There are also a number of special courts: traffic magistrates courts try offenses against the Road Transport Ordinance; special military courts were established in 1954 to try offenses against the Prevention of Infiltration (Offenses and Jurisdiction) Law; a courts martial appeal court was established in 1955 to deal with offenses of soldiers or army employees; a national labor court and regional labor courts were set up under the Labor Courts Law in 1969 to deal with disputes between employers and workers, disputes between parties to collective agreements, claims against pension funds, disputes between a worker and a worker's organization, and claims under the National Insurance Law.

Tribunals, boards, and committees established to deal with special cases or inquiries are frequently headed by judges. The

1967 Commissions of Enquiry Law authorizes the government to appoint commissions to examine and report on matters of vital public interest. The president of the Supreme Court appoints the chairman, who must also be a Supreme Court justice or a district court judge. The chief justice also appoints other members of such commissions. Two notable examples were commissions appointed to inquire into the burning of the al-Aksa mosque in Jerusalem during 1969, and the Agranat Commission, appointed in 1973 to inquire into mismanagement of Israeli operations during the 1973 Arab-Israeli war.

The attorney general of Israel in the Ministry of Justice has extensive power in legal matters related to parliamentary immunity, in indictment of judges for improper actions, in prosecution of offenses against state security in foreign relations, and in matters related to official secrets. He may transfer cases from civilian to military courts or the reverse, or obtain extradition of persons apprehended in Israel after committing offenses in the occupied areas.

The Ministry of Justice is also responsible for registration of title to land in Israel and for other transactions related to landed property. The ministry has continued the practice begun during the Mandate, in which newly settled land is identified and registered according to a precise cadastral survey.

IMMIGRANT SETTLEMENT AND ABSORPTION

The special place of Jewish immigration in Israel's ideology underscores the importance of the Ministry of Immigrant Absorption. The ministry works closely with the Jewish Agency and the World Zionist Organization in carrying out its functions. In effect, there is a division of labor between the ministry and the Jewish Agency, in which the latter encourages and directs immigration to Israel. The agency also assists in absorption of new immigrants once they reach Israel, although at that point the ministry plays the more important role.

Most of the ministry's budget is devoted to housing for immigrants. Official policy is to guarantee every new immigrant family a home somewhere in Israel. The fulfillment of this promise is at times complicated by bureaucratic inconsistencies and administrative problems. Oriental Jews who arrived in Israel at an earlier period believed that housing and employment opportunities offered to them were inferior to those offered to new arrivals from the Soviet Union, such as jobs as scientists or university professors. Young Israeli couples complained that the newcomers from the Soviet Union found apartments with much greater ease than did veteran Israelis.

The ministry arranges special courses for new immigrants to retrain for employment in occupations required in Israel; it assists those retrained and those who already have needed skills to find employment. It helps those with small amounts of capital to establish new businesses, sometimes supplementing their savings with low-interest loans.

Assistance in cultural and social absorption is also an important task. Since few immigrants know Hebrew, the ministry organizes transient absorption centers and hostels, where they are taught the language. It works closely with the dozens of immigrant associations. Many such tasks are carried out cooperatively with other ministries like Education, Health, Agriculture, or Housing.

The Jewish Agency and World Zionist Organization were given a special legal status in a law passed by the Knesset in 1952 and in a covenant signed in 1954 by the Israeli government and the executive of the World Zionist Organization. The law reiterates the fundamental Zionist credo that the state of Israel regards itself as the creation of the entire Jewish people and that every Jew may immigrate to the country in accordance with the law. It notes that the World Zionist Organization led the efforts to establish the Jewish state.

The World Zionist Organization/Jewish Agency is charged with responsibility for immigration and absorption of immigrants. It is the authorized agency for development and settlement, absorption of immigrants from the diaspora, and coordination of Israeli institutions and organizations active in these efforts. A joint committee is created by the law to coordinate activities carried out by the government and the Zionist organization. The law authorizes the Zionist executive to enter into contracts, to acquire, hold, and dispose of property, to enter legal or other proceedings, and to be exempt from Israeli taxation. A prime objective of the law was to facilitate efforts for continuing the tax-exempt status of fund raising in the United States by defining Jewish Agency activities as purely humanitarian.

When Ben-Gurion was prime minister, he frequently circumvented the agency, because he believed it was dominated by the bickering and political manueuvering of the Zionist political parties. He encouraged separate fund-raising endeavors such as bonds for Israel, private gifts to educational institutions, and other projects of interest to him.

HEALTH, EDUCATION, AND WELFARE

Israel's comprehensive social welfare system is administered by the ministries of Labor, Health, and Social Welfare, with plans to combine the latter two in a new Ministry for Social Betterment. Under the direction of the minister of labor, the National Insurance Institute administers an extensive array of social security programs covering a large part of the population. These include old age pensions for men from age 65 or 70, and for women from age 60 or 65, depending on income; pensions for widows and their children; monthly allowances for families with more than one child; maternity benefits; medical treatment and hospital care; payments to the disabled and to families of breadwinners who are killed; and vocational rehabilitation.

The National Insurance Institute is operated by a council of public representatives appointed by the minister of labor and headed by a director also appointed by the minister. National and local insurance tribunals decide contested insurance claims. Appeals from the local tribunals are sent to appeals tribunals headed by district court judges in the civil court system, and final appeals may be made to the Supreme Court.

The social welfare and health network includes extensive services such as rehabilitation, community organization, youth work, services to the blind, and treatment at several government hospitals. These are supplemented by voluntary bodies, which are supported by international contributions. For example, the American Joint Distribution Committee provides hospitals, old age homes, child development centers, and mental health services; the Organization for Rehabilitation through Training (ORT) supports more than seventy technical and vocational institutions; the Women Workers' Council, an affiliate of the Histadrut, pays special attention to child care and education; the Women's International Zionist Organization (WIZO) is involved in child care and education; and Hadassah (Women's Zionist Organization of America) operates the country's largest hospital, internationally known for its health services and research, and other educational services.

The Kupat Holim, the sick fund of the Histadrut, is the country's largest voluntary organization, whose membership includes nearly 70 percent of the total population. It provides free medical insurance to immigrants during their first six months in Israel, maintains over 1,000 clinics, more than 4,000 hospital beds, convalescent and rest homes, laboratories, physiotherapeutic institutes, pharmacies, dental clinics, and a medical research institute. Although not a government agency, its close affinity with the Labor party through the Histadrut gave the Kupat Holim quasi-official status during the era when the country was governed by Labor.

As in other developed countries, a large number of the people in Israel, about one-third, are involved in education, either as teachers or as students. Most educational institutions are government owned and operated under the Ministry of Education and Culture. Special features of the system include division of education for Israeli Jews into secular and religious institutions, both operated by the state. The ministry has a special branch for Israeli minorities, which is responsible for the school system in Arab and Druze areas, where instruction is in Arabic. It also supervises education in the occupied territories, through the military government.

When Israel was established, there was only one university in the country, operating as a private institution with assistance from overseas Jewish contributions. As the number of higher educational institutions has increased and costs have escalated, the country's universities have become increasingly dependent on government financing. Although universities still receive a large amount of private aid, and operate autonomously, the

Ministry of Education and Culture has come to play a more active role in their financing and operation.

INDEPENDENT AGENCIES: BANK OF ISRAEL AND STATE COMPTROLLER

The Bank of Israel, established by parliament in 1954, is one of the two most important independent governmental regulatory agencies. Before it was established, the Anglo-Palestine Bank, later called Bank Leumi, was the banker to the government, the country's bank of issue for currency, and its leading commercial bank. Since 1954, the Bank of Israel has become increasingly responsible for the country's monetary and economic policies. It is Israel's central bank, with the sole right to issue currency and administer, regulate, and direct the currency system. It also regulates and directs the credit and banking system according to government-established economic policies. Its primary purposes are to promote economic stability and to stimulate capital investment. The bank's most difficult task has been in currency stabilization. Since Israel was cut loose from the sterling bloc in 1948, the value of the Israeli pound has declined from parity with the British pound to approximately one-twentieth of its original value.

The Bank of Israel serves the country's banking system as the ultimate credit resource. It can impose credit and liquidity restrictions on the banking system. Through various measures, it can control the quantity of money in circulation and direct the flow of credit to sectors of the economy that it designates as worthy of investment. All new banks and branches of existing banks must be authorized by the central bank. It also supervises the banking system, searching out unsound practices and protecting the public interest. State loans are administered by the Bank of Israel, which represents the country at international meetings related to finance and in agencies like the IMF and the International Bank.

The governor of the Bank of Israel, who is also the government's chief economic advisor, is appointed by the country's president and is assisted by a seven-member advisory board. The bank's independence is indicated by the flexibility given the governor to determine monetary policy based on his assessment of the country's day-to-day economic situation. The only bank decision that must be approved by the Knesset is fixing the country's interest rate. The governor must also report to the Knesset increases in the money supply exceeding 15 percent or more during the previous year.

During most of its history, the Bank of Israel has been free of scandal and charges of nepotism, party influence, and inefficiency. However, it became a center of national attention when Prime Minister Rabin designated a long-time Labor party leader as governor in 1976. The appointment was withdrawn after a police investigation revealed that the appointee had received large sums in concealed payments for fees and commissions in real estate deals, diverting the money to the treasury of his political party.

The second important independent regulatory agency is the office of the state comptroller. This office was established in 1949 to audit ministries, the defense establishment, state enterprises, corporations and companies partially owned by the state, and local authorities. In 1971 the comptroller was also designated ombudsman of Israel, or commissioner of public complaints. The office has exercised a strong influence on government, calling attention to many inconsistencies in policy, overlapping programs, excessive expenditures or misappropriations of funds, and other mishaps which are the bane of a large bureaucracy. In Israel, the authority and scope of this office exceed those of similar institutions in other countries because of the extensive network of government activities.

The State Comptroller Law of 1958 provides for appointment of the comptroller by the president, on recommendation of the Knesset, for a five-year term. The office is responsible only to the Knesset through the Finance Committee, to which the comptroller must report whenever he or the Knesset thinks it desirable.

The comptroller must remain above politics, may not be a member of the Knesset or of any local government, and may not be involved in any business operation. To assure his objectivity, he must not be involved in any undertaking supported by or holding a concession from the government.

The comptroller's annual reports include findings from investigations into ministries, state agencies, and corporations, and reports on local authorities and corporations. The broad objectives of the office are to assure the legality of state financial transactions, to promote accuracy and orderliness in handling government financial documents and records, and to promote efficiency, economy, and ethical behavior in government.

The comptroller has broad powers under the 1958 law, including authority to require submission of regular and special reports on the finances and administrative activities of any government office. With approval of the Knesset Finance Committee, he has the authority to launch a commission of enquiry, including the right to compel testimony under oath.

As the number of government activities has increased and the responsibilities of the comptroller have grown, the staff, with headquarters in Jerusalem, has expanded—from about 100 in 1959 to nearly 500 in the late 1970s. Because of the large number of agencies and offices supervised, inspections are planned so that a number of central units are examined yearly, and other bodies are audited at other regular intervals. Inspections of local authorities are carried out every three to five years and the reports submitted to mayors, local councils, and responsible government ministries. Each year the comptroller's office handles thousands of complaints from the public. When there is a high frequency of complaints about a common problem, they are likely to spark an investigation by the comptroller.

The range of activities of this office can be seen in recent investigations, which included practices in the Israeli Football Association, welfare services for Arabs, and veterinary services. Recent special reports have covered such government institutions as Israel Mining Industries, the Israel Petroleum Company, the Cotton Production and Marketing Board, and the national lottery. Even the Israeli Defense Forces, usually above public criticism, were the subject of a scathing 1977 report by the comptroller containing accusations of wastage, slack reserve–call-up procedures, and poor maintenance of vital equipment. The report concluded that many of the shortcomings contributing to Israel's unreadiness for the 1973 war had not been corrected.

Since 1971, when the comptroller was designated by the Knesset as public complaints commissioner or ombudsman of Israel, any person, citizen or not, can lodge a complaint claiming injurious acts of commission or omission, or alleging excessive bureaucratic rigidity or flagrant injustice. In such cases the commissioner may undertake an inquiry in any way he deems fit, without being bound by the usual rules of legal procedure. If the inquiry reveals that the complaint is justified, the commissioner must report the findings to the complainant. He must also notify the body or official against whom the complaint was lodged to rectify the fault, and that body or person must notify the commissioner of measures taken to remedy the situation.

During the first five years of its existence, the ombudsman's office handled over 30,000 complaints. Its forty professional employees dealt with over 6,000 complaints during 1976. The ombudsman estimated that these represented only about 1 percent of total public complaints, since the vast majority are handled by internal ombudsmen in the various public agencies.

In Israel the number of justified complaints is estimated at around 45 to 50 percent of those received, compared to 20 percent in other countries. Most ombudsmen elsewhere operate in wealthy or well-established countries where complaints are handled by private attorneys. Public familiarity with the ombudsman's office offers citizens reassurance against the excesses of bureaucracy, which the ombudsman himself admits are frequent. The existence of the complaints procedure is often a psychological deterrent to officials and institutions with tendencies to arrogate to themselves excessive or abitrary authority.

CONCLUSION

The administrative apparatus is one force helping to balance the diverse parts of the complex Israeli government system. The spectrum of formal and informal institutions including the Knesset, the political parties, the government administration, the courts, the press, and many interest groups has achieved in thirty years a system of checks and balances assuring the country's Jewish citizens a large measure of political democracy, comparing favorably with the liberal democracies of the West. Despite the absence of a formal written constitution and a Bill of Rights, a political system has evolved and continues to develop in which no one aspect dominates. In the first thirty years of statehood, power has shifted from one institution to another. The evolving balance of power has obviated temptations toward concentration of authority in any one arm of government such as the Prime Ministry, the army, or the civil bureaucracy. Within the administrative apparatus, a system of checks and balances has developed in which an agency, such as the State Comptroller, may restrain a ministry, even the Ministry of Defense. This is no small achievement considering the constant crises facing Israel in domestic, security, and international affairs. The achievement is in large measure the result of vigilance by the informal institutions, especially by the press, which continuously monitors the most minute activities of government—often to the chagrin of officials and bureaucrats. An alert and diverse public often guarantees that government keeps within reasonable bounds in its relations with the Jewish population.

In some areas, the political system has not achieved the goals set out in Israel's Declaration of Independence. Although political democracy for the Jewish population compares favorably with that in Western Europe and North America, Israel's non-Jewish citizens and the non-Israeli Arabs who have lived for more than a decade under Israeli occupation have yet to attain a similar level of political participation in the Israeli system. Failure to absorb Israeli Arabs into the mainstream of the country's democratic institutions is often blamed on the continuous state of war with the surrounding Arab states. Increased awareness and concern about this anomaly on the part of the Jewish majority would help to accelerate government action to improve the situation.

While the advantages of political democracy are enjoyed by all of Israel's Jewish citizens, the country has a long way to go before they all enjoy the social and economic security envisaged by the early Zionist Socialist founders. Since the country was established in 1948, the trend has been away from this goal. Both the security situation and the haste with which large numbers of impoverished Jewish immigrants were taken in have been blamed. But the fact remains that class distinctions have become more pronounced, due not only to the social and economic differences created by immigration, but also to changing values within the mainstream of Israeli society.

The 1977 elections demonstrated how precarious political prediction can be in Israel. They showed that Israeli society is still in flux and that political institutions are not necessarily permanent. Thus it would be rash to make predictions about the future of the Israeli government and society. The safest prediction is that change will continue—that many aspects of the government and society that today seem institutionalized may change, such as relations between Jews and Arabs, between Israel and the Jewish diaspora, and between Israel and its neighbors. The Jewish state of the 1970s may well be unrecognizable by the twenty-first century.

Bibliography

The number of books, articles, and other materials published about Israel is so vast that a comprehensive bibliography would be longer than this entire volume. It seems that the overwhelming majority of items deals with Israel's relations with the Arab world and Israel's foreign relations in general. Surprisingly few books have been published in English about Israel's internal affairs, its politics, or its social and economic problems. The bibliography that follows is selective, concentrating on items that relate to the country's internal affairs and politics. Of course it is impossible to make a clear distinction between internal and external affairs; thus many items that deal with the country's recent history, such as works on the establishment of the armed forces or diplomatic service or biographical studies, include much that relates to foreign affairs, especially to relations with the Arabs. With this caveat in mind, a few items that might be useful as an introduction to Israel's government and politics are included in each of the following categories.

MATERIALS OF GENERAL INTEREST

Israeli Government Publications

Facts About Israel. Jerusalem: Information Division, Israeli Foreign Ministry. An annual summary of useful data about state and society.

Statistical Abstract of Israel. Jerusalem: Israeli Bureau of Statistics. Annual statistical summary.

General Publications

Israel Pocket Library. Jerusalem: Keter, 1973-74. Series of booklets compiled from material originally published in the *Encyclopedia Judaica.* Series includes volumes on geography, Jerusalem, Zionism, history (until 1880), history (from 1880), immigration and settlement, economy, society, anti-Semitism, archaeology, Holocaust, religious life, education and science, Jewish values, democracy, and an index.

Orni, Efraim, and Efrat, Elisha. *Geography of Israel.* 3d ed. Jerusalem: Israel University Press, 1971. General geographic description.

Patai, Raphael, ed. *Encyclopedia of Zionism and Israel.* 2 vols. New York: McGraw-Hill, 1970. A comprehensive series of articles.

Sachar, Howard M. *A History of Israel from the Rise of Zionism to Our Time.* New York: Knopf, 1976. Excellent comprehensive history of Israel through the 1973 war.

ZIONISM AND THE PRESTATE ERA

Bell, J. Bowyer. *Terror Out of Zion: Lehi and the Palestine Underground, 1929-1949.* New York: St. Martin's Press, 1977. An account of Jewish underground military organizations in the prestate era, including Menachem Begin's IZL.

Elon, Amos. *Herzl.* New York: Holt, Rinehart and Winston, 1975. Well-written biography of Zionist movement founder, his trials and tribulations.

ESCO Foundation for Palestine. *Palestine, A Study of Jewish, Arab and British Policies.* 2 vols. New York: Kraus Reprint, 1970. A comprehensive and basic work originally published in 1947.

Halpern, Ben. *The Idea of the Jewish State.* 2d ed. Cambridge, Mass.: Harvard University Press, 1970. A sympathetic study of the origins and development of the Zionist idea.

Hertzberg, Arthur. *The Zionist Idea.* New York: Meridian, 1964. Symposium of thirty-seven Zionist writers from 1850 to the 1950s, with an introductory essay by the author.

Herzl, Theodor. *The Jewish State.* New York: Herzl Press, 1970. Translation of Herzl's original booklet, with an introduction by Joseph Adler.

Laqueur, Walter. *A History of Zionism.* New York: Holt, Rinehart and Winston, 1972. Comprehensive history of the movement, its origins, and diverse ideological trends.

Naamani, Israel T.; Rudavsky, David; and Katsh, Abraham I., eds. *Israel: Its Politics and Philosophy: An Annotated Reader.* New York: Behrman House, 1974. Compilation of essays and writings by a broad spectrum of Israelis, from Zionist to anti-Zionist, including Israeli Communists.

Stein, Leonard. *The Balfour Declaration.* New York: Simon and Schuster, 1961. Study of the origins of the Balfour Declaration and its use during World War I.

Sykes, Christopher. *Crossroads to Israel.* New York: World Publishing Co., 1966. A British writer's history of events during the Mandate, leading up to creation of Israel.

Weizmann, Chaim. *Trial and Error.* Philadelphia: Jewish Publication Society, 1949. Autobiographical account of events leading up to the creation of Israel by Israel's first president and leader of the Zionist movement during the Mandate.

ISRAELI SOCIETY: THE PEOPLE; THE ECONOMY

Antonovsky, Aaron, and Arian, Alan. *Hopes and Fears of Israelis: Consensus in a New Society.* Jerusalem: Jerusalem Academic Press, 1972. How consensus develops in Israel.

Arian, Alan. *Ideological Change in Israel.* Cleveland: Case Western Reserve Press, 1968. Discusses voting ideology, ideology in the *kibbutz,* and changes in ideology.

Benvenisti, Meron. *Jerusalem: The Torn City.* Minneapolis: University of Minnesota Press, 1977. Arab-Jewish relations in Israel's capital, as seen by the city's Jewish deputy mayor.

Curtis, Michael, and Chertoff, Mordechai S., eds. *Israel: Social Structure and Change.* New Brunswick: Transaction Books, 1973. Collection of essays on urban, *kibbutz,* labor, economic, and ethnic problems.

El-Asmar, Fouzi. *To Be an Arab in Israel.* London: Frances Pinter, 1975. Autobiographical experiences of an Israeli Arab writer.

Elon, Amos. *The Israelis, Founders and Sons.* New York: Holt, Rinehart and Winston, 1971. Well-written account of Israel's development and problems, as seen through the eyes of different generations.

Jiryis, Sabri. *The Arabs in Israel.* New York: Monthly Review Press, 1976. An account of the Arab minority in Israel by a nationalist who left the country.

Kanofsky, Eliyahu. *The Economy of the Israeli Kibbutz.* Cambridge, Mass.: Harvard University Press, 1966. A critical economic survey.

Kraines. Oscar. *The Impossible Dilemma: Who is a Jew in the State of Israel?* New York: Bloch, 1976. Detailed discussion of the legalities and controversies surrounding this question.

Lerner, Abba P., and Ben-Shahar, Haim. *The Economics of Efficiency and Growth: The Case of Israel.* Cambridge, Mass.: 1975. Critical account of Israel's economic development or lack of it.

Leslie, Clement S. *The Rift in Israel: Religious Authority and Secular Democracy.* New York: Schocken, 1971. Discussion of religion in education, the army, politics, and everyday life.

Luttwak, Edward, and Horowitz, Dan. *The Israeli Army.* New York: Harper and Row, 1975. History of the Israeli armed forces from the prestate era to after the 1973 war.

Patai, Raphael. *Israel Between East and West: A Study in Human Relations.* 2d ed. Westport, Conn.: Greenwood, 1970. Discussion of relations between Oriental and Western Jews.

Perlmutter, Amos. *Military and Politics in Israel: Nation-Building and Role Expansion.* London: Frank Cass, 1969. Role of the army in state and society.

Rubin, Morton. *The Walls of Acre: Intergroup Relations and Urban Development in Israel.* New York: Holt, Rinehart and Winston, 1974. Arab and Jewish relations in an Israeli city.

Seligman, Lester G. *Leadership in a New Nation: Political Development in Israel.* New York: Atherton, 1964.

Tiger, Lionel, and Shepher, Joseph. *Women in the Kibbutz.* New York: Harcourt, Brace, Jovanovich, 1975. Refutation of some common perceptions about the *kibbutz.*

Wilner, Dorothy. *Nation-Building and Community in Israel.* Princeton, N.J.: Princeton University Press, 1969. Application of some general observations about immigrant settlement to specific cases.

ISRAELI GOVERNMENT: POLITICS; PARTIES

Arian, Alan. *The Elections in Israel.* Jerusalem: Jerusalem Academic Press, 1972. A collection of essays analyzing various influences on voters.

Baker, Henry E. *The Legal System of Israel.* Jerusalem: Israel University Press, 1968. Detailed legal discussion of Israel's basic constitutional structure.

Brecher, Michael. *The Foreign Policy System of Israel: Setting, Images, Process.* New Haven, Conn.: Yale University Press, 1973.

_____. *Decisions in Israel's Foreign Policy.* New Haven, Conn.: Yale University Press, 1975. Although these two volumes deal with foreign policy, they give valuable insights into decision-making processes in Israel, how leaders perceive the world, and how they react.

Czudnowski, Moshe M., and Landau, Jacob M. *The Israeli Communist Party and the Elections for the Fifth Knesset, 1961.* Stanford, Cal.: Hoover Institution, 1965. Description and history of Communist party development.

Deshen, Shlomo. *Immigrant Voters in Israel: Parties and Congregations in a Local Campaign.* Manchester, Eng.: Manchester University Press, 1970.

Elizur, Yuval, and Salpeter, Eliahu. *Who Rules Israel?* New York: Harper and Row, 1974. Popular account of diverse individuals in the Israeli establishment.

Fein, Leonard. *Politics in Israel.* Boston: Little, Brown, 1967. Introduction to the political system of Israel.

Isaac, Jean Real. *Israel Divided: Ideological Politics in the Jewish State.* Baltimore: Johns Hopkins University Press, 1976. Description and analysis of the hawk-dove spectrum after the 1967 war.

Medding, Peter Y. *Mapai in Israel: Political Organization and Government in a New Society.* Cambridge: Cambridge University Press, 1972. History and development of Mapai until its integration into the Labor party.

Shapiro, Yonathan. *The Israeli Labor Party, 1919-1930: The Organization of Power.* Beverly Hills, Cal.: Sage Publications, 1976. Although it deals with the prestate era, it is useful for understanding today's Labor alignment.

Wagner, Abraham R. *Crisis Decision-Making. Israel's Experience in 1967 and 1973.* New York: Praeger, 1974. Detailed study of how the government makes decisions.

Zidon, Asher. *Knesset: The Parliament of Israel.* New York: Herzl Press, 1967. Detailed technical study of the Knesset and how it operates.

BIOGRAPHY, AUTOBIOGRAPHY, AND REMINISCENCES

Allon, Yigal. *The Making of Israel's Army.* New York: Universe Books, 1970. An account of military doctrine by a former military commander and political leader.

Bar-Zohar, Michael. *Ben-Gurion: The Armed Prophet.* Englewood Cliffs, N.J.: Prentice-Hall, 1968.

Ben-Gurion, David. *Israel: A Personal History.* New York: Funk and Wagnall, 1971. Autobiographical history.

Dayan, Moshe. *Story of My Life: An Autobiography.* New York: William Morrow, 1976.

Eban, Abba. *Autobiography.* New York: Random House, 1977.

Kolleck, Teddy, and Kolleck, Amos. *For Jerusalem—A Life.* New York: Random House, 1978. Personal account by Jerusalem's mayor and his son of the city and of Israeli politics.

Meir, Golda. *My Life.* New York: Putnam, 1975.

Peres, Shimon. *David's Sling.* New York: Random House, 1971. Personal account of arming Israel.

Prittie, Terence. *Eshkol: The Man and the Nation.* New York: Pitman, 1969.

Weizman, Ezer. *On Eagles' Wings. The Personal Study of the*

Leading Commander of the Israeli Air Force. New York: Macmillan, 1977.

PERIODICALS

The Jerusalem Post—International Edition. Weekly edition containing items from the English-language daily. Covers political events in Israel.

The Jerusalem Quarterly. Published quarterly by the Middle East Institute in Jerusalem. Contains useful articles on politics in Israel.

Journal of Palestine Affairs. Published quarterly by the Institute for Palestine Studies in Beirut, Lebanon, and Kuwait University. Includes documentation, press summaries, and articles from an Arab perspective.

Middle East Journal. Published quarterly by the Middle East Institute, Washington, D.C. Contains useful articles, bibliography, and chronology.

New Outlook. Published eight times a year in Tel Aviv, under the auspices of the Jewish-Arab Institute, Givat Haviva, Israel. Frequent useful articles on Israeli political, economic, and social matters.

Index